DRIVING T
GREAT NORTH ROAD

DRIVING THE REAL GREAT NORTH ROAD

Andy Bull

Scratching Shed Publishing Ltd

Cover photography: AdobeStock
Interior illustrations: Andy Bull

Typeset in Warnock Pro Semi Bold and Palatino
Printed and bound in the United Kingdom by

SAFE HANDS · QUICK FEET · STRONG IDEAS

Unit 600, Fareham Reach, Fareham Road
Gosport, Hampshire, PO13 0FW

For Richard Manwaring,
who never fails to laugh at my dad jokes

The Author

As a travel writer, Andy Bull has trekked across America with obsessive fans of James Dean, Marilyn Monroe and Elvis; rediscovered the ancient pilgrim route from London to Walsingham; and explored the former republic of Salo, northern Italy, where Mussolini made his last stand.

He has hung out in Lubbock, Texas with Peggy Sue, the subject of the Buddy Holly classic; and toured the locations in the Shipping Forecast.

He has written for *The Times, The Daily Telegraph, The Independent, The Mail on Sunday* and *The Tablet,* and published books including *The Mountain Bikers' Guide to the Lake District; Secret Margate; Walking Charles Dickens' Kent,* and a textbook for trainee reporters, *Multimedia Journalism: A Practical Guide.*

The Great North Road

Edinburgh

TELFORD'S ROAD, 1828

Morpeth

Newcastle

Durham

Darlington

THE YORK ROAD

Wetherby

York

Doncaster

Newark

Grantham

Stamford

Alconbury Hill

THE OLD LONDON ROAD

Royston

Ware

Hatfield

London

Contents

Contents

I

GREAT NORTH ROAD
Hicks Hall
to Alconbury

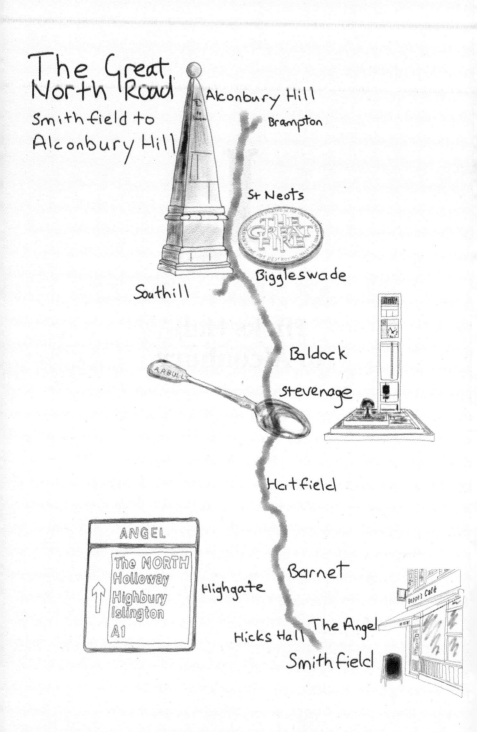

The Great North Road

Smithfield to Alconbury Hill

Alconbury Hill

Brampton

St Neots

THE GREAT FIRE

Biggleswade

Southill

Baldock

Stevenage

A.R.BULL

Hatfield

ANGEL

The NORTH
Holloway
Highbury
Islington
A1

Highgate

Barnet

Beppe's Café

The Angel

Hicks Hall

Smithfield

I was in a Volvo garage in Welwyn, listening to a salesman trying to sell me a car, when my mind and eye wandered.

Across the road, on this quiet Hertfordshire stretch of the B197, was a street sign reading: Great North Road. Surely not? The A1 was over there a-ways, and that was the Great North Road. Wasn't it?

I was pondering this puzzle as the salesman droned on. Eventually his spiel trailed off. 'Anything more you'd like to know?' he asked.

'How come it says Great North Road over there?'

He paused, only just managing to mask his irritation that I hadn't asked something about the car. But, as I'd listened earlier to him telling me all about the operation he needed on his knee, I thought he could indulge me a little.

He looked over at the sign, and then back to me.

'Bypassing', he said. 'This was the main road I don't know when. You can follow it a fair old way north and south of here.'

And then, probably beginning to suspect I was a time-wasting tyre-kicker, he gave me his best price, and we both winced. Me at the price, him because of his knee, which he rubbed under the table.

Then he stood up and, planting his bad leg straight, heel pressed to the floor, did a little dance of pain around it, the bad leg staying put while on the other he hobbled round in a circle. I once saw Billy Connolly do something similar in a routine, impersonating a Glasgow drunk trying to walk. Not wanting to smile at a man in pain I masked my grin by repeating the price he had quoted, sticking a ? at the end.

On account of his knee, he could only manage a nod, so I said I'd have to think about it, bid farewell to Wounded Knee,

3

and left. But I didn't think about it. I thought about the Great North Road instead.

I'd heard it claimed that the A1, aka The Great North Road, is the UK's Route 66. Really? I once drove Route 66, which many Americans think of as the Mother Road, and it is a joy: a two-lane backwater running through small-town America from Chicago to Los Angeles.

I've never found much charm on the A1, with its ubiquitous town bypasses and ever-extending motorway-grade stretches racing from London to Edinburgh. And, as I joined the rush-hour traffic streaming south on it that afternoon, it definitely didn't feel anything like Route 66.

I looked ahead at the clogged lanes, as we slowed and drivers anxious to get home started chopping between them, bringing a foghorn whoop of warning from a truck steaming up on the inside. And I wondered... what if the Great North Road was not the A1? What if, instead of being obliterated when all those bypasses and motorway sections were built, the old road had merely been relegated? Tucked away, out of sight?

And, if so, how much of the old road could I drive today? I needed to find out. And then came Covid lockdown, and I had all the time in the world to pore over old and new maps in search of the answer.

1. To Begin at the Beginning

It's a mix of meat-traders' bloodied white aprons, medics' green scrubs, and truck drivers' hi-vis orange jerkins in Beppe's Cafe this grey Smithfield-Market morning.

Sky, buildings, and cobbles are painted the same shade of gloom. If Farrow and Ball put it in a paint tin, they'd call it London Sludge.

Only Beppe's stands out, a yellow beacon of warmth on a cold, grey morning. It's a cosy narrow corridor of a place, two-seater tables up against the windows on one side, the counter on the other. Yesterday I wouldn't have been able to sit in here, looking out though steamed windows to wet cobbles. It was takeaway only, because of lockdown restrictions. Today I can, though for how long, who knows.

But, for now, I can look out at a slice of London life that goes back over a thousand years. The medics queuing for their takeaway coffees are the professional descendants of many generations who have sawed bones at St Bart's Hospital, over the way, since it was founded by Henry III in 1123. The other brand of butcher goes back even further. There was a livestock market on the cobbles between Beppe's and the hospital from the tenth century. Up until the 1850s, those animals were brought here on the hoof, down the Great North Road, for sale and slaughter.

A lot of the artics lined up around the market halls today, like piglets on a sow's teats, have brought their chilled Aberdeen Angus carcases the same way.

On the other side of the market in St John's Street, at a point called Hicks Hall, is the historic start of the Great North Road. Well, one of them. There are a couple more, but I'll come to that. For now, I'm seeing Beppe's as base camp, a good point at which

5

to plan my ascent of the Great North Road, and explore the various points at which travellers set off.

It's a great comfort to find Beppe's has survived the lockdowns that seem to have killed so many other little businesses.

During my lockdown research I almost gave up on the idea of tracing the old road. Scrolling through the many sites and forums for admirers of it, I found most of them said it was dead. One post on a thing called the 'Travellers' Club' was typical:

'Slowly and saddening for many, the Great North Road of folklore has died. The inns, taverns, cafes and truck-stops that gave it character have gone. For much of its route, the A1 passes through areas with little to see from the road. Now, much of the A1 and A1(M) are little different to any other main road with their Motos and other large operators.'

But, hang on, they seemed to be making the mistake I had, of assuming that the A1 and the Great North Road are synonymous. So I dug further, and it quickly became clear that the A1 is certainly not the Great North Road. Comparing maps down the decades showed me that realignment, re-numbering, re-routing and extensive upgrading have meant that the A1 bears little relation to the original highway.

At a quick reckoning it looked to me that no more than a quarter of the modern A1 follows the route of the authentic Great North Road.

That road sign by the Volvo garage was no fluke. In lots of places, all the way up the country, long stretches of road no longer a part of the A1 are still named the Great North Road. So the old road is there, but heavily disguised. It's hidden, re-numbered as, among others, the B197 that I encountered at Welwyn, the A602, and the B656.

On and on the old road goes, all the way to Edinburgh, hidden on the map in plain sight. It takes in relatively quiet A roads, extensive stretches on B roads and, on occasions, is down-graded to an unclassified lane. And while the modern A1 bypasses the many towns and villages that for centuries earned their living from the road – servicing first the postboys who carried the mail, then the mail and stage coaches, and finally the truck drivers and early motorists – it rolls right through the middle of them.

But it wasn't enough that the old road existed. If driving it proved to be an arid experience: passing through boarded-up buildings in run-down towns; bouncing along rutted, potholed and neglected country sections lined with abandoned motels and forgotten petrol stations, then I might as well stay at home.

There was only one way to find out whether the Great North Road was dead, or an English and Scottish Route 66, our very own Mother Road. I'd have to travel it.

But, first things first, where should I begin? I discovered I had three options.

Option No 1 was Hicks Hall where, for much of its history, the Great North Road began. But, when the men at the Ministry of Transport determined the route of the A1 a hundred years ago, they chose a spot just to the west, in St Martin's le Grand. And there was a third contender further off to the west in Lombard Street.

I decided I needed to take a stroll around, and assess the options. But there was something else I needed to bear in mind. In coaching days the various companies serving towns up the Great North Road didn't actually start their journeys from one of these three points. They first picked up passengers at designated inns nearby, and each company had its own preference. I'd have a look at a few of them, too. But, first, there was the little matter of Beppe's egg, bacon, sausage and beans to be addressed.

Actually, the lockdown London was just emerging from was the second, not the first. And, like movie sequels, this one wasn't a patch on the original. For one thing, the first had good weather. This one dragged on through winter. As I walk south from Beppe's through West Smithfield I feel like I'm crawling out of a bunker after a nuclear winter.

There are only one or two of us popping our heads out to look around and see what's left. Any pubs still in business? Any other decent caffs? Or had only the monoliths, the Starbucks and Wetherspoons, made it to the other side?

It's an eerie experience.

When I was a kid, there used to be an improving strand on the BBC at teatime called *Tales from Europe*. Most of those tales were dry as dust. But there was one that really stuck with me. It was about a boy who wakes up to find he is the only person left in the world. Everyone else has disappeared. He can do whatever he wants, go anywhere he likes. Stroll into a sweet shop and eat everything in it. This sounded fantastic. But the reality soon dawned for that boy. It was lonely. Like it is now, just after lockdown.

But, to look on the bright side, things could only get better. Couldn't they? I held out hope that, as I travelled up the Great North Road, the country would be coming back to life.

I cut over to High Holborn where, at No. 270, stood a coaching inn called The George and Blue Boar. In its heyday there was no busier transport hub. This was Heathrow Terminal 3 blended with Spaghetti Junction and topped off with Victoria Coach Station. It was demolished in 1864, after railways had destroyed the coach trade.

The railway age left the Great North Road as empty as the streets of this post-lockdown London, to be revived again only at the birth of the motoring age, early last century. The six-storey, grey Portland Stone-clad building now on the site of The George and Blue Boar dates from the 1920s, and was the Holborn Telephone Exchange. It's BT offices now, but looks grubby and neglected.

Among the many coaches that set out from here was The Stamford Regent. The wonderfully-named Victorian writer W. Outram Tristram, in *Coaching Days and Coaching Ways*, looked back at what it was like to catch that coach from here, with its celebrity coachman at the reins, in the mid-nineteenth century. Picture the scene. It's well before dawn on a freezing, foggy London morning, not unlike the one I am experiencing today:

The Stamford Regent stands ready for her flight; four chestnuts with a good deal of blood about them seem anxious to be off; ostlers are giving the finishing touches to the toilet. Afar off in a dim doorway the celebrated Tom Hennesy draws on his gloves, and says sweet nothings to a pretty housemaid, with her black hair out of curl.

I feel I have to interject a 'Woof!' at this point. The reason being, I picture this bloke Hennesy as the spitting image of Lord Flashheart, as portrayed by Rik Mayall in *Blackadder*.

But, to continue:

The incomparable Tom Hennesy languidly mounts on to his box. He chews a piece of sweet lavender given by the pretty housemaid – assumes the whip as a marshal does his baton, and darts a deathly glance over his left shoulder at the lingering fair.

'Let 'em go,' he says, 'and look out for yourselves.' The ostlers fly from the chestnuts' heads – the four horses spring up to their collars – the guard performs 'Oh, dear, what can the matter be?' on his bugle in a manner which would elicit an enthusiastic encore at an evening concert, and we are out of the coach-yard almost before we know it.

Off they thunder towards Smithfield.

Flashheart is still making his narrator swoon: 'Tom Hennesy is a master of his art. His manner on the box – all great artists are mannerists – is so calm, so quiet, as to be almost supercilious. But he has to keep a sharp look out, for he is driving through Egyptian darkness. The weather indeed reminds us of Homer's Hell; and as for the cold, it would make a snipe shiver in an Irish bog.'

Another old coaching inn stood between Holborn and Smithfield, in Snow Hill, and I walk to it next. At least this one has a plaque: 'Site of the Saracen's Head Inn, Demolished 1868'.

There had been an inn here since at least 1522, but it also lost its trade to the railways, and was demolished, replaced with a tall terrace that included Snow Hill Police Station. A five-storey grey art deco building sits in the inn's narrow slot now. Today, barriers and bags of clay and rubble suggest it is getting another makeover.

Charles Dickens describes the Saracen's Head in *Nicholas Nickleby*. It is from here that Nicholas departs up the Great North Road for Yorkshire, and the bleakness of Dotheboys Hall, with the tyrannical schoolmaster Wackford Squeers and a clutch of scared little boys. Dickens writes of a narrow yard, flanked by its coffee shop and booking office, above them galleries of bedrooms. It is 'at the very core of London, in the heart of its business and animation, in the midst of a whirl of noise and motion.'

I walk east to St Martin's le Grand, just to the north of St Paul's Cathedral and the site, from 1829, of the General Post Office. Another inn, Sherman's Bull and Mouth, was nearby. The Edinburgh coaches left from here. So did the Glasgow and Leeds coaches, which would follow the Great North Road for most of their journeys.

Today it's a wide street lined with more anonymous grey buildings; St Paul's just glimpsed down a narrow alley to the south. There is no plaque for the post office, but there is one for the inn, recording that it was demolished in 1888.

This is a very significant place in the history of the Great North Road. It marks the decision to abandon the historic start at Hicks Hall, because St John's Street and the narrow route to

Islington were too tight for the numerous coaches that now used it. Instead of threading their way north west through Smithfield, they now headed directly north up St Martin's le Grand to Aldersgate, meeting the original route at The Angel, Islington.

And when, in 1921, the men from the Ministry of Transport charged with charting the route of the newly named A1 sat round a table and, Ouija board-like, put their hands on a pencil to see how the spirits would draw the route up the map, it was from St Martin's le Grand that they set the starting point. So, right from the start, the A1 and the Great North Road were not one and the same.

There is one last location to look at before I head back to Smithfield, and start up the old road. It's a bit further east, in Lombard Street. It was here, from 1670 until it moved to St Martin's le Grand in 1829, that the original General Post Office stood. I walk up Cheapside and Poultry to the usually busy junction with Cornhill, Threadneedle Street, Princes Street, and Lombard Street, where the Bank of England, the Royal Exchange and the Mansion House rub shoulders. Today it's deserted, except for a gaggle of cyclists who flock past a lumbering bus, like yellow-jacketed parakeets mobbing a heron. Post Office Court, just down Lombard Street on the right, is the only reminder of the old General Post Office.

Let me get a few things straight before we go on, about the postal service, and stage coaches and mail coaches.

There had been a postal service of sorts in Britain from 1516, the brainchild of Henry VIII, but its use was restricted to the king and his court. Charles I opened the postal service to the public in 1635. There were 26 postal towns along the Great North Road, and postboys carried the mail between them on horseback. Inns developed roughly every 10 miles to accommodate them, and provide a change of horses.

Postboys regularly fell prey to highwaymen, and the service was inefficient. It often took more than twice as long for a letter to arrive at its destination as it did a passenger on a stage coach. In 1782 a Bristol theatre owner called John Palmer, who frequently travelled on stage coaches, came up with the idea of a system of mail coaches, which could combine carrying the post with paying passengers. He suggested it to the post office and, despite resistance and several years' delay, it was adopted. By 1797 there were 42 routes covering the country, with the London to Edinburgh mail coach introduced in 1786.

Around the same time there was a vast improvement in the quality of the roads, with the introduction of the turnpike system, under which local authorities were required to keep roads in their area in good shape and, in return, could charge those who travelled on them. All except, that is, the mail coaches, which went free. And that caused quite a bit of ill feeling among the operators of private stage coaches, which struggled to keep their prices competitive.

The mail coaches were glamorous beasts, as were drivers such as Tom Hennesy. Even the process of the mail coaches setting off each night from the general post office was considered exciting. Thomas De Quincey, author of *Confessions of an Opium Eater*, also recorded life on the road in *The English Mail Coach*. In it he sketched the scene at Lombard Street.

He tells of how, at about 7.30pm, 21 mail-coaches loaded up with their passengers at their respective inns, clattered down the streets I have just walked to assemble at Post Office Yard to receive the mail bags. At exactly 8pm they set off again, racing through the night.

He writes, possibly with his senses enhanced by a little substance abuse, of how:

On any night the spectacle was beautiful. The absolute perfection of all the appointments about the carriages and the harness, their strength, their brilliant cleanliness, their beautiful simplicity – but, more than all, the royal magnificence of the horses – were what might first have fixed the attention.

The dope really seems to have kicked in when he goes on to say:

Horses! Can these be horses that bound off with the action and gestures of leopards? What stir! What sea-like ferment! What a thundering of wheels! What a trampling of hoofs! What a sounding of trumpets! What farewell cheers.

What about another opium pipe?

Lombard Street brings me neatly to another thing you need to know about the Great North Road. Which is, that it has a rival: the Old North Road.

Mail coaches heading north from Lombard Street had a couple of options. They could either dice their way west up the narrow streets to Smithfield and Hicks Hall, or head in the opposite direction, going to the eastern end of Lombard Street and turning left into Gracechurch Street, to leave the city via Bishopsgate.

The Old North Road forges a separate way out of London, following Roman Ermine Street, now partly the A10, but re-joins the Great North Road at Alconbury, just north of Huntingdon, from which point the two routes head off north together.

Which might lead you to ask: of the two routes out of London, which is the real Great North Road? That has always been the subject of great dispute. Charles Harper, writing in *The Great North Road* in 1901, underlined the passion with which proponents of the rival routes argued their corner when he said: 'Like different forms of religious belief... these two roads eventually lead to one goal, although they approach it by independent ways.'

There is an argument that the Great North Road is an imposter, a Johnny-come-lately, a new-fangled invention dating back merely to the Middle Ages, and as such should be called the New North Road. The true ancient road being the Old North Road.

At this point I turn to the calm tones of brilliantined, pipe-smoking Christopher Trent. Well, that's how I picture him, anyway. I've got a copy of a lovely old book he wrote in 1955. It's got that irresistible, slightly musty secondhand-bookshop smell and I keep picking it up to sniff its pages. I think of Chris as a sort of *Blue Peter* presenter of old, and in his *Motorists' Companion on the Highways of England* he explains calmly the pros and cons of the rival roads.

He says that while the Great North Road: '...has grown up from the tracks which served the flourishing settlements of Eastern England of the Middle Ages', the 'Old North Road... dates from Roman times when Ermine Street, one of the first of the Roman paved highways, was built to connect the growing commercial town of Londinium (London) with Lincoln and York, the advance base of the Roman legions.

> The Roman road became derelict when the Saxons overthrew Roman Britain so that the medieval road on which the coaching road and the modern trunk road [the A1] are based followed its course for only a relatively small proportion of its total length.

And that's in the Midlands and North, as I'll experience later on. When Chris was writing, he was able to recommend the older route out of London, saying:

> Many regular travellers to the north prefer the line of the Old North Road at least for part of its course, especially from London to a point a few miles beyond Huntingdon, and maintain, probably accurately, that they find it the quicker way.

I don't do quick, I do interesting. But I will need to find out whether anything of the 1950s appeal of the Old North Road survives today. Later, I'll also need to explore a couple of other alternatives to the main route: the York Road, offering an alternative path between Doncaster and Darlington, and Telford's Road which, in 1828, was designed to replace the route between Morpeth and Edinburgh, but never caught on.

For now, though, I'm forgetting about the Old North Road and swearing allegiance to the Great North Road, and that means heading back to Smithfield, and the site of Hicks Hall, so that I can begin at the beginning. But, before I set off again, I'm going to give it a few weeks so everywhere will be open once again.

2. Hicksville

– Smithfield to Islington –

I'm standing on the north side of Smithfield Market. Charterhouse Street runs across to my left and right, with the narrow entrance to St John's Street ahead of me. Until the nineteenth century I would have been standing on the very edge of the City of London. Today this is still a border of sorts: between the ancient institutions of market, hospital and the Old Bailey law courts a little further south – which feels very central London – and formerly low-rent but now hugely fashionable Clerkenwell.

Today this old border is lined, on the north side of Charterhouse Street, with the bars and restaurants that have elbowed out the meat traders. In 2027 the market behind me will be shunted off to Dagenham, and the elegant Victorian halls turned into what's described as a 'cultural centre'. Meh.

Until the Reformation, two great monastic houses owned the land on either side of St John's Street, and ran hostelries for travellers on the Great North Road. The monasteries have

15

survived in some guise. To the east is the Charterhouse, a monastery of the Carthusian order, established in 1371. To the west, at around the same time, the Knights Hospitallers established the Priory of St John, from which the road gets its name.

In the eighteenth century, such was the danger of the route ahead, that solo travellers on foot or horse would gather at this junction until taken on in convoy by the armed guard stationed here, and escorted to Islington. Coach travellers were safer, protected from footpads by the whips of coachmen such as Tom Hennesy. After its narrow entrance, St John's Street opens out into a long, slim oval, in the centre of which stood Hicks Hall, a courthouse. Nowadays there are just a few spindly saplings on a traffic island to mark the spot. It could be worse: last century a public lavvy stood here. But, from 1612 to 1782, the courthouse dominated the space.

Hicks Hall was also the point from which distances were measured along the Great North Road, and was therefore its official starting point.

Milestones along the road bore the number of miles 'from Hicks Hall' or 'from where Hicks Hall formerly stood' until the end of the nineteenth century.

By the 1770s St John Street had become so busy with herds of travellers, cows and sheep, that lawyers, defendants and witnesses found it impossible to force their way through. So the courthouse was moved a little north to Clerkenwell Green.

The tall, flat-fronted buildings lining this oval were built as workshops, warehouses and small factories in the nineteen and early twentieth centuries. One, Farmiloes, who were lead and glass merchants, still bears the name embossed on the pediment of this fine example of Victorian commercial architecture, with its Italianate palazzo-style frontage in Portland stone, white brick and polished granite. It, like many others, is home to offices. Not that there's anyone in the offices for now.

There are also a lot of restaurants: St John, Vinoteca All Day Dining, the Taste of Silence, where you eat in total darkness. Another Victorian warehouse is occupied by a digital production company called Mediamonks. See what they did there? An estate agency offers 'outstanding loft apartments' elsewhere in the street for £780,000, penthouses for £1m.

The two monastic communities built hostelries along St John's Street, some of which became coaching inns. A whole string of others sprang up as travel increased and, by the early seventeenth century, this was an important centre of the stage coach and carrier business. John Rocque's map of 1746 shows a whole line of inns, their deep yards running back from the street.

I look for any reminders of those days, and find one at No. 16, where the Cross Keys Inn stood, probably from at least 1637. It closed in the 1880s but is remembered in the embossed cross keys high up on the front of the building.

I find another name-only reminder just up the street at an alley called Hat and Mitre Court, which was once the courtyard of an inn of the same name. I turn in beneath an archway, past rubbish hoppers belonging to the restaurant that replaces the inn at No. 88, and end up at a screened-off outdoor dining area beneath the towering, ancient brick wall built to guard the boundary of the Charterhouse.

Across the road at No. 57 I find a stronger link with the past. The Victorian pub here bears the name of the medieval inn it replaced: the White Bear.

Daniel Defoe, in his novel *Moll Flanders*, features The Three Cups, another lost inn featured on John Rocque's map. He has his heroine, who he describes as 'well-known at Hicks Hall, the Old Bailey, and such places' con a stage-coach traveller outside the inn. He has Moll say:

I placed myself at the door of the Three Cups Inn in St. John Street. There were several carriers used the inn, and the

stage-coaches for Barnet, for Totteridge, and other towns that
way stood always in the street in the evening, when they
prepared to set out, so that I was ready for anything that
offered, for either one or other... People come frequently with
bundles and small parcels to those inns, and call for such
carriers or coaches as they want, to carry them into the
country; and there generally attend women, porters' wives
or daughters, ready to take in such things for their respective
people that employ them.

Moll poses as a porter's wife, and a woman who is to travel with
a small child entrusts her with a large bundle she is carrying.

As soon as I had got the bundle and the maid was out of
sight... I walked away.

In the bundle she found 'a very good suit of Indian damask, a
gown and a petticoat, a laced-head and ruffles of very good
Flanders lace, and some linen and other things, such as I knew
very well the value of.'

I reach the junction with the Clerkenwell Road and turn left
and left again into St John Gate, a much-restored survivor from
the religious house that stood here. There is a museum tracing
the history of the organisation, one that dates back over 900
years, which became the volunteer St John Ambulance Brigade.

The gate was built in 1504 as the new south entrance to the
Grand Priory of the Order of the Hospital of St John of
Jerusalem. The original gatehouse was burned down by Wat
Tyler, leader of the Peasants' Revolt, in 1381, along with the
priory. They were targeted because the prior, Richard Hale, was
also Lord High Treasurer of England, and hence responsible for
the collection of the hated Poll Tax.

The Knights of the Order of St John, also known as the
Knights Hospitaller, were charged with aiding pilgrims to
Jerusalem and ensuring their safety, and will have sheltered

travellers here. The gate was heavily restored, after centuries of neglect, in the nineteenth century.

The gatehouse has had many uses since the Reformation. From 1701 to 1709 it was the childhood home of William Hogarth – he of *A Rake's Progress* and other searing social comment – when his father Richard ran it as a coffee house. Samuel Johnson – Dr Johnson of dictionary fame – worked here in the 1740s when it was the offices of *The Gentleman* magazine.

In 1831 it became St John Hospital and in the 1870s was bought back by the revived Order of St John, becoming the headquarters of the order and its subsidiary, the St John Ambulance Brigade.

From here St John Street becomes more nondescript and scruffy. I pass a scrappy triangle of green before the blue balconies of the Brunswick Estate and a little parade of shops. And it occurs to me that, at a dull point in a journey like this, some travel writers would introduce their sidekick.

I'm thinking Don Quixote and Sancho Panza. Bill Bryson and Stephen Katz. Dr Johnson and Boswell. But with them it was a relationship of, respectively, straight man and funny man; smart guy and good-hearted buffoon; adventurer and narrator.

I run through some other double acts I might try to emulate: Morecambe and Wise, Del Boy and Rodney, Wallace and Gromit, Jeeves and Wooster. There you've got a main character who thinks he's smart, and a sidekick who is actually the smart one or, at least, the not-quite-as-dumb one. Which partner in those double acts do I want to be?

I decide I'd rather be neither.

After all, not every traveller has an actual, physical companion. Michael Portillo goes solo on his endless TV train journeys, stoically ploughing a Michael-no-mates furrow in his lemon-yellow jacket and mulberry trousers, with just his ancient copy of George Bradshaw's railway guide for company.

Maybe there's a hybrid I can work up. Someone with Katz's

thirst and appetite – always up for sampling the fare in the old coaching inns and transport caffs I intend to frequent – combined with Bradshaw's knowledge. Except Bradshaw is not exactly a fully-rounded character. More a sort of Railopedia to be consulted when necessary. And anyway, why have just one sidekick for the whole journey?

Better to let one tag along when they've got something relevant to add, then drop them off before they get annoying. When I think about it, I've already got Tom 'Lord Flashheart' Hennesy. He'll be worth meeting up with again somewhere up the road. I have some others in mind.

For now, as I walk through the dull bit to The Angel, Islington, let me introduce you to John Byng, who trotted on his pony along the Great North Road in the 1780s and 90s.

He recorded the long journeys he undertook in *The Torrington Diaries*, rating all the inns and innkeepers, the towns and villages, the stretches of road, and the travellers he met along the way. He found plenty not to like. The bed was damp, the food overpriced, his luggage got lost. The guide at some historic church or grand country house was drunk, or snooty, or both. And he suffered perpetually from a bad stomach, which meant seeking out an apothecary at every stop. He was like an obsessive *TripAdvisor* reviewer, always ready with a one-star review.

The ByngAdvisor, I'll call him. He was little-known during his lifetime, but has developed a certain following since, particularly among those who get a bitter pleasure out of reading withering put-downs.

In Byng's day we'd have left London by now, and for the ByngAdvisor that could never be soon enough. His verdict on the capital was typical of his put-downs. He called it 'that emporium of wickedness and foolish fashions'.

No change there then.

He adds: 'Happier and happier do I find myself as the miles lengthen from London.'

So by now there ought to be the beginnings of a smile on his face.

As I walk up St John's Street I can hear the ByngAdvisor chuntering in my ear: 'I think I have for many years stated my haste, in spring, to get out of London (with pleasure I could quit thee for ever) seizing every opportunity to renovate myself by country air.'

He moans about the noise and the crowds, he longs 'to be no longer deafen'd by accounts of the opera' and society gossip, gloating tales of scandals enacted, and of nobility brought low, which are spread by those who demonstrate 'presumption without wit or good works'.

It is surprising to him – but not to anyone who suffers him for more than five minutes – that no one wants to accompany him on his travels: 'I love quiet, an abstinence from company, and over-conversation. But who are of my wishes? None that I know.' Hating London as much as he did, it must have really pissed him off when he died there, in 1813.

As Islington gets closer, and things smarten up a bit, I mentally press mute on the ByngAdvisor. Because I have seen a sign: a road sign. Beneath the word 'Angel' it reads:

The NORTH
Holloway
Highbury
Islington
A1

And I know I'm on my way.

3. The Lion, the Angel, and the Monopoly Board
– Islington to Archway –

I want to introduce you properly to my Uncle Charlie, who made a fleeting appearance in Chapter 1. Charlie's no longer with us. Nor was he ever my uncle. But I feel like he might have been.

Charlie, or Charles George Harper to give him his full name, knew more than anybody about the Great North Road. He lived from 1863 to 1943, and wrote extensively about the road as he found it in his lifetime, and its history. His two-volume guide *The Great North Road* was first published in 1901, and updated editions appeared regularly until 1922. Another of his books, *Stage-coach and Mail in Days of Yore*, vividly conjures up the time of Tom 'Flashheart' Hennesy and others.

He's another of my companions, and has a lot to say. But he can be a bit negative. I mean, when I was looking for the start of the old road, he really put me off with this: 'It were vain, nowadays, to seek any of the old starting-points from London.'

He was wrong.

Now, when I consult him about Islington, he comes on again with his vain-it-is-to-seek line. Here he goes:

Time has wrought sad havoc with Islington's once rural aspect, and with its old coaching inns. That grand coaching centre, the Peacock, has utterly vanished, and so has the picturesque Queen's Head – gabled, Elizabethan – wantonly destroyed in 1829; while the Angel... has since retired from business as a public-house, and is now a tea and lunch place, in the hands of a popular firm of caterers.

What Charlie couldn't bring himself to say was that the Angel had become a Lyons Corner House; a chain that was the McDonalds of the first half of the last century. Time and fashion have moved on. It's now a Wetherspoons. Rejoice! Or, at least a part of the old place is. Another bit is a branch of the Cooperative Bank.

Now, say what you will about Tim Martin, the Wetherspoons boss who seems determined to steal Al Murray's act as the Pub Landlord, but he certainly looks into local history when he chooses a location and a name for yet another of his pubs. Then he puts that history in framed posters on the walls, so that those who need a pint with their breakfast can close one eye and read all about it.

The Angel, as in the location rather than just the pub which lends its name to it, marks a key point in the history of the Great North Road. Here, the old route I have been following combines with the contemporary A1, but only for the 3 miles to Archway. At Angel, routes from both St Martin's le Grand and Hicks Hall combined to head north, making this the coaching equivalent of the M1's London Gateway services.

I'm beginning to think Uncle Charlie was not much of a judge of pubs in general, or of former coaching inns on the Great North Road in particular. He seems to have entirely overlooked a genuine survivor from Islington's days as the first service station out of town. It's the Old Red Lion, at No. 418 St John's Street. The present building might be Victorian, but there are several accounts of a tavern called the Redde Lyon being on this site since 1415. Which would make this the oldest surviving pub in London.

The first documented reference is in 1544, but they go for the earlier date in the inscription etched in black high on the building's red brick gable, and add a vinyl banner: 'Celebrating 600 years of history'.

In the fifteenth century there was little more than this inn and a place called Goose Farm here, on what was then a much larger Islington Green, now reduced to a pinched triangle of sparse grass, park benches and London plane trees just up the road. If they got here late in the day, drovers taking herds to Smithfield, and travellers afraid of robbers, would stop overnight.

There were pens where herds of sheep and cattle could be safely sheltered. This area, known as the Sheepcote, and the land the Red Lion stood on, was owned by St John's Priory, which also controlled the approach to the market.

Other inns followed during the seventeenth and eighteenth centuries including, by 1614, The Angel, which bore a portrayal of Gabriel, the Angel of the Annunciation on its sign. He's the one who told Mary she was to become pregnant with Jesus. It's quite a way from that to a beer and a burger for £6.95. This quickly became the largest, and best-known, coaching house in Islington. William Hogarth, who is said to have frequented both inns, drew the busy yard at The Angel in a 1747 work called *The Stage-Coach, Or The Country Inn Yard*. Previously, in 1736, he had included The Red Lion – then a small brick house with three trees in its forecourt – in a painting called *Evening*.

The Red Lion, which acquired its present form in 1899, has links to radical politics spanning the best part of a century. In the nineteen-hundreds, when Russian Communist Party members including Vladimir Lenin and Joseph Stalin lived in exile in the area, various revolutionary splinter groups held meetings in rooms above this pub. By one account, Lenin once bribed the landlord to let him stick his head in the shaft of the dumb waiter which ran between a meeting room and the kitchen so he could eavesdrop on whatever was being plotted.

Later, in the 1980s, the Revolutionary Socialist League, also known as the Militant Tendency, the entryist cuckoo that laid its egg in the Labour Party's nest, also met at the Red Lion. I like to think that, in his quieter, post-Labour-leadership days, Jeremy

Corbyn (MP for Islington North since 1983) might pop in occasionally for a Dandelion and Burdock spritzer, which he barters for a jar of his famous marrow jam. There's no sign of him when I nip in, but I do find a warm, dark-red cave of a place, a true haven of a pub, with a theatre upstairs. If I had any plotting to do, I'd definitely do it here.

As Uncle Charlie mentioned earlier, The Angel has been knocked about a bit over the years. But the pale terracotta building with distinctive corner cupola opposite the tube station is a true London landmark.

Its place in social history was sealed in 1935 when The Angel Islington was included on the London *Monopoly* board, leading its owners to declare it was 'the widest-known hostelry in the world'. They could make that claim thanks to the fact that Victor Watson, who worked for the game's manufacturers John Waddington, and his wife Margery, had a rather nice tea at the Joe Lyons that then occupied the site, and decided to include it on the board.

The A1 bears left at Islington Green, and continues as Upper Street, the way narrowing to pass between gentrified early Victorian terraces as it makes its way to Highbury Corner, where it swings left around Highbury and Islington tube station to follow the Holloway Road. Holloway comes from the fact that, in coaching days, this was literally a hollow way: a muddy track, sunken through overuse, through the fields.

Seeing as we are on the A1 for a short stretch, we ought to talk about how the modern road came into being a century ago. And we can do that over a cup of tea in a true London survivor: The Hope Workers Cafe at No. 111 Holloway Road, or maybe over a Holloway set breakfast: egg, sausage, beans, black pudding, bubble, two slices, tea or coffee.

The Roads Board had been working away at classifying Britain's highways since 1913. The work was interrupted by the First World War, but was picked up again in 1919 by the newly-formed Ministry of Transport. The vast increase in road traffic following the war made it essential that a network of high-quality long-distance routes be established.

Central government had little idea what roads there were around the country, what state they were in, or even an accurate record of mileage between towns. So roads needed to be assessed, and placed into categories reflecting their relative importance.

There were a lot of vested interests. The Michelin map, tyre and guidebook company got involved, and its founder, André Michelin, wrote four papers explaining the French system and proposing a similar one for us. Main routes should be given an N classification, he said, as in route nationale over the channel, starting to the north of the capital with the main, most important roads running out from London like the spokes from the hub of a wheel, then going round clockwise.

In the event, the men from the ministry went for A rather than N, but the French-style hub and spoke system was retained, and the idea of starting from the road headed due north. So the Great North Road became the A1, followed by the A2 though Kent, the A3 through Surrey, and so on.

By August 1921, the plans were in place, but it would be another year before the ministry got round to telling the public about the new road numbers, and for local authorities to start adding them to road signs.

Which meant that, while the A1 certainly existed on paper, as a brave new highway soaring from capital to capital, on the ground it was much less than that. At least in the early years, it was still no more than a string of short roads linked together, with motorists traveling along them like the runners in a relay race.

The road from London carried the A1 baton to Hatfield, where it was handed over to another local road, to be carried via Welwyn and Knebworth to Stevenage. Then the road from

Stevenage to Baldock took over. And so on, for 400 miles, all the way to Edinburgh.

The operators of commercial vehicles – who would be footing a substantial part of the bill for the many road improvement schemes through taxes on their vehicles – were anxious to know what they would be getting for the £28million (£1.4bn today) they would be contributing to. In April 1921 the minister of transport, Eric Geddes, gave the Commercial Motors Users' Association a progress report and detailed briefing, published in its journal, *Commercial Motor*. He said: 'We are today on the threshold of a vast improvement in roads. For the first time, the maintenance as well as the improvement on a national basis of through routes... has been adopted.'

He went on: 'Without this expenditure I cannot think what the state of our roads would have been... for the first time, we now have a national system of through roads.'

Now, given that 2021-22 marks the hundredth anniversary of the birth of the A1, I'm wondering if any sort of official celebration is planned. After all, the fiftieth anniversary of the opening of the M1 was marked, in 2009. The *Daily Mail* wished it a happy birthday, a book of screen-prints of its finest junctions was published, and posters sold at the Victoria and Albert Museum.

So I ring up the Department for Transport to ask. There is silence on the line. Then they ask me to put the question in an email and they'll get back to me. A few days after they say: 'We are unsure on this and would recommend contacting National Highways'. I do, but they are none the wiser.

So, I conclude, not only will there be no telegram from the Monarch, there won't even be a plastic beaker of warm white wine at the ministry. It looks like it's down to me to mark this historic anniversary.

Anyway, at least in 1922, the string of linked-together local routes meant that the A1 was pretty much like the American

Route 66: a Mother Road running from town to town as it made its way up country. But, ironically, the designation of the route as the A1 marked the beginning of its destruction as a great driving road. The programme of bypassing towns in the 1930, made necessary by the weight of traffic thundering through them, killed the thousands of businesses that relied on travellers.

From 1960, the conversion of long stretches into motorway hastened its decline. That process continues. It's only a matter of time before the A1 becomes an entirely different entity to the Great North Road.

Enough of the big picture, let's be on our way.

Uncle Charlie, with some justification, dismissed the Holloway Road as 'a very commonplace thoroughfare indeed [with] long reaches of mean streets and sordid by-roads [that] combine to render the exit from London anything but pleasurable.' Apart from a couple of imposing art deco cinema buildings, and a black plaque commemorating 'Joe Meek, Telstar Man' the Holloway Road is much as Charlie found it.

I pause by that black plaque. It's outside the 24-hour Holloway Express grocery at No. 304, and remembers a man you might call the English Phil Spector. Meek, an extraordinarily gifted record producer and pioneer of electronic pop music, turned the flat above this shop into a curious ad-hoc recording studio. Despite having the singer in the bathroom, the drummer in the bedroom and other musicians on the stairs, he turned out three number-one singles here. While the musicians performed, Joe would speed up, slow down, distort and manipulate the tape to achieve an otherworldly quality best experienced on the 1962 instrumental 'Telstar' by The Tornados.

Despite his genius, Meek was a deeply troubled man, hounded by the police over his homosexuality – then illegal – and in fear of the gangster Kray twins who wanted to take over management to The Tornados. The murder of a rent boy he knew sent him spiralling into paranoia and madness. The descent culminated in his shooting dead his landlady, who ran what was then a leather shop downstairs, before turning the gun on himself. Meek, who had a fascination with the occult and an obsession with the spirit of the American singer Buddy Holly, carried out the murder-suicide on 3 February 1967, the eighth anniversary of Holly's death. Joe was just 37.

Anyway. On to Archway Tavern, and a much happier musical memory. The pub features on the gatefold sleeve of the Kinks' *Muswell Hillbillies* LP from 1971. The band members lounge against the bar of this cavernous Irish boozer, their long hair and loon-pants making them look like visitors from another world, compared to the little men in flat caps who pack the smokey interior.

As I approach I can't be sure it has survived lockdown. On the tall narrow corner wall above one door is a sign that has lost most of its letters. At the top is says GUI. Beneath that, a man climbs up to a clock face with the aid of a seal and an emu, while a toucan looks on. Below him the lettering reads MILLEN I IME. Which I work out must be 'Guinness Millennium Time', and date from the turn of the century.

A little to my surprise it is open, but the pub no longer sports the dark wood and intricately etched mirrors it had in the photo on that album cover. It's altogether open plan, pale and airy these days, hard to relate to the picture I gazed at as I listened to Ray Davies sing of coming from Muswell Hill but dreaming of places he had never seen: New Orleans, Oklahoma, Tennessee.

4. The Big Red Lorry went up the Hill
– Archway to East Finchley –

'The big red lorry went up the hill.'

That was the opening line in my first school reading book. It had me hooked. I wanted to know what happened next.

But then. Oh dear. A chicken comes in. The story isn't about the big red lorry anymore. And it's only about the chicken for one line. Then it goes on to something else. I can't even remember what, it was so boring.

That put me off reading for a good two years.

But, anyway, back to the lorry, and the hill. I'm looking up that hill now. Or how I pictured it from my reading book. The one in my childhood head is exactly like the road that climbs up to Highgate from Archway.

This is another key point on the Great North Road. A parting of the ways, since 1813, when a new route was cut from here, avoiding Highgate village and the 400ft climb to it (the first big challenge the old road threw at horses hauling stage or mail coaches).

I'm standing in front of the Archway Tavern, at the point where the roads divide. To the left of the pub the old route, Highgate Hill, the B519, runs up to the village. To the right of the pub is Archway Road, the continuation of the A1. It runs straight and true, passing beneath the iron archway that gave the area its name, climbing at a shallower gradient, cutting 100ft off the climb and half a mile off the route to Edinburgh. So it was an easy choice for the men from the ministry when they plotted the course of the A1 in 1921.

The new road was intended to be in a tunnel, but it collapsed during construction, so instead it runs in a deep cutting, passing beneath the archway, which is actually a bridge built to carry the B540 Hornsey Lane over the new road.

This view up Archway Road has always taken me back to that first reading book, and the big red lorry going up that hill. It would have been a British lorry, of course: a Scammell, a Bedford or a Foden. Grinding through the gears and belching black smoke. But no matter, because the road, which has squeezed through a succession of cramped high streets up to now, has room to breathe. It's a dual carriageway, so all the cars, all my favourites – the Rover 100s, Jaguar Mark IIs, the Austins and Morrises – could sail past, harried occasionally by the rare Jensen Interceptor or Aston Martin BD5 that wanted to fly past them.

Today, I won't be walking up the Archway Road. I'm quite happy to end my 2.7 mile dalliance with the A1 – a road I won't see again until Baldock, 35 miles away – and take the original Great North Road up Highgate Hill.

The hill has always been a significant London landmark. From the top you can look back right across the capital. The summit marks the limit at which you can hear the sound of Bow Bells, making it the border of Cockney-land.

It's the point at which the siren call of the city caused Dick Whittington to 'turn again'. Just up Highgate Hill there is a curious memorial: The Whittington Stone. It's a stone cat crouched behind protective iron bars, formed into a dome like a parrot cage, and is sadly in need of a coat of paint. The cat is looking over its shoulder back down the hill. It's had the tips of its ears knocked off, so it's probably just as well the cage now protects it.

The story is that, here, in the fourteenth century, Dick, a young apprentice, was fleeing ill treatment from his master in the city and taking his cat with him. On Highgate Hill he heard the bells of Bow church calling him back, with chimes that foretold greatness, and three terms as Lord Mayor, if he did.

The Whittington Stone is on the pavement, close to the pub named after it, a one-storey white-boarded affair where two drinkers are anxiously peering through the windows five minutes before opening time. Locals know this pub as The Cat, and by some accounts an enterprising past landlord put mummified feline remains in a glass case, claiming them to be what was left of Dick's pet.

Just beyond it is the great hulking Whittington Hospital, a black cat on its notice board alongside the NHS logo.

The view back over London from here was the clincher for Whittington. He saw the spires of London's many churches and the silvery Thames and could not leave. Many have been captivated by this view over the centuries.

In *Coaching Days and Coaching Ways*, W. Outram Tristram describes The Stamford Regent, which had set out from the George and Blue Boar in High Holborn in the pitch dark, getting here shortly after dawn, and the expectation engendered in his fellow passengers as they anticipated that view:

> We see it in due course, as our steaming team breasts the ascent to Highgate. The sun springs lurid from a cloud of yellow mist. The great city lies before us, the coverlet of the fog but half withdrawn from her disturbed sleep.

The only annoying thing for Outram Tristram is that they all feel the need to wax lyrical about it: 'The dawn from Highgate is doubtless a grand sight. But it unfortunately inspires my next neighbour on the box seat with the idea that he is a Constable [as in painter, not copper] – this always occurs. He determines to paint the salient landscape – this always occurs too.'

The view also inspired Ray Davies, that uncrowned Poet Laureate of London, who in 'London Song', sings of how, on a clear day, you can see right down to Leicester Square, Crystal Palace, Clapham Common and Streatham Hill. Whenever he sees it: 'I feel that I'm a Londoner still'.

Today, the weather is against me: dull and foggy. I even duck along Hornsey Lane to try looking back from that archway over the A1, but the fog is just as thick. Suicides have led to the erection of a great 12ft galvanised steel fence alongside the archway's balustrades, the top curved over to further deter climbers. I peer through a gap and see a yellow halo hovering over the carbuncle towers that have disfigured the city, but not much else.

Highgate Hill has a couple of other places in history. Francis Bacon – philosopher, statesman and amateur scientist – was travelling up in a carriage on a winter's day in 1626. Snow covered the ground, and it suddenly struck him that it might be possible to preserve meat by freezing it. Keen to put the theory to the test, he stopped at a farmhouse and bought a chicken, stuffing the cavities with snow.

Fortunately, the bird was dead at this point.

Unfortunately, Bacon, who had become frozen to the bone while stuffing it, became suddenly and alarmingly ill. He was driven straight to Lord Arundel's House in Highgate and put to bed. Unfortunately again, the bed was damp, which proved fatal. Bacon died a few days later.

The Victorian actor Joseph Grimaldi, greatest comic of his day, had a dangerous encounter of a different kind on Highgate Hill in 1807, but with a happier ending. Footpads haunted the hill at night, and would grab their victims from behind, clapping a plaster soaked in pitch over their mouths to stifle screams while they went through their pockets.

Grimaldi was grabbed, and his muggers discovered a valuable-looking watch his admirers had given him two years earlier. On its dial was a portrayal of Grimaldi's face in the character he adopted when singing a popular comic song, 'Me and My Neddy'. The robbers recognised Grimaldi from the portrait, returned the watch and let him go.

Things get smarter the higher I climb. I pass Georgian terraces and reach Highgate village: a yellow-brick pimple of poshness standing out on the greasy brow of suburban North London.

At the summit are surviving coaching inns: on the right the Duke's Head, still with the arched entrance to its coach yard, on the left the Angel. The hill is topped by the flat tarmac of Pond Square. There is no pond and this is not a square, but it was once the village green. Now, it's all delis, cafes and flower shops in this smart, elevated little enclave. Thanks to the 1813 road bypassing it, Highgate survives as a reminder of what the villages that once lined the Great North Road must have been like.

Then the road bends right to begin its descent, and there's no more looking back. On the left is another inn, the Red Lion and Sun. In 1832, as a young man, Charles Dickens lived with his family in a house just over the road from the pub, his local. In writing *Nicholas Nickleby* six years later, as mentioned in chapter one, he had his hero's coach continue through here on its way to his grim new life as a schoolmaster at Dotheboys Hall.

As North Hill, the old road runs down to meet the A1, at a junction dominated by a multi-pump Esso station. But I ignore the new road, crossing over onto what is now the A1000 to continue along the old Great North Road, and drop down to East Finchley. In 1921 the road I am now on was designated the A1. It was only in 1960 that the A1 was switched to the road which runs off to my left, built to bypass Barnet.

Tucked in low on the left, just before East Finchley underground station, is the first of two more coaching inns, the Old White Lion. At the second, The Bald-Faced Stag, I decide upon a sneaky wee diversion, inspired by the fact I've been humming the Kinks greatest hits to myself all the way down the hill: 'Sunny Afternoon', 'Dead End Street', 'Victoria', the perfect sound track for this London stretch of the Great North Road.

Opposite the Bald-Faced stag is a road called Fortis Green, and less than half a mile up here I reach the heart of the Kinks's story. Ray and guitarist brother Dave were born and grew up in No. 6 Denmark Terrace, right across the road from a pub called The Clissold Arms.

Theirs was a musical home, with a piano in the parlour, to which Ray's parents Annie and Frederick would weave back from The Clissold Arms with a gang in tow for a singsong. Here, in 1964, Ray and Dave worked out the chords to 'You Really Got

Me', the song that first put them at the top of the charts. It's a modest, homely little house, at the end of a terrace.

It's twenty years since I last came here, and I want to see if it's as I remember. The pub has acquired a brown plaque beside the entrance, headed 'Ray and Dave Davies' which declares: 'Site of first public performance of Ray & Dave Davies, founding members of The Kinks, in December 1960,' when Ray would have been fifteen. The back bar that used to have one or two items of Kinks memorabilia on the walls has been transformed; vastly extended to house a Greek restaurant, and the bar across the front of the pub is now The Kinks Room.

I buy a pint and ask if I can eat in that room, but it turns out a funeral wake is about to be held there. I'm allowed to nip in quickly before they arrive, and take in the board with the first verse of 'Lola' on the wall, above a copy of that 1970 single; the gold and platinum discs for a greatest-hits album, *The Kinks Collection*; a whole load of framed photos and portraits; and an upright piano like the one in the Davies' old home.

I make way for the funeral party and order lunch – grilled octopus and chips and very nice thank you – in the restaurant. When my meal comes I ask the waiter if Ray Davies ever comes in. He looks blank, so I add, 'You know, The Kinks?"

'Oh yes,' he says, 'he was in before Christmas playing music in there,' he nods towards the Kinks room, 'with a group of people.'

I think it's fair to say that if Ray wanted to pop in today for a quiet drink, there's not too much chance of him being mobbed.

On my way back to the Great North Road I look out for No. 87 Fortis Green, the home Ray bought following marriage to his first wife, Rasa, in 1964. It's Rasa's falsetto that you hear on the backing vocals of 'Sunny Afternoon'. It's a white stuccoed 1820s semi, set back from the road. Almost all Ray's songs from that golden period were written here, on the white piano that stood in the front room.

Things ended badly at No. 87. Ray attempted suicide when he and Rasa split up in 1973, and left the house. But I prefer to remember the good times and, as I'm walking back down Fortis Green to the Great North Road, I'm humming perhaps the finest song written in that house: 'Waterloo Sunset'.

5. Drive Time

– East Finchley to Hatfield –

It's drive time. Contrary to any impression I might have given so far, I'm not walking all the way to Edinburgh. It's time to pick up the pace. So, when I return to East Finchley a couple of weeks later it's in the car, to drive on the A1000, as this stretch of the Great North Road is now numbered, almost all the way to Hatfield.

Any traveller would have done well to get a move on in the eighteenth and nineteenth centuries. East Finchley was then a hamlet on the edge of Finchley Common, 1,500 desolate acres that Uncle Charlie called a 'wide-spreading expanse of evil omen'. Here, highwaymen lay in wait, the most famous being Dick Turpin.

Until 1952 a large and ancient tree, Turpin's Oak, stood beside this rucked-carpet of a road. In contrast to the previous, pinched stretch along Finchley High Road, the old forest road still has the ups and downs, bends and a scattering of trees from its days as a rural route. It became the custom for travellers to fire at Turpin's Oak as they passed, to warn any lurking robbers that they would put up a fight. There's no trace of that tree now, but it stood on the corner of Oak Lane, opposite St Pancras and Islington Cemetery.

Executed highwaymen were hung on gibbets along the route as a warning to others. One of those gibbets may have stood at Tally Ho Corner, which I reach after a crawl through relentless traffic, passing over the A406, North Circular Road, and then filing round the traffic-clogged triangle of North Finchley's one-way system.

The introduction in 1805 of a rudimentary police force, the Bow Street Horse Patrol, to guard the road from Highgate to Barnet helped put an end to the days of highway robbery. That, plus the switch from gold to paper money, which could be easily traced, and the enclosure of the common in 1816.

Then it's on through the unforgiving suburbs via Whetstone to High Barnet, another great staging post on the north road, where one of the most famous of the old inns, The Green Man – rebuilt in the twentieth century and now a Savill's estate agents' – was a welcome sight for coach travellers who had suffered the eleven jolting miles from London.

Here, Tom 'Flashheart' Hennesy would strut his stuff, as W. Outram Tristram writes:

The Green Man at Barnet is now to me like the star, seen, or not seen, by the mariner, and in due course I see it, and alight at the first opportunity. But not before Tom Hennesy. In front of the Green Man at Barnet his languidly sedate manner goes. For here too he is a great favourite with the fair. Looks quite the coaching Lothario, as he lounges against the bar, his beaver [hat] adjusted rakishly, his melting glances fastened, now on his next team already fuming in the traces, now on the Barnet Hebe [goddess of youth].

The Green Man may be no more, but across the road its deadly rival, the Red Lion, has survived. The two did all they could to steal each others' trade, as Uncle Charlie writes:

The landlord of the Red Lion thought nothing of forcibly taking out the post-horses from any private carriage passing his house, and putting in a pair of his own, to do the next stage to St Albans. This, too, free of charge, in order to prevent the business going to the hated rival.

The Green Man's host responded by giving 'a glass of sherry and a sandwich, gratis, to the travellers changing there.' So the Red Lion took the gloves off and 'engaged a gang of bruisers to pounce upon passing chaises, and even to haul them out of his rival's stable-yard.'

The ByngAdvisor, my hyper-critical occasional companion John Byng, stays at the Red Lion, and inevitably gets off on the wrong foot, demanding: 'Bring instantly some tea, and some thin dry toast;' adding as a piece of advice for other travellers that they should consume: 'Never anything butter'd, or you get stale butter.'

Byng feels he'd get altogether better treatment if he were rich: 'Were I a man of fortune, my letters and servants should precede me: and then, at my arrival I should sup in the best parlour. Drink of my own wine and sleep in the best bed upon my own sheets and pillow.' I believe that's how King Charles III travels.

Today, the Red Lion bills itself as a carvery-style family restaurant. It's a great Portland Stone-faced place that could be mistaken for a branch of Barclays Bank if it weren't for the model of a red lion that walks a short iron gangplank suspended out over the street.

There is a strong Dickens connection at the Red Lion, and also at The Mitre, a lovely old inn that I shall be walking over to in a moment.

While Dickens was dining at the Red Lion, a member of the Barnet Board of Guardians is said to have told him about a workhouse boy who asked for more food at dinner time. That germ of an idea sparked the plot of *Oliver Twist*, and Barnet is a significant location in the book.

Oliver, having fled the workhouse, reached Barnet exhausted and starving after a week on the road. It looks like his luck has changed when a seemingly kind boy, the Artful Dodger, befriends him. In fact the Dodger is about to draw him into servitude of an altogether darker strain.

Dickens writes:

He had been crouching on the step for some time: wondering at the great number of public-houses... gazing listlessly at the coaches as they passed through, and thinking how strange it seemed that they could do, with ease, in a few hours, what it had taken him a whole week of courage and determination beyond his years to accomplish: when he was roused by observing that a boy, who had passed him carelessly some minutes before, had returned, and was now surveying him most earnestly from the opposite side of the way.

The Dodger buys Oliver a loaf, and then:

The young gentleman turned into a small public-house, and led the way to a tap-room in the rear of the premises. Here, a pot of beer was brought in, by direction of the mysterious youth; and Oliver, falling to, at his new friend's bidding, made a long and hearty meal, during the progress of which the strange boy eyed him from time to time with great attention.

That inn is, by some accounts Ye Olde Mitre, just up and across the road from the Red Lion, at No. 53 High Street. The Mitre – timber-framed, low and rustic – is the oldest pub in Barnet, dating from 1553. Today it's a very friendly local that has survived lockdown but, when I pop in, is soon to lose its very popular landlord of 13 years, Gary Murphy.

I'd been following him through the pub's Facebook page, and seen his accounts of how tough lockdown has been for his and other pubs. He ran up debts of almost £10,000 in the first five weeks, and £6,000 worth of beer went off in the Mitre's cellars. Later he wrote on Facebook: 'This is my reality – a £40,000 deficit if we are not allowed to open until Easter [2021].' At the height of the lockdown he launched a national campaign: 'No Pub, No Rent', to urge pub companies to give tenants a rent holiday while they were forced to close.

Gary struggled through ever-changing rules on social distancing, added outdoor seating when that was required, reconfigured things inside as the numbers of people who could sit together shifted, and kept the business going. But, finally, he got fed up and sold the last five years of his lease back to the pub's owners, Greene King.

When I pass through, restrictions have eased enough for me to order a drink to my table, but life is not yet back to normal. Gary's very cheery and is telling some regulars that the pub will carry on with a new tenant. I wonder whether there oughtn't to be a plaque to him on the front of the pub, as there might also be for Charles Dickens.

Time to drive on.

The old route through Barnet regains the name Great North Road after I bear right at the wishbone junction by St John the Baptist church and soon, finally, the buildings drop away and I am free of the suburbs. There's no traffic and I can put my foot down, sailing high along on the ridge of Enfield Chase, past another fine old coaching inn, the Duke of York, before I slip under the M25 and in to Potters Bar.

Nothing to see here. The Great North Road runs right through along the High Street, but Potters Bar got little trade in coaching days because it was halfway between the main staging posts of Barnet and Hatfield, so I press on.

In the approach to Hatfield the old road has been knocked about a bit, the alignment changed several times since medieval times. The present road sweeps west, then curves east to reach Hatfield, but if I keep my eyes open at the hamlet of Bell Bar I can pick up Bell Lane, the old alignment of the Great North

Road, which used to pass much closer to stately Hatfield House than it does today.

I spot my turning, and follow the route of the old road, now a muddy lane that loops round clockwise to the clutch of houses that make up Bell Bar. The old road emerges at the far side of the hamlet, where, alongside an Esso garage, it crosses the A1000 and continues as Woodside Lane to the boundary of Hatfield Park.

Originally, the Great North Road ran straight ahead for three miles across the expanse of Hatfield Park, but there are now double gates and a lodge. I'd thought I might be able to walk on through, down the die-straight gravel track I can see beyond the gates. It looks very tempting on the map, slicing through the estate and bisecting the vista that runs from the front of the house across to Bell Bar. But no. A very clear 'Private: No entry' sign, and a lady watching me from a window in the lodge, persuade me to drive on.

The route I wanted to follow was diverted in 1784 to a slightly more southern path across the park, but that's blocked off as well, the boundary of the estate secured behind a high, mesh and barbed wire fence.

Seventy years later, a much more radical realignment shifted the road right out of the park. The owner of Hatfield House, Robert Cecil, Lord Salisbury, exchanged land for the railway, which was then being built, with the proviso that the turnpike road should get orf his land. And that's the route I have to follow, heading south-west down Wildhill Road.

Uncle Charlie comes over all egalitarian about this, saying that Salisbury and family were forced to avert their noses because the road 'brought wayfarers between the wind and the nobility of the Cecils... Accordingly the road was diverted at the instance of the then Lord Salisbury, and the public no longer offend him, his heirs, executors, or assigns. And now, for ever and a day, those who use the road between Potter's Bar and

Hatfield village must go an extra half mile. This is indeed a free and happy country.'

There used to be a coaching inn here, The Greyhound – now a private house called St Michael's – where the ByngAdvisor stayed. His account reveals that, while he takes his own discomfort and misfortune very seriously, he delights in the suffering of others.

Byng learns from the ostler that a man he refers to as Mr T. has been badly hurt when the stage coach he was travelling in overturned, and is recovering from his injuries upstairs in bed. Byng writes: 'I ascended to his bed room; and found him recovering from an accident he was happy to relate, and at which I could scarcely refrain from laughter'.

He goes on:

The coach was broken down near this inn door, and Mr T. fell under five female passengers with not much damage; (the horses running off with the fore wheels;) when the roof breaking in, sent an upper cargo upon him, which added to his former load, bruis'd him, and cut his head so much as to confine him here for several days.

So, this poor bloke has been crushed under the weight of five women, then had the boxes on the roof crack his skull open. Hilarious.

At Welham Green, just outside Hatfield, I come across the first true transport caff I've encountered. I park on the expanse of mud beside it, and head in.

As a kid I loved transport caffs, and insisted on stopping at them on family drives, much to my mum's discomfort. My favourite was Uncle Tom's cabin, in the New Forest, but anywhere with some trucks outside would do. Sometimes mum would put her foot down and refuse to go in, on the grounds – incomprehensible to me – that the place was filthy.

If I did persuade her to enter, my order was always the same: Coca Cola and a sausage roll: the flaky-pastry sort with rubbery pink meat oozing out of it. Even as a child I had sophisticated tastes. And today, for old time's sake, I order exactly that.

6. Lord Peter Wimsey, and the Curious Case of the Abominable S-bend
– Hatfield to Stevenage –

For motorists headed north up the A1(M), all Hatfield amounts to is a long low tunnel under the Galleria shopping centre. A point of mild interest, perhaps, in the context of a very dull stretch of identikit motorway, but far removed from the real old Hatfield a mile to the west, on the Great North Road.

The old road winds along the perimeter of Hatfield Park, to be joined on the edge of town by the Great Northern Railway. Salisbury's deal – getting the road off his land in return for letting the railway slice through the town – was great for him, not so good for the townsfolk. It left what is now Old Hatfield perched precariously on a narrow strip of land between estate and rails.

At the roundabout beside the visitors' entrance to Hatfield House I leave the A1000, which sails on through town bearing the name Great North Road but which is in fact a bit of an imposter. To keep to the real old road I go one click more around the roundabout for The Broadway, and park. I'm by a former coaching inn, The Salisbury Hotel, an orange-brick affair with barley-sugar-twist chimneys, which became a restaurant and is now offices. Samuel Pepys stayed here in 1661 and confessed in his diary that, while on a walk 'I would fain have stolen a pretty dog that followed me, but I could not, which troubled me.'

A comment which leaves it unclear whether he was troubled

because he wanted to nick the dog, or because he was unable to do so.

The Great North Road took a left turn in front of this old inn, but its course is gone, over-written by the little car park I'm using, a church and a doctor's surgery. I will pick up the old road again in a minute, but first I walk on down The Broadway to Fore Street.

On the corner is The Eight Bells, another *Oliver Twist* location. It is said to be the pub where Bill Sikes and dog, Bull's-eye, find temporary refuge after his brutal murder of Nancy. Dickens certainly stayed there in the 1830s, but then, he's been in more pubs than the boss of Wetherspoons. Dickens wrote:

> It was nine o'clock at night, when the man, quite tired out, and the dog, limping and lame from the unaccustomed exercise, turned down the hill by the church of the quiet village, and plodding along the little street, crept into a small public-house, whose scanty light had guided them to the spot. There was a fire in the tap-room, and some country-labourers were drinking before it.
>
> They made room for the stranger, but he sat down in the furthest corner, and ate and drank alone, or rather with his dog: to whom he cast a morsel of food from time to time.

When Sikes leaves he finds the mail coach from London standing outside the post office. Coaches brought news. A small crowd has gathered and he overhears the guard and a passenger discussing the murder he has just committed.

I head on up Fore Street, where the rustic Tudor houses beside the inn seem to have sunk into the pavement, which laps up against their bowed windows. The houses get grander the further I climb, until Fore Street ends at the remnants of the Palace of the Bishops of Ely, which Henry VIII snaffled at the Reformation. Henry's daughter Elizabeth was imprisoned here by her sister, Mary. And it was here that Elizabeth learned Mary was dead, and she was now queen. Robert Cecil built his Jacobean mansion alongside it, and two corner towers topped with chocolate-drop domes peek out above the high wall between the house and the graveyard of St Etheldreda's church. The churchyard is spread out on a summit like a green picnic blanket, pegged down around the edges by rows of black and white Tudor cottages.

It's a charming spot, as is the rest of what the railway and new road have spared of old Hatfield, but Uncle Charlie found a very different place a century ago. He wrote: 'Hatfield village touches the extremity of wretchedness, just as Hatfield House marks the apogee of late feudal splendour.'

I find a very concrete metaphor for that relationship when I walk back down Fore Street and turn right past the Eight Bells into Park Street. Today, it's a pretty little road lined with whitewashed cottages, but they duck beneath a weighty brick viaduct, which strides through them as it takes the formal approach to Hatfield House skimming over their rooftops.

I turn down an alley just past the Horse and Groom – a seventeenth-century coaching inn – to emerge on the A1000, which is now back on the course of the old road. I walk past a multi-storey carpark and nondescript offices to a roundabout. Here, the modern motorist has to turn left or right, but the old route runs straight ahead, before an abrupt halt at the railway line.

Once, the road doglegged left then right here to cross via a bridge. It was a famous hazard on the old road, which novelist Dorothy L. Sayers called 'that abdominal and unexpected S-bend across the bridge at Hatfield,' in her Lord Peter Wimsey story 'The Fantastic Horror of the Cat in the Bag'.

I'll get to why the bridge is no longer there in a moment, but first, let's savour Sayers's glorious evocation of what it was like to drive the Great North Road in the golden age of motoring. She wonders why anyone bothers with other roads when 'all the time the Great North Road winds away like a long, flat, steel-grey ribbon – a surface like a race-track, without traps, without hedges, without side-roads, and without traffic.' In the story she describes a chase between motorcyclists up the old road, which almost ends in disaster at this bridge:

> With the sun and wind behind them, two black specks moved swiftly. To the yokel in charge of the hay-wagon they were only two of 'they dratted motor-cyclists,' as they barked and zoomed past him in rapid succession...
>
> At that abominable and unexpected S-bend across the bridge above Hatfield, the Norton [motorcycle] man, in the pride of his heart, turned to wave a defiant hand at his pursuer. In that second, the enormous bulk of a loaded charabanc loomed down upon him from the bridgehead. He wrenched himself away from it in a fierce wobble, and the Scott [motorcycle], cornering melodramatically, with left and right foot-rests alternately skimming the tarmac, gained a few triumphant yards. The Norton leapt forward with wide-open throttle. A party of children, seized with sudden panic, rushed helter-skelter across the road. The Scott lurched through them in drunken swerves. The road was clear, and the chase settled down once more.

That abominable bridge was Wrestler's Bridge, built in 1850. Now, just a Mecano-like footbridge allows pedestrians to trace the old route. Why? Because in 1966 the bridge collapsed. Rather than rebuild it, the authorities took the opportunity to iron out that kink in the road. So, now, motorists heading north must turn right back at the roundabout, then take a counter-clockwise loop around the top of Hatfield.

But if you walk across the bridge you find that the road on the other side is still called the Great North Road. It presses on to the left of the railway lines as it always did. It's a quiet little cul-de-sac today, with a nice old brick-cottage of a pub, The Wrestlers, after which the bridge was named.

I walk through what Uncle Charlie called 'an area of motor

repair-shops and garages, with their squalid advertisements'. This is still garage-land, with Volkswagen, Isuzu, SEAT and Audi lined up along the original route through town, which reaches the A414 and turns west for the modern A1(M).

But I don't have to join the motorway. At the roundabout above it I can go one exit further around onto the A6129, which takes me alongside the new road for 800 yards until another roundabout lets me exit left, pass over the motorway and continue on the old road into Stanborough.

But in Stanborough, at another roundabout, I have a choice, between the route the Great North Road took until 1833, and the one that succeeded it.

The successor is the B197, which runs just to the east of the modern road. It's a bit of a star, and I'll be following it all the way north through Stevenage to Baldock. It is the real Great North Road for 17 miles. But, before 1833, that title belonged to the other option at Stanborough, the B653, which heads off west across country, as if it has lost its way. The first stretch of the B197 is also home to that Volvo dealership, where I first began to wonder whether the Great North Road still existed today.

The change was made in order to straighten out a stretch that ran for a mile west before doglegging right at Brocket Corner to descend to the village of Lemsford. Here it shadowed the estate wall of another grand house, Brocket Hall, crossed the River Lea and climbed out of the valley once again. So, as I knew the newer bit of road with Volvo on it, I decide to take the older route.

I pause in Lemsford, a cluster of cottages around the narrow bridge over the river Lea. On the right before the river is the red-brick Sun Inn. On the left after it is a pub called the Long and the Short Arm, which sounds like half of an old joke about short arms/deep pockets. Here, the route of the Great North Road as it was before 1833 runs through what is now the pub car park and up a wooded incline to bang its nose against the A1(M). This was Brickwall Hill, named after the brick wall of the estate.

I'd seen this spot on the map and had planned to walk the now abandoned stretch of old road up Brickwall Hill. However, no fewer than three signs warn me to keep out, to halt, to not even think about it. So I do the next best thing, and stand looking over the five bar gate at the back of the car park, up the overgrown track which runs along the perimeter of the Brocket Hall estate.

There is a darkly romantic story about this stretch of the road, concerning Brockett Hall, Lady Caroline Lamb, and Lord Byron. Lady Caroline was the wife of the hall's owner, the 2nd Viscount Melbourne, Prime Minister from 1835–41. Caroline, who collected literary lovers, had affairs with men of letters including Byron. She coined the description of Byron as being 'Mad, bad and dangerous to know'. Nevertheless, she entertained him regularly at Brocket hall, once holding a birthday banquet for him at the house, during which she had herself served, naked, on a large silver dish.

'What's for afters?' he asked.

Anyway, one day in 1824, Lady Caroline drove out of the park to encounter a funeral cortège processing along what was then the Great North Road. When she learned the coffin contained her former lover, she collapsed. His remains were being taken to the family vault in Hucknall Torkard, Nottinghamshire, burial having been refused at Westminster Abbey. Lady Caroline experienced a mental breakdown that blighted her life and died four years later. She was buried in the graveyard of St Etheldreda's, the church on the hilltop that I visited back at Hatfield.

Thwarted in my pursuit of this bit of the old route, I drive up out of the village and cross the A1(M) to pick up the B197 again. In about a mile, at Ayot Green, I get another chance to take a look at the pre-1833 route. Here I cross back west over the A1(M) and turn left onto a surviving stretch of the older road.

This is a lovely spot. Ayot Green is well named: cottages line the edges of a wide expanse of mossy grass, shaded by veteran oak and chestnut. I take a sharp right and follow the old road to a dead-end by The Waggoners, a former coaching inn now a 'rustic, real-fire pub with modern European bar food and inventive French cooking in the restaurant'. I approve. It's good to see an old coaching inn given a new lease of life. The road is lined with the cars of walkers who are taking a stroll over the golf course in the grounds of Brocket Hall.

The road has been climbing to this point but, from here, as I re-join the B197, it begins the long descent down Digswell Hill towards Welwyn, the road cut deep, running as a sunken avenue between rugged banks. I leave the B197 at Welwyn, taking London Road, which winds down into a cloistered little town. Until 1927, this was the route of the Great North Road, twisting into what is now known as Welwyn Village or Old Welwyn to distinguish it from the twentieth-century new town of Welwyn Garden City.

It's like gliding down a slide, the road passing the White Hart and levelling out. It looks like the steepness of the hill I have just descended raised issues of animal cruelty in coaching days. An old RSPCA sign high on a house wall warns coachmen: 'Please slacken hame [the collar in a harness] or bearing rein when going up hill' and warns 'complaints of cruelty will be forwarded to the secretary at headquarters'.

Old Welwyn feels like a living museum, or a film set. I half expect Miss Marple to putter past in a Morris Minor. It certainly hasn't changed much since the coaching days. Along with the White Hart it has: a baker that has been in business since 1838; a shop – Hill and Co – that specialises in building and restoring violins, violas and cellos; and a thirteenth-century inn, now called the Wellington but, until 1816, The White Swan.

Now, the White Swan was clearly a venerable inn, but the ByngAdvisor takes issue. Here he was offered 'an old fusty tart of last year's fruit,' but rejected it: 'I open'd the lid, and closed it tightly down for the next comer. No tricks upon travellers.'

The diarist Samuel Pepys fared better: 'We supped well, and had two beds in the room and so lay single, and still remember it that of all the nights that ever I slept in my life I never did pass a night with more epicurism of sleep; there being now and then a noise of people stirring that waked me, and then it was a very rainy night, and then I was a little weary, that what between waking and then sleeping again, one after another, I never had so much content in all my life, and so my wife says it was with her.'

The old road climbs back out of Welwyn to re-join the B197, which crosses the A1(M) and takes me on a long, traffic-free swoop through Woolmer Green and Knebworth to Stevenage.

As I drive I'm thinking about that joke I made about Byron, Lady Caroline and 'what's for afters?' My kids would tell me that's a dad joke. As in bad. Just as dad dancing is bad dancing. And you definitely wouldn't want a dad bod. Now, I don't know about you, but this denigration of dads is beginning to make my fingers itch. Dadism should be as unacceptable as sexism. So, the fightback starts here. I vow to continue proudly slipping dad jokes into this book until the bitter end.

7. Mods, Rockers and Mochas
– Stevenage to Biggleswade –

Speaking of dad jokes, you might think this is another one, but bear with me. In the early days of the Beatles, when they excelled at repelling inane press-conference questions with witty wordplay, Ringo is asked if he's a Mod or a Rocker. 'Neither,' he says, 'I'm a Mocker.'

A good joke, I think you'll agree. Spoken not by a dad, but a young Beatle, and hence showing that what might sound like a dad joke can actually still be funny. It comes to mind in the queue at the Greggs in Stevenage's Town Square, where I'm after a Steak Bake. Two blokes in biker's leathers have ordered drinks, and as they are placed on the counter they are asked 'Who's the Mocha?' To which one of the bikers says 'That's me'.

I know one dad who, in my position, would have tapped him on the shoulder and said: 'Actually, I think you'll find you are in fact a Rocker.' I don't do that. I like my teeth too much. But I take the very fact that I've thought about it as a warning: dad joking could be dangerous.

Anyway, I'm in Greggs because I need some sustenance after my tussle with the road system getting in to Stevenage. I could go all Alan Partridge at this point and reel off all the numbers of the roads that tried to knock me off course, but I won't. Suffice it to say that, against all odds, I've stuck to London Road, navigating overpasses, underpasses, roundabouts and gyratories to reach Danestrete.

As the name – but nothing else about the location – suggests, this is the route of the Roman road through Stevenage, which the Great North Road followed. Here, squeezed between a Matalan and a Holiday Inn, I have driven as far as I can. Beyond here a giant Tesco Extra blocks the way, the route of the Great North Road running straight through it. So I park.

I sit in the Town Square to suck the meaty gravy out of the superheated flaky pastry sachet that is my Steak Bake. Stevenage represents a brave new world. It was founded in 1946, the first of the New Towns built in a ring around London. But, like the futuristic illustrations in a 1950s sci-fi comic, it looks pretty dated now. This square must have been daringly modern when completed in 1959. At its centre is a raised oblong pool, in which the blocks of colour beneath the shallow water are bisected by black lines. I wonder if Mondrian had a side line in paddling pools.

From it rises a 60ft clock tower – or 'campanile' in the 'constructivist abstract style' as Historic England prefers to call it. The tower is a four-storey frame of concrete-wrapped girders, like the hose-drying towers they have at the back of fire stations. A galvanised ladder with protective loops runs up to the clock. It looks as if it ought to lead to a high-diving board jutting out over the pool. A banner on the borough council building across the way reads: 'Congratulations Lewis'.

That's Lewis as in Hamilton, Stevenage's favourite son, who had recently won his seventh Formula 1 driver's championship, matching Michael Schumacher's achievement. I've checked to see if Lewis has anything to tell me about the Great North Road and learn that his regular childhood road journey from here was actually over to Ware and then down the Old North Road to Rye House Kart Raceway at Hoddesdon for training, a stretch of road I'll be exploring later.

Fortified by my Greggs, I press on, back up Danestrete to Tesco. To trace the next bit of the old road I have to go in, walk to the back where the Costa cafe is and follow the rear aisle past household and homeware to the other back corner of the store.

I do that, just for completeness, then go back out to the car park and walk north, where an elaborate metal footbridge approximating to the old route takes me over the four lanes of the A1155 to Ditchmore Lane. What a contrast. From modern and bustling to old and overlooked. And then the narrow lane opens out into the wide High Street of old Stevenage, a place, once lined with inns, that lived off the coaching trade.

That all ended in 1850, when the railway arrived. From 21 coaches a day to none. As Uncle Charlie puts it: 'Stevenage is the first of the many wide-streeted towns and villages whose emptiness proclaims the something missing that was provided for by all this vast roominess. Its one street, lining the old road, was originally laid out so spaciously for the purpose of affording room for the traffic for which, once upon a time, it was not too spacious. It is all too wide now.'

Nothing much has changed since then. Old Stevenage feels

like a backwater: overlooked, rarely visited, but nevertheless full of interest. There's quite a tale at No. 37 High Street. Here, in 1742, the coffin containing the body of Henry Trigg was 'buried' in the rafters of this house. The coffin is still there, but the body has since received a conventional burial. No. 37 became the Old Castle Inn, then a bank, and is now the Dental and Implant Centre.

The story goes that, one night, Trigg, a wealthy Stevenage grocer, encountered body snatchers digging up a coffin from St Nicholas's church. Determined this should not happen to his remains, he bequeathed his estate to any friend or relative who would ensure his body was 'decently laid [in the recipient's house] upon a floor in the roof.' His brother, Revd Thomas Trigg, did so. There his remains lay, until 1999, when the Nat West moved into the building and decided Trigg's bones had to move out. The ByngAdvisor has his own tale to tell:

> Passing thro' Stevenage I recollected a trick of an inn-keeper there (often practised I believe); *viz*, that finding many people dissatisfied with his house, and wishing another to be set up; another inn quickly open'd against him, which, tho' the worst, got much custom. In a course of years it was discovered to be kept by one of his waiters, who daily accounted to him.

I believe that, today, crappy restaurants do something similar, cloning themselves under a range of names on food-ordering apps.

I have my own Stevenage tale. Wandering off the High Street I found an Oxfam shop in Middle Row. Do you remember in *Blackadder* when Baldrick proudly shows that he owns a bullet with his name on it? Well, I found a silver teaspoon with my name on it in Oxfam. I pick it out of a tray of odd cutlery and do a double take. But, there it is, written on the handle: A. R. Bull. Spooky, me being Andrew Richard.

Baldrick sees his bullet as a lifesaver. He says to Blackadder: 'You know how they say that somewhere there's a bullet with your name on it? Well I thought that if I owned the bullet with my name on it, I'll never get hit by it.'

I'm wondering what protection my spoon might offer. It may not be a lifesaver, but it will forever be my Lucky Spoon, and accompany me as my official stirrer on my travels from here.

At the far end of the High Street the A602 comes swinging in from the left, and commandeers the route of the old road for a short stretch, but the B197 is released from its grip again after 400 yards or so, and freed to sail on north through Graveley, the A1(M) creeping in from the west. There's a brief altercation with the A505 but the B-road survives that tussle to run free again.

Out of Stevenage it rises to run to the east of the A1(M), and is a fine stretch of single carriageway road that dips for the village of Graveley, where the George and Dragon, a handsome red-brick coaching inn has a sign demonstrating the enterprise that is needed to keep such places thriving: Farm Shop Inside.

The road lifts its head again to flick past a bungaloid Hungry Horse outlet called, dubiously, The Highwayman. This site was once Jack's Hill truckstop, with cafe, fuel pumps, garage and truck park. Round the back is an old building that held drivers' accommodation in the days before cabs had beds in them.

The Great North Road straightens its spine for a stretch on the course of a Roman road before being forced to perform a little loop where it meets the A505, getting dragged to a roundabout over the motorway, but allowed to loop right round, and back onto the B197 for the gentle descent into Baldock.

On the outskirts comes a very grand Art Deco Tesco. Of course, it wasn't always a Tesco. It was built in 1924, inspired by Howard Carter's explorations of Egypt. It is made of crushed orange brick mixed into concrete, and is 150 yards long.

From 1928, the building was home to the Full Fashion Hosiery Company, later Kayser Bondor, which made stockings and underwear. The firm had a slogan that was a lot less snappy than the elastic in its knickers: 'Fashioned or seam free, don't take a risk, then you'll certainly see sales will be brisk!'

Where Tesco's car park is now, there was once an open-air swimming pool, tennis courts and gardens for the staff.

Baldock is a lovely little place: the first of a string of market towns whose centres open out into market squares characteristic of coaching stops. The wide High Street has Georgian houses set well back behind flower-filled gardens. The Great North Road turns sharp right when it reaches Whitehorse Street, just by the George, a former coaching inn, above which the spire of thirteenth-century St Mary's church peeks.

Whitehorse Street was once on the A505, the main route from Oxford to Cambridge, which made Baldock a very busy place. That was before the A1 was moved west, in 1967, and the A505 diverted in a loop to the south, avoiding the town.

Baldock's history as a travellers' town goes way back to the twelfth century. It was founded by the Knights Templar, a Catholic military order responsible for seeing pilgrims safely to Jerusalem. They laid it out as a market town and built the original church in 1150.

It is said that the name Baldock, which the Templars gave their town, is derived from the Old French name for Baghdad: Baldac. The story goes that, having failed to conquer Baldac – then the most prosperous market town in the world – during the Crusades, they named this town after it, as a sort of consolation prize.

Whitehorse Street is a pleasant, old-fashioned shopping street these days. It has Baldock Hardware Store, a traditional ironmongers', into which I'd walk, if I were truly into dad jokes. There, in a tribute to *The Two Ronnies*, I'd ask for four candles. I bet they get that all the time.

There is also an antique clock shop, and, from the wonderful smell that pervades the area, I deduce there must be a coffee roaster in one of the cafés. At the top of the street, the old Great North Road turns sharp left, north-bound once again as the A507, and back on the Roman route.

On the corner of this junction is the White Horse which, in a rare good review, the ByngAdvisor says has 'become a good inn'. Today it offers 'Pizza, Pots, Pints' and has an old white rocking horse chained high up on the frontage.

When Daniel Defoe passed through, in 1724, he found the state of the road here so bad that travellers had to take to the fields, which led to landowners posting guards at the gates onto their land and demanding a toll.

By 1750 that was sorted out, and it's certainly a glorious stretch of road today, rising to a crest, beyond which the flat landscape of Bedfordshire stretches ahead. Behind me, all the rivers ran south to the Thames. From now on, they run east to the Wash.

And with the change in landscape comes a change in my fortunes. So far, on the 42 miles from Smithfield, I have had to travel only 2.7 of them on the current A1. But now, my luck is about to run out. At Baldock Services, Junction 10 of the A1, and at the end of the motorway section that runs from Hatfield, there is nothing for it but to join the dual-carriage road, which was built on top of the old route in the 1950s.

From here it's eight full, flat Bedfordshire miles to Biggleswade. So I switch my brain to cruise control, and tell it to wake me up when we get there.

8. Biggles Flies North

– Biggleswade to Alconbury –

The name Biggles, given by Captain W. E. Johns to his World War I flying ace, ought by rights to be short for Biggleswade. In fact it's not, it's short for Bigglesworth.

No matter, I still think he ought to have been named after this town. It's just the sort of bristling-moustache, retired-colonel sort of place that he would have settled down in, in his twilight years.

If Biggles flew over Biggleswade today in hot pursuit of the White Fokker he would first see the looming infinity boxes of the distribution hubs clustered at its southern fringe. These are cropping up all over the place, painted in gradations from pale blue rising to pale grey, and on a dull day they disappear into the sky.

Biggleswade was bypassed in the Sixties, the A1 now sloping off to the west, but I take the old road, running straight on as the A6001, all the way to Biggleswade's Market Square.

This used to be an open expanse, now the road is corralled through it and the rest is given over to parking, and bus stops, but there is still a market here, every Saturday and Tuesday, as there has been since 1227.

It's a pleasant, bustling spot, still clearly the heart of the town, and lined with shops that could still supply Biggles with gentlemanly staples. But my favourite is the much more on-trend Seasons Kitchen, within the green-glazed tile walls of which are piled all manner of fruit and veg, with bottles and preserves tumbling out of wooden crates. They are advertising Greek and curry nights, plus classes in vegan Middle Eastern cookery and invite me to 'join us on our plastic-free journey'. I'm on board.

Outside is a handy sign, reading: 'Shop. Cook. Eat'. Yep, that's how I've always done it. Maybe add: 'Digest. Evacuate. Repeat', just for completeness.

At opposite ends of the market place are two surviving coaching inns, The White Hart to the south-east and The Crown to the north-west.

The Crown is now a Wetherspoons, and handsomely turned out. To one side is an old shop where, behind the elderly bicycle in the window, are ranks of barrels snoozing in hammocks. It also sports a plaque commemorating The Great Fire of Biggleswade which, I read 'started in the Crown Inn yard on 16 June 1785 destroying half the town.'

I think they need to add a line: 'Sorry about that.'

On the western edge of Market Place is a curious monolith of a building, the great Doric columns along its facade making it look like a Masonic Temple. It's unused, but has the faint outline of the name of its last occupant, Pizza Express, on the peeling white gloss it has been coated with.

It's had various uses since it was plonked here in 1844: courthouse, council offices, dancehall. In 1927, a Mr J Rowe tried to exploit the motoring age on the Great North Road by turning it into a vast garage with seven petrol pumps. That didn't work, and today it again looks like a very big, and very white, elephant.

John Byng's favourite hostelry was the Sun Inn, which stood at No. 13 Sun Street, and is now disguised as a row of five whitewashed houses. The ByngAdvisor always gave it five stars: a substantial place with 24 bedrooms, maintaining 44 horses. It closed in 1836.

Byng was on home territory in Biggleswade, and you wonder why he bothered travelling at all when you hear how great this inn was after a long day on the Great North Road. He writes:

> One grows melancholy in an evening; and I was glad to come into the old shop, The Sun, there to find my cloak-bag, to drink some good tea, to pull off my boots and refresh... Poney [as he spells it] ate heartily his corn, and so did his rider of a nicely-roasted chicken, and plenty of custards, and green currant tart.

After dinner he takes a walk to the church, and I follow in his footsteps. St Andrew's is in Shortmead Street, where the Great

North Road turned right at the end of the High Street to head north once more. In 1200 a miracle occurred at this church, involving a post-mortem traveller on the Great North Road. Hugh, Bishop of Lincoln, who had a palace up the road in Buckden, had died in London, and his body rested here on its way, via home, to burial at Lincoln Cathedral.

The devout filed through to pay their respects, among them a woman with a broken arm who touched the body and was immediately healed, a miracle that helped win Hugh canonisation 20 years later.

John Byng's ancestral home – or, rather, the ancestral home he was robbed of – is four miles away in the village of Southill. Given his moans back at Barnet about being too poor to get decent treatment at the Red Lion, it is a surprise to find he came from an aristocratic family, but it is so: the ByngAdvisor was the younger son of the 3rd Viscount Torrington.

So how come he wasn't rich? Why didn't he have a country estate?

That was just typical of Byng's lousy luck. He did inherit the title, becoming the 5th Viscount in 1812, upon the death of his elder brother George. But George had squandered the family fortune and been forced to sell the ancestral home, Southill Park.

So there was nothing left for John to inherit.

To cap it all, the ByngAdvisor died the following year, before he had a chance to take his seat in the Lords. The house was bought by the brewer Samuel Whitbread, and is still in the family.

I decide to take a look at Byng's estate in Southill so, instead of re-joining the A1 as I leave Biggleswade, I go straight over it. Swapping the A6001 for the B658, I roll over a flat, soggy Bedfordshire landscape through which the roads run on embankments. Southill is a quiet village, built to serve the gentry at Southill Park. That Georgian house is insulated within its blanket of parkland, landscaped by Capability Brown, and I can't get much of a look at it. But the village church is accessible, and holds a fascinating memorial to the Byng family.

It is across from a watery grove where a specialist nursery grows full-size trees in great tubs stuck in the ground.

I've read about the Byng family vault and am ready for something grand, but not this. Walking round the foot of the fourteenth-century church of All Saints, I come to a great brick annex, which was built up against the north side of the chancel in 1733.

There is a high, arched double-doorway, presumably to admit coffins, which is locked. However, at shoulder height on the side wall is cut a curious hole, like a four-leaf clover. It's only a hand's width across, but is nevertheless protected by three iron bands.

It is pitch black inside the vault, but I poke my phone through and fire off some camera shots, then flick through them to see what I can make out. I see ghostly pale-yellow walls, a ladder up to a platform, and – only just emerging from the gloom – a memorial plaque.

This is the ByngAdvisor's final resting place. Among the other Byngs interred here was one you might call the Bad Byng. He was Admiral John Byng, fourth son of the 1st Viscount Torrington, who was controversially executed by firing squad. His crime sounds arcane to modern ears but, in 1757, during the Battle of Minorca against the French, he failed to relieve the British garrison on the island. He had set sail with a hastily gathered bunch of unseaworthy ships and, after a skirmish with the enemy, returned to Gibraltar to get the vessels repaired. He was found guilty of failing to 'do his utmost' to relieve the garrison.

But the plaque tells a different story. It is hard to make out but, once I check records later, I find it reads:

'To the perpetual disgrace
of public justice,
the Hon John Byng Esq,
admiral of the [?] Rue
fell a martyr to
political persecution
March 14th in the year 1757 when
bravery and loyalty
were insufficient securities
for the
life and honour
of a
naval officer'

They obviously still share that feeling in the village. In 2007, on the 250th anniversary of the execution, an event was held to honour their local hero, at which an Admiral Byng real ale was brewed.

It is time to get back to the A1, and I join a dual carriageway superimposed on the die-straight Roman road, following it up the valley of the Ivel, just to the west of river and railway.

I am passing across a great plain, on the very edge of the Fens. I'm tempted to describe the road as featureless but, if I do, I'll clash with the ByngAdvisor, who thought it the finest bit of road in the land.

On one occasion he got into a row with some lady travellers about the standard of this road and the merits of his favourite Sun Inn in Biggleswade. They, he asserted, were not fit to judge because, while 'I travel about, slowly, on horseback, for observation; ladies, commonly, rapidly in a post chaise – and are not supposed to observe.' These ladies tell him the Sun is wretched and filthy, which gets his gander up. To him it is 'one of the cheapest, quietest inns I know.' Then they criticise his favourite stretch of the Great North Road as being 'Horrid! Oh horrid! to the extreme.' Byng stoutly defends the way from Biggleswade to Buckden, and his detailed description of the route in the 1780s gives me a useful comparison with what I see today.

For Byng, 'as a road of fine gravel it is unequalled... you pass the old bridge over the River Ivel, with a pleasing view of the river, and its frequent navigation. A mile of flat road, thro' enclosures, with a distant view of Warden, and Northill churches to the left, and of the Sandy Hills to the right, leads into Lower Caldecote hamlet; hence a twining road of another mile to above Beaston hamlet, where you have a charming look of Sandy church and village.'

He has a point when he talks about needing to travel slowly, and observe, in order to appreciate the Great North Road and the countryside it passes through. He, trotting along on his 'poney', is better placed than me in my car, but on my frequent stops, and in my diversion to Southill, I can compare the landscape he saw to the one I pass through. And it is different. I see a great ocean-wide mono-crop of cabbages, fine in their way, but Byng saw much greater variety: 'Every field is cropp'd by peas, carrots, parsnips, French beans, cucumbers... [in] very open fields; and you cannot prevent your horse from smashing the cucumbers.'

That sounds a little careless, given that the cucumbers won't actually have been growing on the 'road of fine gravel'.

The Great North Road never went into Sandy, but ran half a mile from its western flank, through the hamlet of Girtford. There is still a stretch of the old road here, dropping down to turn east and cross the Ivel at Girtford Bridge, but take it now to follow the old route and you end up at a dead end, so I press on.

At Tempsford, the old road ran through the village as Church Street, passing the Wheatsheaf inn and the church. A loop of it survives.

In the 1970s, in his *The Great North Road*, Norman Webster

said of Tempsford that it 'remains a haven of peace and tranquillity. Of old cottages, timbered houses and an old inn, The Wheatsheaf, facing the church; a beautiful church whose ornate tower and nave are of mellowed stone, with an even more impressive interior than its outer aspect suggests... In this village the more ancient features survive.'

Happily, that description holds today, despite the thunder of passing traffic. Just before the loop of old road leads back onto the A1, there is the wooded glade of Tempsford Millennium Garden Sanctuary, created on a strip of land compulsorily purchased when the A1 was driven through to the east of the village, but later found surplus to requirements. It's an unexpected woodland oasis.

I could re-join the A1 here, but I don't. As I want to get off the modern road wherever there is a viable alternative, I take an option favoured by Tom 'Flashheart' Hennesy of the Stamford Regent, among others.

While many travellers – including Byng and Dickens – went on along the route the modern road follows, I have a cunning plan. It is to retrace my steps back down Church Street and turn left over the A1, then left again to travel through open country via St Neots to Little Paxton where, five miles on, this route re-joins the main one.

This alternative way is a great road. Despite not warranting even a B classification, it is a well-engineered single carriageway snaking over gentle rises and falls. It's far finer than the A1, which swerves west just after Tempsford to cross the River Great Ouse before meeting the A421 Bedford bypass at the Black Cat roundabout and grinding north.

However, there was a risk for Flashheart in taking this alternative. The Great Ouse flows just to the west, and regularly flooded its banks, putting the flat farmland under several feet of water for half a mile or more, breaking up the road surface and turning it treacherous. This happened far less often on the main road, but Flashheart relished the challenge of navigating this more dangerous route.

On one occasion the waters set his coach afloat, and flooded into it, terrifying the elderly lady passengers. The men who took the outside seats were little safer, and were drenched by torrential rain. As one passenger recorded: 'The only difference between us and the old ladies was that whilst they got it from below we got it from above'.

My road becomes the B1043, Barford Road, as it reaches St Neots and runs on to the market square. The first travellers to come here were pilgrims. This, another bustling market town, is named after the Cornish monk St Neot, whose remains were brought to the priory church from Bodmin, in 980. I sail on through, the road becoming the B1041 out of town and, at Little Paxton, re-join the modern A1, but it's only four miles before I can leave it again, at Buckden.

Buckden is one of the absolute highlights of the old road. The ByngAdvisor gives it his seal of approval with 'I consign you to the good inn, The George'. The George, with its three-storey slab of red-brick Georgian frontage, stands on the west of the High Street, facing off with its once-deadly rival, the more homely, whitewashed Lion, of 1492 vintage.

Now, smart ladies' clothes shops have joined the face off: Anne Furbank has three elegant widows under the George, while Eloise's lingerie, swimwear and nightwear fixes its eye on potential customers from next door to the Lion. Its gin and gowns versus pints and pants.

Uncle Charlie liked this spot too, describing: 'an easy descent into narrow-streeted Buckden, one of those old 'thoroughfare' coaching villages which imagined themselves on the way to becoming towns in the fine, free-handed old days.'

He goes on:

The huge bulk of the George is eloquent of this, with its 15 windows in a row, and the signs still noticeable in the brickwork, showing where the house was doubled in size at the period of its greatest prosperity. Nowadays the George is all too large for its trade, and a portion of it is converted into shops. As for the interminable rooms and passages above, they echo hollow to the infrequent footfall, where they were once informed with a cheerful bustle and continuous arrival and departure. There was a period, a few years ago, when the North Road Club's road-racing events brought crowds of cyclists and busy times once more to the George, but they are irretrievably gone.

In coaching days the landlord of the George, the inn's namesake George Cartwright, doubled up as a coachman, driving the York Express daily between Buckden and Welwyn, which no doubt improved the chances of passengers on that coach choosing the George over the Lion. Both seem to be holding their own today.

Buckden once hosted a string of kings and queens, but not at the inns. They stayed further up the High Street, at a place enclosed behind a high, crenellated brick wall. This was the Palace of the Bishop of Lincoln from 1186 to 1842.

It's a red-brick Tudor place, now called Buckden Towers, and sheltered beneath two towering firs. I walk over a dry moat and pass beneath the Great Tower into the courtyard. On the wall is a plaque recording famous visitors, which include: Henry III in 1248, Edward I in 1291, Catherine of Aragon (1533-34), Henry VIII (1541) and Catherine Howard in the same year. After them come James I, Samuel Pepys – who I shall re-encounter at my next stop – and the Prince Regent, later George IV.

Today the Towers is a retreat centre named after my kind of saint: St Claret. The Claretians, a missionary order, took possession in 1957, restoring the palace and building the modern chapel that doubles as the Catholic parish church.

It is dedicated to St Hugh of Lincoln, he of the miracle at Biggleswade. There is a statue of the saint in the courtyard, with a plaque that records he was 'Bishop of Lincoln and Lord of Buckden Palace 1186-1200'. He is portrayed with a swan, a reference to the story that he had a pet swan that followed him everywhere, and would attack anyone who approached him.

I find this a remarkable place to stumble upon just off the A1 and when, on my way back to the car, I pop next door to the church of St Mary (Anglican since the Reformation), I find another treasure house.

The church's deep porch was the village schoolroom from around 1600, and the initials that the children scratched into stone and wood can still be seen.

'PULL TURN PUSH' are the hand-painted instructions above the handle of the 570-year-old oak door into the church, and I do. Inside, another ancient door leads up to a room above the porch, known as a Parvis Chamber, which once housed the Bishop of Lincoln's precious medieval library. I look up to see an Angel orchestra. Six carved figures dating from the late 1430s, their wings outstretched, line the roof of the chancel.

There is one last place I want to stop before Alconbury, but before I get to it, I ought to let the ByngAdvisor sing the praises of the stretch of road from Biggleswade:

> From Biggleswade Sun, I have conducted you by a vehicle of truth, to the Buckden George... [along] a road of unusual populousness, fertility, and pleasing views. Ten villages, or hamlets, are pass'd thro' in 16 miles... and at every mile a good public house may be entered in case of storms, or hunger.

He can't resist one final dig at the unappreciative ladies who, he points out, were Scottish. He asks: 'Now what can be compared to this in Scotland?'

Well, I shall see when I get there. But, for now, I have to retrace my steps to the southern end of Buckden and the roundabout that will let me back on to the A1. In a mile I can leave it again on the B1514 for Brampton, and Pepys House.

Just before that house is a very superior milestone in the form of an etiolated pyramid topped with a sphere. It stands on a triangle of green at what was a crossroads, now a roundabout. On one face a hand, styled like those pointing-finger painted signs you used to get in public libraries, indicates over my shoulder to London, the way I have come. The next, as I walk around it, points south to Huntingdon. The third points north.

Pepys House originally belonged to Samuel's uncle Robert, but Pepys spent much of his schooldays here. It's a fine old timber-framed Fenland farmhouse set in a meadow, which Pepys lauded as 'the largest and most flowery spot the sun ever beheld'.

He inherited the residence when his uncle died, and had his parents and sister, Paulina, live here. He visited Brampton regularly all his life, refers to it frequently in his diaries, and obviously saw it as a safe haven.

When, in October 1666, it was feared the Dutch would overrun London, he sent his father and wife here with his treasure. Dad had a girdle round his waist containing £1,300 worth of gold coins and paper money (£312,000 today according to the Bank of England's inflation calculator), with instructions to bury it in the garden. When Pepys came to retrieve it, there was a problem. Dad couldn't remember where it was buried. I bet Pepys was in no mood for dad jokes as he rooted around for it in the dark. Eventually he came across it, but was furious: it has been buried no more than six inches down, in full view of passers-by and their neighbours' windows. The gold was loose and the notes disintegrating. Not only that, several hundred gold coins were missing.

Pepys took his father into the garden again to try to find them but, dad being deaf, he realised his yelling about the gold at the top of his voice might lead his neighbours to pile on in for their share. Eventually the missing coins were found, and Pepys packed them into a basket which he took back to London on a coach, clutching his hoard nervously on his lap.

I follow him back through Brampton until, where he went south on the Great North Road, I turn north on the A1 for the steep climb to Alconbury.

But before I can turn off for that village, I must endure the busiest stretch of new road so far. The A14 swings in from the east, then runs alongside the A1 before sailing overhead and peeling off to the west. Then the A141 joins from the east. Phalanxes of trucks are zooming overhead and flying in from all sides. It's all fresh concrete walls, flyovers, and embankments covered in thousands of little plastic tubes from which a forest will sprout.

It's a relief to turn off for Alconbury, where Great North Road and Old North Road have always met. At Alconbury Hill, the end of this stage, I have covered 84 miles, but only 19 of them have been on the modern A1 or A1(M). Which is a mere 23 per cent. OK, I took a couple of short diversions, but even discounting them, that's still less than 25 per cent on the new road, 75 per cent on the real Great North Road.

II

OLD NORTH ROAD
Lombard Street
to Alconbury

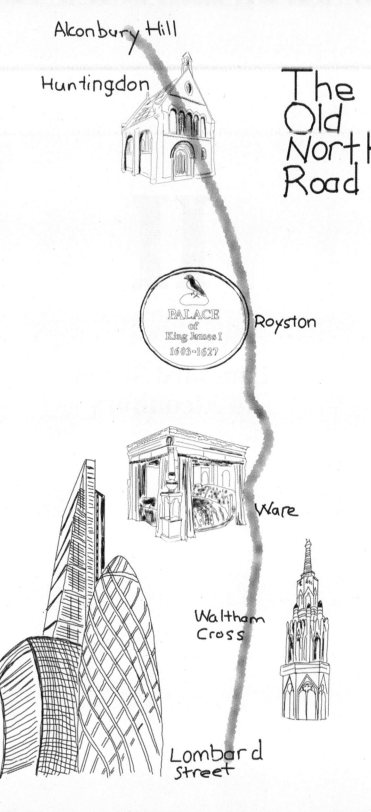

Alconbury Hill

Huntingdon

The
Old
North
Road

PALACE
of
King James I
1603-1627

Royston

Ware

Waltham
Cross

Lombard
Street

So that was one way to Alconbury. The Old North Road offers another. I'm not sure what to expect. How different can it be? Will the original route, as with the real Great North Road versus the A1, bear little relation to the new roads? Will there be bypasses I can avoid by sticking to the historic route, or is it A10 and other unrelenting modern roads most of the way?

I know this was a fine route a century or more ago, when Uncle Charlie championed the Old over the Great. He said that while 'the Great North Road has been forcibly modernised, haphazardly in the past, drastically in recent years,' the Old North Road is 'still the mail coach road, lined with deep green edges and long avenues of old trees. Crest after crest is breasted and still fresh vistas lie ahead. Less worried by traffic it gains on all counts, a startling reminder of what the Great North Road used to be.'

One thing is immediately clear when I start looking at maps: the route follows a remarkably Roman-like straight course out through the City of London and its northern suburbs. In contrast to the Great North Road, which weaves its way north, the Old North Road forges on. The A10 barely diverges from a straight line for the six miles to Tottenham, where it becomes the A1010. There's a little moderate wiggling on the way to Ware, but then come three long straight sections, with a slight shift in trajectory between each one, from there to Royston. And, after that, its straight as an arrow all the way to Huntingdon

Will the drive be boring? Only one way to find out.

71

9. The Carbuncle Kids, and the Palace of Football
– Lombard Street to Waltham Cross –

As I walk east up Lombard Street a great looming presence peers down at me over the buildings to my right. It's the Walkie Talkie, and it's as out of place here as the giant Pilsbury Dough Boy who stomps across the city in *Ghostbusters*. How could developers be allowed to do this to London?

At the end of Lombard Street I pass onto Roman Ermine Street: the Old North Road, and am able to turn my back on this steel and glass Mr Blobby. Today, of course, while it still bears the comfortingly historic name of Gracechurch Street, this has become an ultra-modern city canyon: a north-bound crevasse threading its deep-cut way through the towering concrete cliffs that line the Roman road, now the A10.

There are a couple of name-checks to the past: Belle Inn Yard marks an old coaching inn, Wetherspoons' Crosse Keys takes its name from another, but it is when I turn off Gracechurch Street into Great St Helens that I find a church which has been serving this ancient way since the fourteenth century.

This church had a very distinguished parishioner, someone who travelled frequently up the Old North Road, at least for a few miles, to the theatres in Shoreditch. He was William Shakespeare, and he lived in a house overlooking this churchyard. This is one of the few churches to survive both the Great Fire of 1666 and the Blitz.

Here again, a giant embarrassment is peering down at me. This is the Gherkin, a great green-glass dildo of a building that, for decency's sake, ought to be hidden in a giant underwear drawer. What a shame that bloke Cristo, the artist who specialised in wrapping buildings, is no longer with us. I avert my eyes, and regain my route. Only to be confronted by two more monsters: the Cheesegrater and one so ugly, so big, so new that it doesn't have a nickname yet. It's 8 Bishopsgate, and I decide to name it The Cigarette Lighter. It looks like one of those shiny cylindrical jobbies from the Seventies, the sort airline pilots used in fag ads to light their Rothmans. Even the smaller buildings around here are pug ugly. There's one in Houndsditch that looks like a tin of ham.

But things change quite suddenly once I'm past Liverpool Street Station. The towering city suddenly runs out of thrust. Just before that is another reminder of the old road: St Botolph's church. Appropriately enough for me, St Botolph is a patron saint of travellers.

When Botolph – who established a monastery at Boston (Botolph's Town) in East Anglia in the seventh century – died, his remains were taken to Westminster Abbey, processing through four city gateways on their way: Billingsgate, Aldgate, Bishopsgate and Aldersgate. A church dedicated to him was built alongside each of these, and the last three survive.

It's dark and sombre inside. I sit for a moment, the reverberations from the rumbling traffic sending tremors up through the pew and into my hands. Meaning it's easier to commune with the Old North Road than with God.

As I leave I look back down what is now Bishopsgate at a dense forest of towers, standing in a gang like the carbuncle kids, hoping one day to grow up to be Dubai. I mean, by all means build Dubai in Dubai, but leave us our London. Too late.

Just past the station is a modish residential block, Principal Place 'where the city meets Shoreditch'. Looking back I don't think it's too fanciful to wonder if these towers aren't the anachronism, rather than the fragments of the past I have been seeking out. Given the way the post-Covid world is shaping up, will we really need all these offices?

The landscape does change from here. The tide of the city runs out fast. Old, low London takes over, but it's being pushed back here too.

Old North Road

At Folgate Street, another block has been partially flattened, and concrete is rising. A skip swings in mid-air, an old street sign has been nailed up high on the hoardings around the site. I know this part of the Old North Road from a Madness album: *The Liberty of Norton Folgate*.

Norton Fogate was the nine acres which the canons of St Paul's owned at Bishopsgate, and which was consequently a 'liberty', outside the jurisdiction of the City of London.

The title song's lyrics are about local characters such as 'Old Jack Norris the Musical Shrimp', a semi-vagrant who scratched a living selling shrimps on the street, and sang about his wares, and other 'old fellows, pickpockets, dandies, extortioners and night wanderers,' in their second-hand coats, threads and patches, who are part of the 'dark river of people'. The song echoes to the cries of stallholders and the calls of the music hall, it takes in the past and the present.

Now sadly defunct music magazine *The Word* described it as 'Peter Ackroyd writing for The Kinks, it's Sherlock Holmes in Albert Square, it's a Mike Leigh movie of *Parklife*, its *Passport To Pimlico* meets Brick Lane, and it is Madness's masterpiece.'

It brings this bit of vanishing Old North Road to life.

On the corner of Norton Street and Blossom Street another character is remembered in the name of a pub that is tucked, for now, behind the builders' hoarding. It is the Waterman Poet, and is named after John Taylor, the seventeenth-century Thames ferry-man who was also a pamphleteer, poet, and writer of satirical ballads. He was befriended by characters such as John Aubrey, diarist and man-about-town, and the playwright Thomas Dekker. Taylor went on epic walks around the country, sponsored by rich men who liked to patronise the arts, setting off up the Old North Road. So he's a fellow traveller.

It appears the pub, along with some of the other old buildings behind the hoarding, are going to be incorporated in the new development.

I walk around the block, down Folgate Street into Elder Street, where the old flat-front buildings have survived on the right, away from the development, but on the left the warehouses and little factories are currently roofless, windows gaping to the sky, winches that once hauled goods up to the first and second floors now folded back against the buildings.

Another local character was Shakespeare's contemporary, Christopher Marlowe, author of *Edward II*, *Doctor Faustus*, *The Jew of Malta* and *The Massacre of Paris*. We know from a warrant issued for Marlowe's arrest in September 1589 that he lived in Norton Folgate, in lodgings shared with a fellow playwright, Thomas Kyd, author of *The Spanish Tragedy*. Nearby lived another friend, Thomas Watson. Marlow and Watson were arrested and jailed, pending trial, on suspicion of murder.

The court records show that, in a street then called Hogg Lane, now Worship Street, which runs west off the Old North Road just past Folgate Street, Marlowe was attacked by William Bradley, son of an innkeeper, over an unpaid debt. Watson drew his sword to protect Marlowe, and Bradley was run through and killed. The pair fled but were tracked down, arrested and remanded in Newgate Gaol for a fortnight. When their case came to trial on 3 December, the claim that Watson acted in self-defence was accepted, and the pair were bound over to keep the peace.

I walk a block up Worship Street, where high rises give way to an eighteenth-century streetscape and turn into Curtain Road. Here stood one of London's first two theatres, The Curtain. Marlowe's plays were probably performed here, Shakespeare's certainly were. This is the place immortalised as 'this wooden O' in the prologue to *Henry V*, and where *Romeo and Juliet* got its premiere.

The theatre was long lost, but during excavations prior to building works in 2012, the well-preserved ruins of The Curtain, including two sections of the exterior wall, were uncovered, just off Curtain Road in Hewett Street. The theatre will be preserved, as a residential block called The Stage rises above it. Yep, all the world's a loft-style apartment in modern Shoreditch.

The next turning off Curtain Street is Holywell Lane, the scene of another of Marlowe's crimes. In 1592 he was summonsed for assaulting two constables here. They told the court they went in fear of their lives because of Marlowe. He was fined £20 and again ordered to keep the peace. He died, in 1593, aged just 29, stabbed to death in a fight.

Another couple of hundred yards up Curtain Road is New Inn Yard, where London's first purpose-built theatre stood. This, named simply The Theatre, was taken lock, stock and dressing-up box to become the Globe at Bankside in 1596. This site is also now home to a desirable residential development, protected within a gated courtyard. Around the corner in New Inn Broadway a surviving warehouse building is adorned with a frieze of flowers. A painted Juliet peers down from the gable wall, together with this quote from *Romeo and Juliet*:

My bounty is as boundless as the sea,
My love as deep; the more I give to thee,
The more I have, for both are infinite.

Next door is a new building called The Box Office, which will have a performance space alongside offices.

Madness's lyrics also mention Arnold Circus, a little way on up the Old North Road, which is now Shoreditch High Street, and a place that has entered my dreams more than once. I can't tell you why, but it draws me back. I'm embarrassed to admit this, but I feel like I knew it in a past life. It haunts me, for reasons I can't explain.

It's certainly a place with a history. This was once a terrible spot, a notorious slum called Old Nichol. In 1863 the *London Illustrated News* wrote that life here was 'one painful and monotonous round of vice, filth and poverty, huddled in dark cellars, ruined garrets, bare and blackened rooms, reeking with disease and death.'

It was cleared in the 1890s, to be replaced by the Boundary Estate, the first council estate. The bricks from the old slums were piled into a mount at the centre of the site, covered with earth in a sort of burial mound, and named Arnold Circus after the then-leader of the London County Council. From this point, seven roads radiate out, lined with twenty arts and crafts-influenced blocks of flats, five storeys high, in red brick with decorative pink bands.

I walk down Calvert Avenue, where the little shops have become gentrified along with the rest of Shoreditch. The building bearing the sign Boundary Estate Community Laundry is now a radical bookshop. Across the street, Leila's sells tea in expensive-looking yellow tins, and boxed Madeira cake imported from yer actual Madeira. I climb up the burial mound and sit in the band-stand at the top.

This has always seemed a strange place to me. An eerie place. I have a recurring dream about it. I get the sense that if there were tears in the space-time continuum, there would be one here.

Time to move on through Shoreditch. Above the shops are old signs for an iron works, the buildings now vegan pizzerias, the Hackney Brewery and the Love Vinyl record shop. The street has closed in, it's narrow and cloistered. A steel railway bridge runs low and wide at an angle over the road. Then, suddenly everything folds back, and it's an altogether airier walk past the Ironmonger's alms houses, now the Museum of the Home, and Shoreditch Church, St Leonard's.

A peeling sign announces Revd P. Turp 36 Hoxton Square. He inspired the TV series *Rev* but, I learn, retired in 2018. There are many memorials to Elizabethan actors in the church, and I'd love to go in, but it's firmly padlocked.

I walk over the Regents Canal – once fetid and rank, now virtually Perrier-sparkling and hemmed with loft-living – then

tack one block east off the Old North Road to Stean Street. At
No. 68 the Kray twins, Ronnie and Reggie, were born in 1933,
and lived for their first five years. Their house was bulldozed
along with the rest of the street during slum clearance. There are
mainly low yellow-brick block houses to my right, but on the
left the railway runs on a viaduct, the arches beneath housing
car repair shops. There was a stable opposite their house when
the Krays lived here.

Up to now, walking was the right pace at which to see
things, now I take a bus, the 149, sitting in the finest seat in the
house: front row on top. Up what is now the Kingsland Road
through Stoke Newington, on up Stamford Hill, where fine
houses were built for rich city merchants in the nineteenth
century, then coasting down towards Seven Sisters.

The road widens substantially for the final approach, and
feels like it was once a great highway. You can see why first the
coachmen, and after them the motorists, liked it, compared to
the pinched Great North Road route up to Barnet. On my right
the narrow strip of grass is what's left of Page Green where, in
the eighteenth century, seven elms were planted in a circle
around a walnut, giving this the name Seven Sisters.

I get off by Seven Sisters station, where one half-hearted
tower block juts above the sea of low-rise. It's called Apex
House, which is a misnomer as it doesn't have a clear apex at
all, rather the tower is divided into quarters, each of which rises
to a different height, as if four competing teams of builders just
stopped when they felt like it.

Here, what is now Tottenham High Road is lined with squat
terraces and grubby parades of generally care-warn shops, with
the occasional green shoot: an ethnic bakery or greengrocery
planted by hopeful immigrants from one of the many
communities to have taken root here: Caribbean, Ghanaian,
Albanian, Greek, Turkish, Cypriot, Somalian, Portugese, Polish,
Vietnamese, Filipino and Zimbabwean.

The original village centre is at Tottenham Green. Here, the Old Well, which supplied the then-small community until 1893, stands to one side of the Old North Road, with the High Cross Monument on the other. This was a wayside medieval cross rebuilt in brick in 1600 and renovated again in 1809.

Opposite the police station is a grand old building, now with buddleia sprouting from it. Built as the Tottenham Palace Theatre, it switched from variety to film, to bingo and then worship, when it was given the unlikely name Tottenham Palace Cathedral. Historic England describes its present condition as 'very bad' with rainwater causing significant damage to structure and interior plaster of the Grecian-style auditorium, and 'no solution agreed' with the congregation.

Just past Bruce Grove overground station the A10 peels off west and Ermine Street, the Old North Road, forges ahead as the A1010. This is a significant point: a parting of the ways. Through traffic is funnelled west to the start of a modern, dual carriageway A10 which bears no relation to the Old North Road. New and old routes won't come together again until Puckeridge, 28 miles from my start.

Just past this point is a palace of football.

Tottenham Hotspur's massive new stadium is like nothing on earth. Or, at least, like nothing on earth in this generally ground-down swathe of working-class suburban London. It's like a vast alien space craft has landed, all arcs and curves in glass and steel and grey cladding: designed to inspire awe and wonder. I've heard it described as a beacon of hope; a catalyst for further regeneration in the area. Which would be good.

Just up the Old North Road from the stadium in Edmonton, the road now called Fore Street, is a cavernous pub called Gilpin's Bell, packed with Tottenham fans on match days, which plunges me back to reality and into the history of the old road.

In 1782 William Cowper wrote a poem that told the comic tale of a hapless Cheapside draper in the City called John Gilpin, whose wife decided that they should celebrate their twentieth wedding anniversary at the Bell – which actually stood across the road from the present pub of that name in Fore Street. She goes on ahead in a carriage, John to follow with the wine on a borrowed horse. Unfortunately, the horse proves very wayward and refuses to stop when Gilpin reaches the inn. I'll let Cowper take up the story:

> 'Stop, stop, John Gilpin! Here's the house!'
> They all at once did cry;
> 'The dinner waits, and we are tired';
> Said Gilpin: 'So am I!'
>
> But yet his horse was not a whit
> Inclined to tarry there;
> For why? His owner had a house
> Full 10 miles off, at Ware.

Gilpin eventually manages to turn the horse round but, once again, it fails to stop at the Bell, and his bemused wife can only look on as it takes him right back to Cheapside.

Cowper, who had never been to Edmonton, was told the tale – which may be based on the real-life antics of a Mr Beyer, a linen draper of Paternoster Row – and thought it had potential.

He was right. The average Tottenham fan in the Bell today might not have heard of it, but Cowper's *The Diverting History of John Gilpin* was hugely popular in Georgian England and put Edmonton, and the Bell, on the map. The poem is commemorated in a curious 8ft tall sculpture called the Stone Bell, carved with scenes from the ride, and placed on the pavement outside Fore Street Library in 1996.

After Edmunton, I'm back on the bus to Waltham Cross which, in coaching days, would be where the first change of horses took place. I'll change horses there too, from bus to car.

10. I'll Take the High Road
– Waltham Cross to Huntingdon –

Just after it passes over the M25, the A1010 loops off to the east, skirting Waltham Cross as Monarch's Way, but Ermine Street (aka the Old North Road) goes straight ahead, becoming pedestrian-only just after the old Embassy Cinema and a pub called The Moon and Cross.

The Moon and Cross is another Wetherspoons exercise in branding with a veneer of local history. Normally they get it bang on, but here they've gone off at a bit of a tangent. This pub sits on literary ground. The novelist Anthony Trollope, of *Chronicles of Barsetshire* fame, lived in Waltham House on this spot from 1859 to 1871, during which time he wrote the last three books in the six-volume series. The house was knocked down in 1936.

But the pub name does not refer to Trollope, rather to George Orwell, who wrote an essay in which he described his perfect pub, and called it The Moon Under Water. So that's where the Moon comes from. The Cross is, however, a reference to actual Waltham history, and gave the town, as well as the pub, half its name. A little further on I come to that cross. It sits in a sea of pink and cream concrete paving, like a dropped, inverted cornet in a pool of melted ice cream. The setting puts a bit of a dampener on its impact, but there is a powerfully romantic story attached to it.

In 1290, when Edward I's wife Eleanor of Castile died at Harby, near Lincoln, her funeral cortege took a winding route to Westminster Abbey, where she was to be buried. The king ordered commemorative crosses to be erected at each of the twelve places her body rested overnight, one being a mile from here, at Waltham Abbey. It was placed here, on the main road to

London, rather than at the abbey itself, partly because it would be seen by more travellers, and is one of only three of the crosses to have survived. I love this story of loss, devotion, and a love that transcends the grave.

Forget its modern setting, and the cross is an impressive thing: a 70ft tall hexagonal spire; a three-storey landmark for travellers on the Old North Road. On the main stage are three statues of Eleanor, each standing in a niche under a canopy. They eroded badly and were replaced with replicas in the 1950s.

Immediately north and south of the cross were two ancient coaching inns: the Four Swans and the Falcon. Both are gone, but the one to the north, the Four Swans, is remembered through the four carved swans on a beam straddling the highway: two birds facing left, two facing right, the necks of the lead birds entwined. It's a replica, created in 2007, after the original was destroyed in the 1960s, along with the inn, to make way for a shopping centre and multi-storey car park.

In the nineteenth century a sign used to hang beneath it, declaring 'Ye Olde Foure Swannes Hostelrie 1260', obviously painted by a sign writer who really liked doing e's.

To the south was the Falcon, built in 1617 actually abutting the cross. In the late nineteenth century, the inn was knocked down and rebuilt at a more respectful distance, allowing the cross to stand in isolation, the replacement inn biting the dust in 1974.

The York Mail made its first change of horses since leaving London at the Falcon. Charles Harper, old Uncle Charlie, wrote in *Stage-coach and Mail in Days of Yore* of a slick operation that took 'little more than two minutes' before they were 'off again, on the ten-mile stage to Ware, through the long narrow street of Cheshunt, past the New River at Broxbourne, and along the broad thoroughfare of Hoddesdon.'

To follow that route today is best by car and, when I return a few weeks later to pick up my journey, it's under my own steam. I drive round Monarch Way as it swings back from its diversion around town to meet the northern end of High Street at a roundabout. Here the Old North Road takes the second exit, to continue as the B176.

I drive up a more or less permanent high street through Cheshunt. For mile after mile I am never more than three doors away from a hairdresser, a nail bar or a takeaway. There are road works too. Three stop me in quick succession, but my hopes are rising. Soon the road will run free.

After Cheshunt I pick up the A1170 into Broxbourne where, just to the east of the Old North Road on the other side of Broxbourne Park, is a memorial to the man who made modern highways possible: John Loudon McAdam. It's in St Augustine's church, and describes him as 'the great improver of British roads'.

McAdam's 1816 invention, 'macadamisation', gave us decent roads for the first time since the Romans left. Actually, he was reinventing what they did: raising the carriageway above ground level, and giving it a solid foundation of large stones. This was overlaid with crushed stone bound with gravel, topped with a tar binder, and the surface given a camber, so rain ran quickly off, rather than penetrating and damaging the road.

Just before the centre of the next town, Hoddesdon, the A1170 diverts east, while the Old North Road runs straight on, as High Street, through the little market square. This is the traditional site of one of the great Hertfordshire markets. There are still stalls today, dressed in green-striped awnings, and drivers are crawling along, looking for a place to pull in as close to their chosen stall as possible. Ideally, they'd like to have their veg handed straight through the passenger-side window, so I have to wait for several of them as they crawl along, halt, back up and then squeeze their way into their chosen tight spot. It'd probably save me time if I got out and did their shopping for them.

Then, finally, a few miles after Hoddesdon, the road emerges from the suburbs. Here is the first whiff of countryside, and I am rolling along to Ware, the old road swinging left to run through town as the High Street.

What Christopher Trent wrote in his *Motorists' Companion on the Highways of England* in the 1950s is still true today: 'Ware is the first of the places along the road which really gives the impression of living on and for the country.'

Ware had a bit of a reputation for debauchery, in coaching days, among travellers on the Old North Road. It was all to do with a bed. Not just any bed: not some King, Superking or even Emperor concoction. This was the 10ft by 11ft, elaborately carved and canopied Great Bed of Ware, reputedly designed to accommodate at least four couples. By other accounts it could accommodate twenty or, indeed, 'a troop of soldiers'.

With its red and yellow striped curtains it looked like a hang-out for a sultan's harem. Many of the couples who sampled it carved their names in its stout oak pillars, and no doubt there are many more anonymous notches on its bed posts.

Between 1590 – when it was crafted by Hertfordshire joiner Jonas Fosbrooke – and 1869, the Great Bed moved up and down the High Street, bought and sold by no fewer than five coaching inns.

The earliest reference to it came in 1596, when a German playboy prince, Ludwig of Anholt-Kohten, wrote a little rhyming ditty about it: 'At Ware was a bed of dimensions so wide, four couples might cosily lie side by side, and thus without touching each other abide.' What Ludo appears to have missed, despite his razor-like Teutonic brain, is that if four couples decide to go to bed together, not touching probably isn't the goal.

The bed made Ware incredibly famous. It plays a supporting role in William Shakespeare's *Twelfth Night*, where Toby Belch, encouraging Andrew Aguecheek to dissemble in a letter, tells him to write 'as many lies as will lie in thy sheet of paper, although the sheet were big enough for the bed of Ware'.

The Jacobean playwrights Thomas Dekker and John Webster contrive, in *Northward Ho*, a happy ending in which their hero suggests 'This night let's banquet freely, come, we'll dare our wives to combat in th' great bed in Ware.'

Lord Byron, in *Don Juan*, ponders whether the joys of group sex are worth the demands it places on a person's stamina, writing the (unfortunately Islamophobic) lines:

Polygamy may well be held in dread,
Not only as a sin, but as a bore:
Most wise men, with one moderate woman wed,
Will scarcely find philosophy for more;
And all (except Mahometans) forbear
To make the nuptial couch a Bed of Ware.

There's a Great Bed of Ware Heritage Trail, so I can follow its progress up and down the High Street.

None of these locations survive as inns, but plaques identify the site of the Saracen's Head, the George, the Bull, the Crown and the White Hart. This last, a modest looking, two-storey white stucco place until recently a branch of HSBC, is thought to be the original home of the bed, from 1590 to 1692.

By some accounts, the bed was commissioned by the landlord here as a tourist attraction, after Henry VIII's dissolution of the monasteries and ban on the veneration of saints destroyed the town's lucrative pilgrim trade.

The story is plausible. Ware was on the route from London to Norfolk, and the shrine of Our Lady of Walsingham. This was the most important pilgrim destination pre-Reformation, and Ware was a key staging post on the journey there. Chaucer mentions Ware in his *Canterbury Tales*, as the town where the Cook lived, and the stretch of The Old North Road running through it was known as Walsingham Way.

All the coaching inns where the Great Bed came to reside

were originally pilgrim hostelries. As I walk up the High Street I can look into the many old entrances (or wagon ways) to inn yards on the south side, then called Water Row, that mark them out.

I drive out of Ware on the A1170, crossing the A10 but shunning it again, and climbing to sail along on a lovely stretch of quiet country road through villages that have been returned to tranquillity since the A10 bypass relieved them of traffic in 2005.

I'm beginning to see what those who champion the Old over the Great road were getting at. It's a breeze to drive today, but in coaching days the ups and downs were a challenge. Uncle Charlie wrote that: 'At Ware we change teams at the Saracen's Head, and four fine strong-limbed chestnuts are put in, to take us the rather hilly stage on to Buntingford', but there's a lovely stretch of empty road and some pleasant villages before I get there.

This is a real driver's road, dipping to pass through the twin villages of Thunderidge and Wadesmill, divided by the River Rib, then rising again for a truly exhilarating stretch that feels like motoring along the top of the world

I encounter the A10 again just before the village of Puckeridge, but cross it at a roundabout and turn left to follow the Old North Road, here called Cambridge Road, through the village.

Puckeridge is another pleasant backwater, now the A10 has relieved it of traffic, but right back to Roman times it was an important, and busy, crossroads. Here, Ermine Street met east-west Stane Street just to the north of the present village, where there was a Roman town. That cross-route has now been pushed to the south of Puckeridge, as the A120.

The village coaching inn, the Crown and Falcon, dates back to 1530 and survives as a friendly local. Among past guests was Samuel Pepys, and his diary entries show how tough this road could be for travellers in the seventeenth century.

On 18 September 1661 he arrived on horseback with his wife, who came a cropper around here: '...the way about Puckridge very bad, and my wife, in the very last dirty place of all, got a fall, but no hurt, though some dirt. At last, she begun, poor wretch, to be tired, and I to be angry at it, but I was to blame; for she is a very good companion as long as she is well.'

Then, on another trip on 9 October 1662: 'We got to Ware before night: and so I resolved to ride on to Puckeridge, which we did, though the way was bad, and the evening dark before we got thither.' He needed the help of other travellers to find his way to the inn. Next morning, he is in a bad way: 'my feet so swelled with yesterday's pain, that I could not get on my boots, which vexed me to the blood, but was forced to pay 4s. for a pair of old shoes of my landlord's and so ride in [his] shoes to Cambridge.' If only he'd had *TripAdvisor* to vent on.

After Puckeridge, new meets old and the A10 runs north, now faithfully following the line of Ermine Street and the Old North Road, except for loops around villages such as Buntingford, where Pepys had another bad experience, at the George and Dragon.

In his diary for 14 September 1663, he writes: '...to Buntingford, where my wife, by drinking some cold beer, being hot herself, presently after 'lighting, begins to be sick, and became so pale, and I alone with her in a great chamber there, that I thought she would have died, and so in great horror, and having a great trial of my true love and passion for her, called the maids and mistress of the house, and so with some strong water, and after a little vomit, she came to be pretty well again; and so to bed.'

Pepys seemed to get over his distress pretty swiftly though, because the entry goes on: 'I having put her to bed with great content, I called in my company, and supped in the chamber by her, and being very merry in talk, supped and then parted, and I to bed and lay very well.'

Old North Road

Today Buntingford is a fashionable little commuter town, blending the new – shops on its high street include Replenish and Reuse, and the Cheese Plate – and the old: several inns, among them the seventeenth century Black Bull.

But not all of the once-numerous inns survive. If Mrs Pepys got sick in The George and Dragon today she'd risk throwing up over an estate agent: it's a branch of Hunters. Across the road in the former Angel Inn they pull teeth rather than pints, this being a dentist's but, in a panel of terracotta tiles just above the entrance you can just make out: 'THE ANGEL INN'.

The Angel is rather quaint – a bit like a Victorian station-master's house, with dainty pale-cream brick, and orange and black arches around windows and door – but it has a much older, fifteenth century heart. There is a little pitched-roofed clock tower above the coach-yard entry, from which the blue face of a rare, sixteenth century, one-handed clock looks out. There is a little door above it, which looks as if it ought to open on the hour so a man carrying a bell can trundle out and ring the chimes.

At the north end of the village, Ermine Street rejoins the A10 once again, for another fine die-straight stretch past prairie-like fields over high, undulating ground. There are a couple of hamlets, a few farmyards filled with giant Tonka-toy machinery on a scale to tackle those vast fields and, at Reed, that rarest of rare on the Old North Road, a surviving transport cafe, The Silver Ball. Then comes the dip down to Royston.

The A10 swings off east just before the town centre, so I park and walk down the High Street to follow the old road between a jumble of shops from assorted centuries, and the fifteenth century Old Bull Inn.

At the bottom of the hill was another major crossroads, where Roman Ermine Street encountered the prehistoric east-west route, the Icknield Way. This point was once marked with a great stone cross, but today just the rough-hewn, red millstone grit boulder that stood at its base remains. This is the Roisa Stone (hence Royston), the square-cut mortice hole in it once taking the tenon of the long-lost cross.

A few doors beyond the crossroads, in Kneesworth Street, is Old Palace, showing a stern, stony face to the road. It has two great muscular chimney stacks, and a sign saying 'Palace of King James I 1603-1627'.

James, already King James VI of Scotland, stayed in a house on this site in 1603, while on his way down the Old North Road to be crowned James I of England. He liked what he saw and rented it as a hunting lodge for a year, before deciding to build something grander, and demolishing it and two adjacent inns to realise his ambition. The king came often to hunt, but the house was not large enough to accommodate his full court, so offered something of an escape from kingly cares.

James's successor, Charles I, was less interested in hunting, but had one enforced stay in Royston during the Civil War when, captured by the Parliamentary Army, he was briefly held prisoner here in June 1647. He would be executed two years later, after which the house fell into disrepair.

Kneesworth Street becomes Old North Road as it leaves town. My route is no longer on the A10, which has peeled off north-east for Cambridge. It's now via my old friend the A1198, which follows Ermine Street faithfully north. Coach traffic made good headway here, after the mud, floods, ups and downs encountered by Pepys further south.

In his evocation of coaching days, Uncle Charlie writes of how they 'come on to the galloping ground that brings us smartly, along a level road, to Arrington Bridge [over the here-diminutive river Cam], a pretty, retired spot, with a handsome inn and an equally handsome row of houses opposite.'

That inn, the Hardwicke Arms, is once again in a 'pretty, retired spot', the distant A10 now doing all the heavy lifting.

The pub takes its name from Earl Hardwicke, owner of

seventeenth century Wimpole Hall, which stands in parkland just to the east of the road and is now in the care of the National Trust. According to Uncle Charlie, being so close to this aristocratic pile, and hence being patronised by so many superior sorts, led the inn to be rather snooty about their coach customers.

He has this account of the frosty welcome received:

'Will you please to alight?' asks the stately landlady of the Hardwicke Arms inn and posting-house, with perhaps a little too much air of condescension towards us, as coach-passengers. We of the stage-coaches – nay, even those of the mails – occupy only a second place in the consideration of mine host and hostess of this, one of the finest inns on the road. Their position, hard by my lord of Hardwicke's grand seat of Wimpole, spoils them for mere ordinary everyday folks.

Charlie's passengers haven't eaten since lunch at Waltham Cross: 'It is now more than half-past seven o'clock, and we have had no bite nor sup since two. Therefore we alight at the landlady's bidding and hasten into the inn, to make as good a supper as possible in the twenty minutes allowed.'

Inevitably, they get ripped off: 'Half a crown each, in all conscience, for two cups of tea, and some bread and butter, cold ham and eggs! We climb up to our places, dissatisfied. Soon the quiet spot falls away behind, as our horses get into their stride.'

I'd like to see if things have changed at the Hardwicke Arms, but the place has yet to reopen after lockdown when I pass through.

At Caxton, the A1198 loops west around the village, but I drive straight on along the Old North Road. Here, the George and the Crown – both lost – did a brisk trade from the road but, after the coaching era, Caxton declined. In 1863, a traveller described it as 'a small, rambling village, which looked as if it had not shaved and washed its face, and put on a clean shirt for a shocking length of time.'

Then it's back on to the A road for what Uncle Charlie called 'that grim relic', Caxton Gibbet, on which the bodies of the executed were displayed, and which 'rises dark and forbidding against the translucent evening sky.'

This bleak stretch of road was a chilling place for coach travellers. Even after displaying the bodies of the dead ceased to be thought a reasonable part of their punishment, the gibbet was maintained.

William Cobbett, a journalist and political reformer who published *Rural Rides* in 1820, records: 'Just on the most dreary part of this most dreary scene, stands almost opportunely, Caxton Gibbet, tendering its friendly one arm to the passers-by. It has recently been fresh-painted, and written on in conspicuous characters.'

This was probably a then-modern replica designed to chill and intrigue travellers, and perhaps to advertise a pub built alongside it, called The Gibbet Inn.

Cobbett hears bad reviews of this place, and its landlord. His coachman tells him that the inn belongs to a Mr Cheer, a man whose meanness belies his name and who could never be accused of 'the sin of making people either drunkards or gluttons.'

He goes on: 'Certainly the spot, on which he has built his house, is one of the most ugly that I ever saw. Few spots have everything that you could wish to find; but this, according to my judgment, has everything that every man of ordinary taste would wish to avoid.'

The pub is gone, but a replica gibbet still stands. It is alongside a McDonalds, built here to take advantage of the junction with the east-west A248. What was it Cobbett just said about things you'd want to avoid?

There's a lot of traffic here for the first time since Royston, but it's all on the cross route. Once over the roundabout, I'm really rolling again. The road is empty, and I have that wonderful sense of discovery you get on the very best road trips. Zipping along, beating the traffic, telling myself I've found a route no-one else knows about.

At Papworth Everard, the A road loops away again, but the Great North Road passes straight through the village and then drops down to Godmanchester, which guarded a ford over the River Ouse in Roman times. On the north bank is Huntingdon. I find the river very swollen, brimming up against its banks as if about to spill over and swamp the low land, and reminding me of the perils of travel in past centuries.

11. Flashheart's Graveyard
– Huntingdon to Alconbury –

Once across the bridge from Godmanchester, the Old North Road runs up Huntingdon High Street, straight through town, to emerge at the far end as Ermine Street.

Not that I can drive up it now. These days there is a ponderous ring road that encircles the town like a flaccid balloon. So I park and take the footbridge over from Godmanchester, which runs alongside the old bridge, on which there are nicks in which pedestrians once had to cower.

William Cobbett thought this a lovely spot. He wrote:

Above and below the bridge, under which the Ouse passes, are by far the most beautiful meadows that I ever saw in my life ... Here are bowling-greens of hundreds of acres in extent, with a river winding through them, full to the brink. One of these meadows is the race-course; and so pretty a spot, so level, so smooth, so green, and of such an extent I never saw, and never expected to see... I think it would be very difficult to find a more delightful spot than this in the world. To my fancy (and every one to his taste) the prospect from this bridge far surpasses that from Richmond Hill.

There is a former mill on the Godmanchester side of the bridge, and a handsome, ivy-covered inn, the Old Bridge Hotel, on the Huntingdon one. The ivy is kept neatly trimmed, like designer stubble. The southern end of the High Street has been blocked off, and is reached by crossing that ring road.

The kernel of Huntingdon is a lovely old town. For Cobbett: 'It is one of those pretty, clean, unstenched, unconfined places that tend to lengthen life and make it happy.' 'Unstenched': I like that. I wouldn't mind being described as unstenched.

At the southern end the buildings are modest, a mix of old and new, and get grander as I get closer to the Market Place at the centre. On the way, local boys Samuel Pepys and Oliver Cromwell get a pub each, but only Cromwell is granted a museum, housed in the former grammar school where he, and Pepys, were both pupils. It's a former almshouse, and a curious old building, a little like a truncated church with, toward the road, a blocked-up doorway beneath a gable that rises to a bell tower and, to the side, a pair of filled-in, two-storey Norman arches. It's clearly been knocked about a bit.

A plaque fills me in on Cromwell, a man I'm going to encounter repeatedly as I continue north. Huntingdon was his birthplace (in 1599) and family home for his first thirty years. He became a soldier in the Parliamentary army at the outbreak of the Civil War, rose through the ranks to become a great commander, and played a key role in the trial of the king he helped depose, Charles I, in 1649.

The king dispatched, Cromwell modestly took his place, becoming Lord Protector and even installing his son as his successor. As The Who sang: 'Meet the new boss, same as the old boss.'

They give me a Cromwell trail leaflet in the museum, which guides me through town, passing the old coaching inns on the way, to the site of the church of St John the Baptist, now gone, where Cromwell and eight of his children were baptised.

The grandest inn is the George, which also has a Cromwell connection. It was built in 1574 and later bought by his grandfather, Henry. Ironically, the king Oliver Cromwell deposed made it his headquarters in 1645.

The George stands, around its galleried courtyard, on a huge corner site where High Street meets George Street. The courtyard is a fine feature, and hosts Shakespeare productions each summer; just the sort of setting Elizabethan plays were originally performed in.

Uncle Charlie's travellers didn't get here, exhausted, until 10pm, but there was no respite. Before their coach sets off again, they can only 'take the opportunity afforded by the change of filling our pocket-flasks with some rich brown brandy of the right sort, and invest in some of those very special veal-and-ham sandwiches for which good Mrs Ekin has been famous these years past.' Today the closest I can see to veal and ham on the menu is in the 'Signature pies' section, so I have a Beef and Ruddles Ale one. I half expect it to have been signed by the chef, but no, it comes un-autographed.

The other surviving coaching inn, the sixteenth-century Falcon on Market Hill, also has a Cromwell connection. He used it as a recruiting centre for his Roundhead New Model Army, the one that went on to defeat the Cavalier Royalists.

It's much smaller than the George, little wider than the arched entrance to its stable yard, but just as interesting, a dark cave of a place with high-backed settles, and a great oak bar bearing 15 hand pumps. Oh how I'd love to have the time, and the liver, to work my way along those: through Hobgoblin, Sunbeam and Forty-Niner to Beijing Black and Kinver Noble Golden Ale, via Oxford Gold and EPA.

Upstairs is a tea room, from which the bay window above the arch in its white rendered facade is a perfect spot for people watching.

Uncle Charlie tells me of a sad human footnote to the demise of the coaching days in Huntingdon, one that is 'melancholy in the extreme to contemplate'. This is where Tom 'Flashheart' Hennesy ended up. Once stagecoaches no longer travelled from London to Stamford, or indeed anywhere else, he was out of a job. If video killed the radio star, then rails killed this star of stage.

Charlie writes of his sad end:

Why, this man dandy of the Stamford Regent! the knight of the crooked whip, the adored of barmaids, the idol of schoolboys, horsily inclined, for eighty-nine miles of the finest coaching road in England, came down from mere natural force of circumstances – circumstances in a real sense over which he had no control – to what?

To driving a two-horsed bus from Huntingdon to Cambridge.

Hennesy, and other coachmen, were now:

Heeded by no one; buried away in obscure corners of out-of-the-way counties; driving buses; hanging about inn-yards, where formerly their very footfall produced clumsy reverences from drunken postboys; melancholy, blue-nosed phantoms of their former selves. Seldom surely has there been so cruel a revolution!

Time to move on. I get the car and circumnavigate Huntingdon's ring road to pick up the B1044, Ermine Street, aka the Old North Road. It takes me, rising steadily all the way, through the villages of Great Stukeley and Little Stukeley, towards the summit of Alconbury Hill, where it becomes the B1043.

I've covered 63 miles on the Old North Road and am about to reach the point at which it joins the Great North Road. It's time to decide which is best.

In terms of how much of the original road I can drive, and the extent to which it diverges from the modern A10, The Old North Road does well. Just as the A1 is very definitely not the Great North Road, the A10 is not the Old London Road. After the first six miles I don't touch the A10 again for over 22 miles, when I reach Puckridge. After that there are two short stretches on the A10, totalling eight miles, until, from Royston, I never touch it again. So, 14 miles on the A10 out of 63. That's 22 per cent, which is comparable with the historic route of the Great North Road.

The first mile of the Old North Road through Shoreditch is richer in historic interest than anything on the other route, but the rest of the suburban section is more of a grind, with far fewer points where I wanted to stop and explore. However, once past Ware, the Old North Road is unsurpassed as a drive. But, again, there are fewer interesting old towns on it and, although sticking to the old route of the Great North Road is more of a challenge, it offers more rewards for doing so.

So, I guess that if I'm just out for a drive, I'll take the Old, but if I want to really explore all the riches of England's past, I'll take the Great.

No matter. From here, the routes are united, and I can't wait to see how this next section compares.

III

GREAT NORTH ROAD
Alconbury
to Doncaster

The Great North Road

Alconbury Hill to Doncaster

Doncaster

Scrooby

Pilgrim Fathers
SCROOBY

Retford

A1
CROMWELL
NOTTS · C · C ·

Tuxford

Cromwell

Newark

THE BEEHIVE
FREE HOUSE

Grantham

Colsterworth

Stamford

Norman Cross

STILTON

Stilton

Alconbury
Hill

To London 64 Miles

Alconbury Hill is where everything comes together, and also where everything changes. The Great North Road and the Old North Road meet and forge on as one, on the path of Ermine Street, as the B1043. And, as they do so, they drop down on a long slow descent into the once-waterlogged fenland, and a whole new economic landscape.

Up to now, everything along the old road has been thriving. From here, I see the sort of decay I remember from America's Route 66: abandoned businesses, others just clinging on; villages once made rich by the road plunged into poverty once they were bypassed, and the scars still showing.

But it's not all doom and gloom. Things improve markedly as I press on to the heart of England. At Stamford I discover one of the finest towns on the Great North Road, with a wonderful old coaching inn and, at Grantham, another. They started life in, respectively, the twelfth and thirteenth centuries as pilgrim hostelries.

Along the road I find the 400-year-old apple tree that inspired Newton to formulate his theory of gravity, the one-time late-night rendezvous-point for bands returning from gigs in towns up and down the old road, and a fortress that was once the Key to the North.

Much of this section is off the A1. I do a quick tally of the amount of old versus new road I will encounter from Alconbury Hill to Doncaster, and find that only 28 per cent of the route is on the A1. Out a total of 108 miles, 77 miles, or 72 per cent, of the Great North Road is not on the A1. And, all the way from Newark to Doncaster, there is an unbroken 34 miles stretch away from the new road.

12. Stilton, and a Whiff of Decay
– Alconbury Hill to Stamford –

I'm standing at an historic spot, beside a forgotten monument to the Great North Road. It's an elaborate stone milepost, known as The Obelisk to coach drivers, at the summit of Alconbury Hill.

It is sandwiched between the new road and the old, on a grubby, narrow grass verge, shielded by a galvanised crash barrier and behind knee-high black-iron railings. It's a late eighteenth century, Grade II-listed pillar of pale limestone, topped with what its English Heritage listing describes as a 'shaped cap with ball finial' but looks to me like a giant chess pawn. It was shifted here when the A1(M) motorway came through.

Blink and you'll miss it, dwarfed as it is by the big metal sheds of the Crossways Distribution Centre on the other side of the old road. It bears, on its north-east and north-west faces, the same pudgy hand and fat pointing finger that I saw on the skinny pyrimid at Brampton. It's hard to make out the mileages now, but under the grime and the lichen it tells me that it is 65 miles to London on the Old North Road through Huntingdon, Royston and Ware; 68 miles by the Great North Road through Buckden, Biggleswade and Hatfield.

I've actually travelled 84 miles on my route from Hicks Hall, but then I've been doing some wandering off the road along the way.

While today's road powers up to this point in a cutting that makes the hill a doddle, it was too steep a climb for horse-drawn coaches on the Great North Road from Buckden, quite a grind for the trucks of the first half of the twentieth century, and an icy, exposed and treacherous stretch for everyone in winter.

So coaches on the Great North Road swung left at the bottom of the Alconbury Hill, on what is now an unclassified lane, to skirt the western edge of Alconbury village and reach the point I am standing at via a gentler gradient.

A famous – not to say notorious – old inn called the Wheatsheaf once stood here on the summit of Alconbury Hill, just to the west of the milestone, where six lanes of traffic whizzes now. It fell into decline during the nineteenth century, was rebuilt in the 1920s, then flattened by the A1 motorway in 1998.

This was a bleak spot. A traveller called Francis Jeffrey wrote in 1831: 'Tonight it snows and blows, and there is good hope of our being blocked up at Alconbury Hill, or some of those lonely retreats, for a week or so, or fairly stuck in the drifts.'

The ByngAdvisor gave the Wheatsheaf one star. He had booked dinner at 3 o'clock but, despite arriving half an hour late, found: 'Dinner not ready! We were rather peevish at the delay – for the half hour before dinner is always a snappish time. The dinner was better than I expected in this filthy inn which, to the miseries of a cold alehouse, joins the charges of a London tavern: for two small tench stewed in a black sauce were charged 7 shillings.' That's about £50 today.

It was a dangerous spot too, notorious for highwaymen. Uncle Charlie, in *Stage-coach and Mail in Days of Yore*, says that, at night, a dodgy ostler at the Wheatsheaf would help change the horses on a coach, then run north to a deep, heavily wooded hollow called Stangate (or Stonegate) Hole. There he would hold the coach up as it came down the hill.

Apparently, he was often just pointing a candle stick at his victims but, in the dim lights of the coach, it looked very like a pistol, and driver and passengers generally decided to take no chances. It must have been a bit like when a Magnum-toting Clint Eastwood asks you: 'Do you feel lucky?'

The development of the 14-mile stretch of road from Alconbury to Water Newton indicates how things had to change as traffic increased on the Great North Road. A dual carriageway was built in 1958. Then, in 1964, came a two-mile A1 bypass up Alconbury Hill. In 1998 the bypass was redeveloped as the six-lane A1(M) we see today.

But, brilliantly, the old route survived all those changes, as the B1043. Which means I can go sailing north on it today. It's a lovely road, wide, fast and empty as I coast down the long, gentle descent to Sawtry and Stilton.

Just as the road flattens out I come across the first remnant of the old road's glory days: a half-forgotten travellers' rest. Tucked back in a break in the trees on my right are clustered a Pace Mobile service station; Spiceland, 'finest Indian buffet and takeaway'; and Redwings Lodge.

This really does remind me of the sort of place you get on Route 66: a clutch of bypassed businesses clinging on beside the old road. Spiceland, ('seven days a week, 72 dishes'), occupies a low white building whose three red-painted gables are a clue that it was once a Little Chef, in the days when they were dotted along every major road in the country. Them and Happy Eater.

But the rotund figure of the Little Chef that once graced the chain's signs got slimmed down by a health-conscious ad-agency, and the Happy Eater was ridiculed for its logo, on which a red-faced cartoon character pointed down his throat in a way that suggested he might be trying to make himself throw up the meal he had just eaten.

Little Chef ate Happy Eater, which then went into a period of decline, its remaining restaurants bought by Euro Garages and converted into Starbucks and Greggs. There are plenty of those along England's highways, but not on old roads like this. Most of the transport caffs are gone too, leaving those who drive the A1 for a living eating from caravans parked in lay-bys created when kinks in the old road's alignment were ironed out.

Once down Alconbury Hill, my road levels out onto a very flat and low-lying plain which, until 150 years ago, was a watery world. There's a clue to that in the name of the next village,

Sawtry, which means 'the salt-sellers' landing place'. Salt would be brought 100 miles upstream from the eastern coastal saltpans, through the Fenland waterways, to be offloaded here, in what is now the land-locked heart of England.

What a porous isle this was before the fens were drained. Someone who can tell us what this area was like at the start of the eighteenth century is Celia Fiennes, a remarkable woman who rode on horseback through England between 1685 and 1712.

Celia was feisty: a pioneer travel writer, riding at a time when travel for pleasure was unusual, and a woman travelling alone almost unheard of. She rode, as she says in her journal, 'to regain my health by variety and change of air and exercise'.

At Sawtry, Celia writes: 'We came in sight of a great water on the right hand about a mile off which looked like some sea, it being so high, and of a great length. This is part of the fenny country and is called Whitlsome Mer.'

Actually it was Whittlesey Mere, which was drained in 1851. Celia says it was 'three mile broad and six mile long,' and that 'in the midst is a little island where a great store of wildfowl breeds. There is no coming near it in a mile or two, the ground is all wet and marshy, but there are several little channels run into it which by boats people go up to this place. When you enter the mouth of the mer it looks formidable, and it is often very dangerous by reason of sudden winds that will rise like hurricanes in the mer but... there is abundance of good fish in it.'

That fish was packed into barrels and sent to market in London.

Celia never intended anyone beyond her family to read her journal, and it was only published after her death, as *Through England on a Side Saddle*, in 1888. A revised edition followed in 1947, and it has remained in print ever since. She makes a worthy companion, and it will be an honour to have her along for my journey. I think she'll get on very well with my other imaginary friends, Uncle Charlie and the ByngAdvisor.

Great North Road

After 11 miles coasting along at my left shoulder, the A1(M) cuts across the alignment of Ermine Street, the main street through Stilton, blocking off the original approach to the village. But I can follow the B1043 as it switches to the western side of the motorway, and then double back to the village. Stilton was one of the greatest coaching villages, its broad main street once a true artery of the nation. It's almost as wide as the motorway that rumbles past, just behind the houses.

Today, just one great institution from Stilton's glory days has survived: the magnificent Bell inn. The rest is decidedly downbeat: a succession of unkempt, struggling businesses still holding out the hope that travellers will chose to stop here. Stilton is an English version of the defeated little towns I found on America's Route 66.

Uncle Charlie writes lyrically of how, once, the 'many-voiced Babel of travel... surged and swayed round this teeming coaching centre, now lying silent and deserted as the grave' and concludes, putting the fatal knife in: 'it is very certain that no place more representative of the Coaching Age Decayed than Stilton is to be found on Earth.'

Like many of the towns and villages on the road, it had no role once the coaches stopped rolling through. In some, travellers still came, by rail, but not at Stilton: 'For here the Great Northern Railway has diverged from the line of the old road, and by doing so has turned a vast coaching emporium into a corpse of a town – if town indeed Stilton could by any stretch of language ever have been called. It was rather, in its best days, a village clustering about two magnificent inns, the Angel and the Bell, which still stare at each other stonily across the Great North Road.'

Today we have to scrub the 'magnificent' from the Angel. What Charlie says was once a vast barracks of a place with 300 horses is now the Angel Spice, a bedraggled Indian restaurant that can't begin to fill the shoes of the once-grand inn.

Across the street, however, The Bell is still imposing: a block-long, honeyed-stone place that is a living embodiment of the term 'old world coaching inn'. It deserves to be on a postcard, a chocolate box, to be made into a jigsaw puzzle. The various entrances offer: Hotel and Galleried Restaurant, Village Bar, and Bistro.

Thrust out high above the street on a wrought iron gantry hangs its vast painted inn-sign: a bell in vivid orange with gold detailing, beneath the one word: Stilton.

Two union jacks flutter alongside a vintage yellow and black AA Hotel sign, and a fresh stone lintel above a doorway registers that the hotel was 'Aedificatum AD 1642, refectum AD 1989'.

The D in Aedificatum (meaning built or building) appears to have been corrected from what was initially carved as a B. Can't get the stone carvers these days.

Refectum, which I had expected to mean 'restored', seems to translate as 'meal'. Maybe the builders made a meal of it, cocking up more than the carving of that lintel.

I pop in and find a seat beside the blazing log fire in what I'm pleased to discover is a very homely, thriving place. I had feared the coaching inns of the Great North Road would be shadows of their former selves. Or maybe mere ghosts. But no. The Bell is one of eighteen owned by the Coaching Inn Group, and I'll find another later on my travels. They may have saved and revived far fewer of these inns than Wetherspoons, but theirs are decidedly more up-market.

A group of ladies are ordering from a very complex and comprehensive coffee menu. It takes them a while. Will it be a macchiato or a cortado? A mocha, or a flat white? A latte or a cappuccino? Me, I just want a cuppateano. Milk no sugar.

When I hear the word Stilton I naturally think of cheese. And Stilton is indeed the place the crumbly stuff was first made, and sold right here at the Bell. A plaque beside the entrance records the fact under the heading 'The birth of Stilton Cheese', crediting the landlord from the 1720s, Cooper Thornhill, with creating 'a substantial and enduring market for the product'.

Even Daniel Defoe, writing that he was offered a spoon with which to eat the mites in his chunk, didn't put people off. However, Stilton's claim to be the home of the cheese was fiercely disputed until recently. It was claimed all Stilton cheese was actually made by a relative of Thornhill in Melton Mowbray, 36 miles away, and that Stilton cheese had never actually been made here.

However, in 2009 a local historian, Richard Landy, uncovered compelling evidence that it was. He discovered a recipe dated 1722 for a pressed, cooked cream cheese, which was called Stilton, attached to a letter written to Richard Bradley, Cambridge University's first professor of botany. The letter confirmed the cheese had been produced and sold at the Bell. It was not, however, the blue-veined stuff that is the most common modern variant of Stilton, but a white version.

Which means the Bell can now rightly claim to be the birthplace of Stilton. Never mind, Melton Mowbray, you've still got the pork pie.

You can buy Stilton at the Bell today, and I do. The waitress tells me they don't have as big a selection as usual 'because someone' and she says the 'someone' as if that someone might be within earshot, 'turned the fridge off and we lost a load.' I buy a chunk of the white, and ask if it's made locally. Sadly, it's not. Now there's a gap in the market for some enterprising local dairy farmer.

There is a definite cheesy theme to Stilton. The Talbot pub has stained glass windows featuring a great wheel of it and, while The Stilton Cheese Inn may he awaiting a new owner, the Stilton Foot Clinic does brisk business. Here they treat a very nasty infection, Stilton Foot, which causes lower extremities to develop blue veins, go white and crumbly, and give off a decidedly cheesy odour. It's caused, obviously, by eating too much blue Stilton.

In case it's not obvious, that was a joke. But there is a Stilton Foot Clinic.

It wasn't just human travellers who passed through Stilton. Flocks of geese and herds of oxen did too, and the Angel had a busy side-line in shoeing cattle for their trek on to Smithfield.

Coming out of Stilton, the B1043 hops almost immediately back over the motorway to become the A15 at Norman Cross, and the old Great North Road resumes its progress along the eastern flank of the modern A1(M). From here, the old road is now unclassified, a yellow lane on the Ordnance Survey map, but in reality still a broad highway. Before taking it, I stop in Norman Cross, where a bronze imperial eagle spreads its wings atop a towering column of stone, marking a curious piece of history.

In 1797-1814, during the Napoleonic Wars, the navy built the very first prisoner of war camp here, to house 4,000 French captives. The eagle-topped column is a memorial to the 1,770 who died while incarcerated. It was erected beside the Great North Road in 1914, but moved to stand alongside the A15 in 1998, when the A1(M) came through.

Somehow or other, determined steeple-jacking thieves stole the bronze eagle in 1990, but it was replaced in 2005.

Until recently a Premier Inn stood on the site of the camp but, when I passed through, it had just given up the ghost. It stood quarantined behind tall security fencing, freshly stripped of its insignia.

Conditions were insanitary. At the camp, not the Premier Inn. Uncle Charlie says that some prisoners 'lost their minds', a few escaped, often to die in the ditches of the fog-bound landscape. To get by, many made toys and ornaments from wood, straw, and bones from their rations, to sell to travellers on the great road who stopped to gawp at them.

Some were allowed out on parole, but could not stray from the highway, and had to return before dark. Any found out at night could be shot on sight. The Post Office offered a reward of £5 to any mail guard who did so, which had the unintended consequence, for several farm labourers, of being peppered with shot as they walked home at night.

For the first time today, the modern road rather messes with the route of the old. Two miles past Norman Cross I am forced to turn sharp left and pass under the A1(M), then through the hamlet of Haddon and on, due west, along a narrow lane with very wide verges. Two miles on, the lane becomes a green way and I turn right to reach the A605, then right again to regain my route north, at Peterborough Services. Here I have no option but to take the A1, which loses its M at this point, but it's only three miles before I can regain the old road, at Water Newton.

This is a lovely spot where, in contrast to much else on this stretch of the road, there is not a whiff of decay or neglect. Water Newton used to be an island in the marshes, and the Great North Road ran right beside the church of St Remigus, which I reach by walking down a track, through the garden of the very desirable former rectory, to the thirteenth century church on the bank of the River Nene. It's a peaceful spot, the broad river running through a weir and lock where a mill once stood. Rowing boats bob in a boathouse, and the grassy banks offer a perfect picnic spot.

Daniel Defoe wrote, in the 1820s, in his *A Tour through the Whole Island of Great Britain*, that the course of the old Roman road was still visible here, and was called the 40 Foot Way. It isn't traceable today and, if the Ordnance Survey is to believed, Defoe got it wrong, Ermine Street fording the river to the south of Water Newton to run away across-country to the east.

But there are other reminders of Roman times. In the church here is a Roman coffin, and there was a Roman town, and extensive pottery kilns, just to the west of the present village. In 1975, ploughing uncovered a remarkable collection of fourth century Roman Christian liturgical silver – the oldest discovered anywhere in the world – and evidence that there was a church here almost a millennium before the present building pointed the way to heaven.

Water Newton is on the first of a series of loops off the A1 where the old road survives, here as a narrow lane. There was never a coaching inn in the village, meaning no money was to be made from the road, and its loss had no financial consequences.

The next loop is less than two miles away, at Stibbington. Here, a business from the motoring age soldiers on. At the Stibbington Truck Stop the little while bungalow housing the Stibbington Diner stands marooned in a vast, muddy lorry park. Overnight there are ranks of trucks lined up here, curtains drawn in the cabs, the hum of their refrigerator units merging with the roar of traffic on the A1.

The good old Stibby Diner keeps the tradition of the big trucker's plateful going. How about steak, sausage, bacon, mushrooms, fried egg, chips and peas? Or a burger as tall as the Burj Khalifa? And, for the diet-conscious... actually, scrub that.

On winter Sunday mornings the Great North Road Vehicle Gathering is held here, and you can admire the sort of cars that ruled the old road, plus a lot of exotic American ones that didn't.

That thought brings me to mentally list some of the cars I'd like to be driving up the Great North Road today. Among them would be: a Mark III Cortina, ideally in sunshine yellow with a black vinyl roof; a Vauxhall Cresta in maroon and cream; a Mark II Jag in grey with red leather seats; an Anglia with its radical and never-to-be-repeated reverse-angled rear window; and one of those police Riley Pathfinders with a bell, not a siren. I'd also go for a stubby-snouted Sunbeam Rapier like my friend's dad had, and a sexy little Triumph Spitfire like my university girlfriend's.

South down this loop of the old road, just before it re-joins the A1, is Wansford Station, on a line closed in the Beeching cuts of the 1960s, but now home to the preserved Nene Valley steam railway. Queen filmed the video for the single 'Breakthru' on the seven-and-a-half mile stretch of track here, and I watch a behind-the-scenes film on YouTube. It all looked very silly: the band miming on a flat-bed truck; a steam train crashing through a polystyrene wall built over a tunnel entrance; and a pouty girl running after a bare-chested Freddie Mercury.

Down at the station, I find a rather nice old Wagon Lit dining car among the preserved rolling stock. Personally, I'd do my video in that.

Less than a mile after I have to re-join the new road I can turn off once again, for the village of Wansford, which is tucked down on a bend in the River Nene, where the old road runs as the B671 through an affluent village of soft stone cottages, venerable old Land-Rovers, and shops offering vintage Vivienne Westwood, fresh roasted coffee and leather handbags straight from Tuscany. It's a friendly little place, where Jim and Colette welcome you to the Cross Keys, and the Paper Mills pub and Country Lounge cafe offer, respectively, gastropub cuisine and coffee and cake.

The typically wide street of this former coaching village leads to a very narrow, 13-arch stone bridge, built in 1557 over the Nene, the waters of which run surprisingly clear and powder blue.

It was because of this bridge, which was considered dangerous in coaching days, and treacherous once early motor traffic was trying to squeeze across it, that the village got one of the first bypasses, in the 1920s.

Uncle Charlie tells the story of how the Stamford Regent almost came to grief here. Not in the hands of Flashheart on this occasion, but an equally impetuous young coachman, driving horses that were a little too lively for their own good, and their passengers' safety.

The coachman misjudged the approach as the horses flew

at the bridge, the coach struck it, and the horses performed a panicky dance, after which they rushed back the way they had come. This completely disorientated the passengers, who were startled to find themselves, back at the door of the Haycock Hotel, which they had left a few minutes earlier.

Wansford, sustained by the paper mill after which the Paper Mills pub is named, and other industry, proved affluent enough to survive the loss of the great road. Even the Haycock Hotel, as big and formal as a county courthouse or town hall, is spruce and busy. The ByngAdvisor, however, was unable to enjoy his stay here.

A dodgy traveller's tummy meant he couldn't eat the slap-up meal presented to him: 'A good supper came in; of which I was scarcely allowed to eat; for fear of spasms: the finest peas, which, at their first appearance, are much to my liking, were denied to me; tarts likewise; custards ditto. This was very right, but very hard! Nor dare I venture for some time till the memory of my last spasmodic night be blown away.'

I don't like the sound of a 'spasmodic night'. It conjures up images of bedclothes sent flying across the room by unwanted eruptions. Elizabeth I stayed here while heading up the Great North Road for Stamford, and Lord Burghley's place; as did Mary Queen of Scots, when on the way to her execution at Fotheringay Castle.

Wansford is sometimes called Wansford-in-England due to a bonkers old tale, in which a local farmhand who fell asleep on a hayrick, or haycock, during a flood was carried downstream on the River Nene. He was way out east at Wisbech, in an area known as the Hollands, when he woke up and asked someone on the riverbank where he was. On being told 'Hollands', he assumed he had floated right across the North Sea. Asked where he had floated down from, he told them he came from 'Wansford in England'. The Haycock Hotel is named after the story.

Once over the bridge the old road climbs up to the new, but

in under four miles I can turn off on the B1081 for Stamford. Here I re-join Ermine Street, which I parted company from just before Water Newton, and which runs alongside Burghley House and Park.

Burghley House, built by William Cecil, secretary of state to Elizabeth I, is a Tudor treasure house. Elizabeth would have felt very much at home during her visits here: Cecil modelled it closely on her favourite home, the Thames-side Richmond Palace, which has not survived.

I came across an article about Burghley House in a colour supplement just before my trip. It told me all I could possibly want to know about the Rock family, which owns Burghley. Three paragraphs in and I had already encountered Cosmo, Dido, Crumble and Orlando. Apparently, two of those names belong to Rock family dogs, but I struggled to work out which.

Now, if I had the surname Rock, and was naming my sprogs, I'd have gone a different way entirely: Blackpool, and Adult-orientated, would be among my choices. And maybe a double-barrelled moniker for the heir: Thrash-Metal Rock.

Orlando, I learn as I read on, is chairman of Christie's. So, not a dog then.

Celia Fiennes visited Burghley House. She had a number of themes in her journal. Nosing about stately homes, many of which were newly-built at the time, was one of her abiding interests, as was the quality of beer she found along the way, and the freshness of fish served at the inns. She also relished a gruesome tale, as I discover a little further north.

Here, Celia was impressed by the house and grounds: 'The situation is the finest I ever saw on the edge of the hill... you ascent to the house thro' the midst of rows of trees on either side of a very broad glide or visto that looks finely to the river and to the adjacent hills, a distance clothed in fine woods; the town of Stamford appears very fine on the left hand and most noble woods on the right.'

Celia found the house was filled with remarkable art. However, she disapproved of the way the figures in many of the paintings 'were all without garments or very little, that was the only fault, the immodesty of the pictures especially in my lord's apartment.'

I head on to Stamford, that 'very fine' town, where I've booked lunch at the George.

13. Ram Jam Thank You Ma'am

– Stamford to Grantham –

Traffic flows down the Great North Road and collects in a puddle before the bridge over the River Welland in the centre of seventeenth-century Stamford.

The traffic lights here are slow to change. Very slow. Giving me plenty of time to admire one of the finest surviving coaching inns along the whole of the old road. Spanning the street above my head is a gallows sign that declares this to be: The George of Stamford.

The George shows its best face to the Great North Road: the three-storey limestone block built in 1597 by Lord Burghley, owner of the big house just down the road. But hospitality on this site stretches way back beyond that date, to 1173 at least. Here stood the House of the Holy Sepulchre, a monastic hospice. Knights of St John of Jerusalem stayed on their journeys to Jerusalem, to fight in the Crusades.

There was also an almshouse, the Hospital of St John the Baptist and St Thomas the Martyr, which catered for pilgrims and the local poor and sick, and a church. The courtyard garden behind The George was once the churchyard.

When the traffic finally moves I park around the corner in Station Road, which cuts through the medieval site, and head inside for lunch. I've been looking forward to the George, and it doesn't disappoint. Two rooms either side of the Great North Road entrance, one labelled YORK, the other LONDON are reminders of the days when travellers to north and south waited here for one of forty daily coaches.

They don't let you in that way today. Instead you trek to the very back of this block-deep building and up to a reception point, where they funnel you through the courtyard garden to either restaurant, bar or lounge. It's only noon on Monday but the place is packed, further testament to how coaching inns can still thrive. Uniformed staff are flying all over the place. We must have one each, but they can't keep up with the demands of guests. I just about get a perch in the lounge for a cheese sandwich, and the wait for its arrival gives me a chance to nose into the York and London rooms. One's a bar, and I envy those who have managed to grab a table there.

Sandwich finally delivered and despatched, I explore Stamford a little. This is my kind of town: one of the finest on the old Great North Road, a place with 600 listed buildings, and several fascinating stories.

I follow the old road across the bridge over the River Welland, the waters of which sport a brushed-aluminium look created by the gentle breeze over its slow-flowing depths. Stamford gets its name from the 'stone ford' the Romans used to cross the river. Upstream, the river wishbones around the Town Meadows, a willow at the fork, alongside which a dad is teaching his daughter to fish. Then it flows beneath my feet to run between banks of former wharves, and new apartment blocks designed to look like them.

Stamford is another of the towns that, in the Middle Ages, were inland ports. Access to the North Sea down the Welland meant it became the key market place for the medieval wool trade, and was rich.

It is the first sizeable town since, respectively, Biggleswade,

45 miles south on the Great North Road, or Huntingdon, 30 miles away on the Old North Road: between three and five hours on a jolty carriage travelling at around 10 miles per hour, through lonely and sometimes dangerous country.

Charles Dickens features such a journey in *Nicholas Nickleby*. Nicholas, Squeers and the poor frozen, starving schoolboys pass through Stamford at night. He writes:

> The night and the snow came on together, and dismal enough they were. There was no sound to be heard but the howling of the wind; for the noise of the wheels, and the tread of the horses' feet, were rendered inaudible by the thick coating of snow which covered the ground, and was fast increasing every moment.
>
> The streets of Stamford were deserted as they passed through the town; and its old churches rose, frowning and dark, from the whitened ground.

It looks a lot more welcoming today. To give you an idea of what a lovely, oldy-worldy place Stamford is, adaptations of both *Middlemarch* and *Pride and Prejudice* have been filmed here. It's like being morphed into Sunday night television. Arrive in a top hat and a frock coat and I'd fit in perfectly.

The soft, weathered limestone is so much a part of the town that the Civic Society has published a book on it, telling owners how to identify which of the six local quarries their house was dug out of, and detailing the twenty-three weathering patterns and processes that can cause damage and deterioration.

The ByngAdvisor, for some reason, didn't like Stamford, telling his journal: 'Stamford is a large but an ill-built town, without shade around it, or manufactory within it.' To cut him a bit of slack, the illness he complained of back at Wansford was still troubling him: 'I stopped for some time in Stamford in search of a stomatic medicine.'

I follow the old road up St Mary's Hill, turn sharp left into St Mary's Street, pausing to admire the black gloss and silver-detailed shop front of Sinclairs ('Fine China and Cut Crystal, Gifts for All Occasions'). Then it's sharp right through cobblestoned Red Lion Square for Barn Hill, just off the old road.

I'm following in the footsteps of Charles I, who came this way in 1645, during the English Civil War, when fleeing the parliamentary forces of Oliver Cromwell. That war raged up and down the Great North Road, and Cromwell, who I encountered at Huntingdon, is going to become a bit of a theme as I head north. Two years before Charles slunk through, Cromwell had held Stamford and besieged Burghley House.

On the king's previous visits, before everything went a bit Frank Spencer for him and his reign, Charles had stayed at The George. Now, he came disguised as a clergyman, and hid for a night in No. 9 Barn Hill, home of William Stukeley, vicar of All Saints church just down the hill and, his blue plaque says, 'father of British archaeology'. And Royalist, obviously. Stukeley's house had a section that formed a bridge over the road, containing his library and study.

Charles was able to slip out of the house, and through a gate in the town wall that ran around the garden, to enjoy a few final hours of freedom before hurrying on towards Newark, and surrender, under cover of darkness.

If Stamford feels a little like Cambridge or Oxford, there is a good reason. It once had a university to rival theirs, and I come across that part of its history as I walk back to All Saints, then head for East Street and Brazenose House.

I walk east along Broad Street, once home to the Beastmarket, and past the former Central Cinema, its curving 1930s Art Deco facade an elegant rebellion against all that limestone, to St Paul's Street.

Stamford's two centuries as a rival to Oxbridge began in 1266, when a group of students at Oxford who had left following a protracted dispute between town and gown, founded several colleges and halls here, which thrived. In 1333 another large Oxford exodus arrived, but a petition to the king forced their return. Both Oxford and Cambridge agreed not to recognise degrees awarded at Stamford and, by 1463, the university was closed.

The site of those college buildings is now occupied by Stamford Endowed School, but one reminder survives. Just past Brazenose House is a stone archway, the only surviving element of the college set up by students of Oxford's Brasenose (as it is spelt today). A double oak door is set into the arch.

Until 1890 this door bore the original twelfth-century bronze knocker, a lion's head with a ring in its mouth, which gave the college its name, and which had been brought here from Oxford. But that year the Oxford college bought the house and carried the knocker away, displaying it in its own hall in Oxford. It was replaced by a replica, which survives. It looks less like a lion, more like a sleepy tortoise with a big ring through its nose.

I want to explore one final Stamford story. A couple of hundred yards back past the George, up the hill I drove down, is St Martin's church. Close to it is the site of a former inn, the Waggon and Horses, now a private house. The two locations feature in the story of Daniel Lambert.

Lambert, who weighed over 52 stone and whose waist measured 9ft 4ins, made a career of displaying himself at fairs in London and up and down the Great North Road, promoting himself as 'The fattest man in Britain'. He died suddenly, in 1809 aged just 39, at The Waggon and Horses.

The undertakers had to remove a window and section of wall to get his body out, fit his coffin with wheels, and run a sloping ramp to his grave, which is in an annex to the churchyard. His tombstone bears his vital statistics. The grave is well tended, freshly planted with red geraniums when I visit, and a notice describes him as 'a wonder of nature, a prodigy, and much respected'. They have a life-size model of Daniel in the town hall. Pinned to his chest is a notice: 'Please do not touch me, I do not appreciate it', suggesting he might be a bit less respected today.

Not to be outdone by the Waggon and Horses, the George also claims Lambert as a former patron, and his portrait hangs in the entrance hall. 'Well,' they might say, 'at least we didn't kill him.'

The road out of town is the A606 for a short stretch, before the B1081 reclaims ownership and follows the route of Ermine Street via Great Casterton to re-join the A1, which I'll be on most of the way to Grantham. This is dual carriageway, two lanes each way, thick hedges either side meaning the only view is up the exhaust pipe of the truck in front. And there are plenty of trucks, those in the outside lane travelling at around one tenth of a mile faster than those in the slow, meaning I might as well sit back and let the 6.5 miles roll by until Stretton, and another famous travellers' rest: The Ram Jam Inn. There were few villages between Stamford and Grantham, hence the establishment of large, isolated inns like this.

The lonely Ram Jam stands alongside the old road, with just a petrol station for company. And, far from thriving, it has been closed since 2013. Plans to demolish it have been rejected, but I guess it's only a matter of time before a Starbucks or a Costa rises here.

Beside the old inn, the Texaco Station is still open, a little red-and-white striped cabin of a place and itself a reminder of the motoring past. Between the two is a car park, and after refuelling I pull in for a closer look at the Ram Jam.

Its frontage, just a few feet back from the road, is covered in ivy, its windows blocked with marine ply, the 'Ram Jam Restaurant and rooms' sign forlorn, the whole wrapped in security fencing. I edge along the front, trucks whooshing past at my back, and peer in.

It's 20 years since I last stopped here. Then there was an entrance at the back into a pleasantly old-fashioned coffee lounge. I remember thinking then they could make something of its history. From the Sixties on it was frequented by many musicians, who would make a point of stopping here after gigs in the expectation of meeting up with other bands. The Sixties soul singer Geno Washington named his Ram Jam Band after it.

The significance of the Great North Road for musicians ambitious for success is reflected in the songs that have been written about it. Among them are Sting's 'Heading South On The Great North Road' on his 2016 album *57th and 9th*. He said of the song:

> I couldn't make it in Newcastle. I had to leave home and make that journey 300 miles south to... London, with little more than an old guitar, a bag of dreams and a notebook full of songs.
>
> Well I shared that leap of faith, that leap in the dark, that same journey, with many others from my part of the world – some of us were successful. Eric Burdon and the Animals, Brian Johnson of AC/DC, Mark Knopfler from Dire Straits, Trevor Horn... Bryan Ferry of Roxy Music, Lindisfarne and my dear friend Jimmy Nail... we all had to travel south down the same road.

Mark Knopfler refers to the Great North Road in '5:15 AM', from the album *Shangri La*.

One version of how the Ram Jam got its name – it was originally The Winchelsea Inn – tells of a stunt pulled by the highwayman Dick Turpin. Turpin, who had run up a large bill that he did not intend to pay, is said to have tricked the landlady, a Mrs Spring, by offering to show her how to get both mild and bitter from the same barrel. Drilling two holes in a cask, he got her to 'ram' one of her thumbs into the first hole, and 'jam' the other in the second while he got the taps. Turpin fled, with the landlady unable to extract her thumbs and give chase without losing the precious contents of a full barrel.

Another, more likely origin for the name is that it came from a strong spirit or liqueur sold from 1740 in small bottles to stagecoach travellers. The name is derived, it is said, from Rum John or Rum Johnnie, the term used by English settlers in India for table servants. The drink, and the pub, became as famous as The Bell and Stilton cheese.

The road has been rising gently all the way from Stamford and here I reach more open country, the hedges thin and there is a view over flat Lincolnshire farmland.

With so few hostelries on this stretch of road, some coaches peeled off for villages such as South Witham, which is a couple of miles north, and half a mile west of the Ram Jam, and the A1. The ByngAdvisor did that, and to escape the trucks, I do the same. Byng stayed at the eighteenth-century Angel Inn, which survives at No. 13 Church Street, and is another of the many friendly village locals that refresh my journey. But Byng had yet another problem here. His luggage got lost.

He wrote in his journal:

> At The Angel Inn Coles [his travelling companion] had a smiling appearance, but not so was mine, when I found only two portmanteaus arrived, and that mine was missing, and might be gone to Newcastle; with all my little comforts, and my greater comforts, as my sheets, physick box, etc. The only things that poor R. Crusoe [that's who he sees himself as] had saved from the wreck, were a night cap, and two shirts, and two pair of stockings that were in [Coles's] portmanteau.

A lane takes me from South Witham to the next village, Colsterworth. Here, I am in Isaac Newton country. Newton's family home, a seventeenth-century limestone farmhouse called Woolsthorpe Manor, is in the adjoining hamlet of Woolsthorpe-by-Colsterworth, and is now owned by the National Trust. The other place associated with him is the church of St John the Baptist, which I come to first.

Colsterworth is a funny place, with no sense of its having been a coaching village. The old road runs as the narrow High Street between stone and brick cottages. There's a Co-op and a modern pub, the White Lion, with a Sixties executive-home look. The church is opposite. There's another royal story here. This small village may have such a large church because a former inhabitant was Judith, niece of William the Conqueror. It stands at the bottom of a deep, sloping churchyard. Inside, it is a sombre and powerful place, with herringbone stone work in the chancel revealing its Saxon origins, and Norman arches that survived a thorough Victorian restoration.

Isaac Newton was baptised in the font that stands toward the back of the church in January 1642. One of the church's prized relics is a block of limestone on which Isaac, aged nine, carved a sun dial in 1651. It is now mounted, encased in a marble surround, high in the north wall.

I'm thinking that nine-year-olds hacking graffiti into church walls might have been frowned upon, until I learn that he actually carved this stone at Woolsthorpe Manor, and it was only brought here, by a descendant, during the Victorian restoration.

I head from church to manor house via a convoluted route and a series of right angle turns. There I learn that young Newton made a bit of a habit of drawing on walls. He sketched the church on the kitchen wall in around 1650.

But it's not his Banksy-like abilities as a graffiti artist that bring visitors here, to this handsome Lincolnshire farmhouse. They come for the tree from which Newton saw an apple fall and wondered why it didn't go up. And to see the room where he used a prism to split sunlight into the colours of the rainbow, and explored the nature of light.

The apple tree is still in the orchard, surrounded by a circle of woven fence like a buried wicker basket, and propped up with a wooden crutch. It looks a little past its best, but then it is 400 years old.

It was in one intensively creative period, from summer 1665 to spring 1667, that Newton – who was at university in Cambridge but returned home to escape the plague – developed his theories on calculus, optics and the laws of motion and gravity. He worked obsessively, in solitude, laying the foundations for much of modern scientific knowledge.

There is another, far less inspirational, story about Colsterworth. It concerns the parish priest at St John the Baptist, and a cause célèbre called the Home Office Baby Stunt.

In 1884 the Revd John Mirehouse, driven to desperation by the closure of the cemetery, which left nowhere for him to bury the dead, devised a gruesome ploy. He posted the body of a still-born baby to the home secretary in a box marked 'perishable'. He escaped punishment when an ecclesiastical lawyer gave the opinion that he had committed no offence under Canon Law, and could not be disciplined.

After Colsterworth there is no alternative to the A1, which swings 30 degrees west while Ermine Street curves gently east to Lincoln. I only just manage to squeeze myself into a line of begrudging truckers, who let me get just – figuratively – one buttock on the seat of the A1 for the five miles to Little Ponton, where I slip out onto the B1174 for Grantham, and my stop for tonight.

14. The Key to the North
– Grantham to Newark –

Descending London Road into Grantham it looks like someone has stuck a pin in the town. In fact that's the soaring spire of St Wulfram's Church, which was stabbed here to stop Grantham sliding about on the map. It works. It's still where they left it, down in a broad shallow bowl.

Celia Fiennes says 'tis a long time when you see a great part of the steeple 'ere you come to see the church or town, it lies so in the bottom.' Simon Jenkins, in his *England's 1,000 Best Churches*, reckons St Wulfram has 'the finest steeple in England'. I'm not going to argue.

In *Nicholas Nickleby*, Charles Dickens gives another aspect of the town a five-star rating. He calls The George (yes, another one) 'one of the best inns in England.' And he makes it clear that there were two classes of traveller on the stage coaches of the Great North Road: those who could afford to stop the night at lovely old inns like this, and those who had to rattle on through the night in a draughty coach. Dickens writes that while the quality were warming themselves at The George: 'The remainder wrapped themselves more closely in their coats and cloaks, and leaving the light and warmth of the town behind them, pillowed themselves against the luggage, and prepared, with many half-suppressed moans, again to encounter the piercing blast which swept across the open country.'

I'm going to stay the night at Grantham, but I can't do that at the George. It still presents its proud Georgian face to the Great North Road but, go through what was the arch to the coachyard and you'll see the old hotel's guts have been ripped out. Behind the preserved facade is a giant modern atrium, with shops on two levels, into which muzak is seeping like a narcotic designed to subdue shoppers. When I visit the shops are empty, and a sign on the front says the place is to let.

Uncle Charlie, in *Stage-coach and Mail in Days of Yore*, has his travellers arrive late at night at the George with 'the screaming and grumbling of the skid [brake] and the straining of the wheels' as they drop down to the inn. There, one passenger awakes to find he has missed his stop:

The person thus awakened proves to be a passenger who had booked to Colsterworth, which is a little village we have now left eight miles behind us. He had been asleep, and as Colsterworth is not one of our stopping or changing places, the guard forgot all about him until the change at Grantham.

The passenger and the guard are now waging a furious war of words on the resounding pavements of the sleeping town... If he had been a little bigger and the guard a little smaller, his fury would perhaps make him fall upon that official and personally chastise him.

As it is, he resorts to abuse. Windows of surrounding houses now begin to be thrown up, and nightcapped heads to inquire 'what the devil's the matter, and if it can't be settled somewhere else or at some more convenient season?' The guard says 'This 'ere gent wot's abusing of me like a blooming pickpocket goes to sleep and gets kerried past where he wants to get out, and when I pulls him out, 'stead of taking 'im on to Newark or York, 'e...'

'Shut up,' exclaims a fierce voice from above: 'can't a man get a wink of sleep for you fellows?'

So, as I say, the George is not for me, but I can stay at the Angel and Royal, a little further down the High Street.

The Angel and Royal is a remarkable place, even more impressive than the George at Stamford. The owners took advantage of enforced lockdown closure to undertake an extensive refurbishment, which has ensured it is now as fine an inn as it ever was. Uncle Charlie rates it 'one of the three medieval hostels remaining in England', adding: 'it was undoubtedly one of those Maisons die Roi [king's houses], as they were called, which in days gone by, when the roads still had life in them, were placed at the special service of kings and their retinues... on royal progresses or quelling insurrections.'

I stand across the street and admire it. The soft stone frontage has bays to either side of the old coach entrance, now screened with glass doors, which leads through to the yard. Above the arch, and beneath the oriel window of the royal chamber, a seventeenth-century carving of a crowned angel shines bright gold, the last survivor among many that once adorned the building.

The current inn dates from the fourteenth and fifteenth centuries but, like the George in Stamford, the site previously housed a pilgrim hostelry, run from 1203 by the Knights Templar.

King John held court here in 1213, in the building which preceded this one. In the fourteenth century, Edward III and his queen, Philippa, stayed a couple of times, and plaster corbels of their heads commemorate that stay.

In 1483, in the great *Chambre de Roi* above the entrance, now a restaurant, Richard III signed the death-warrant for Henry Stafford, Duke of Buckingham, for high treason. Buckingham had helped Richard claim the throne earlier that year, Edward IV's heirs being declared illegitimate, but had then led a revolt against the new king. They have a copy of the warrant on display at the top of the stairs, just outside the room. Alongside it are portraits of all the kings who have stayed here.

It's certainly the most atmospheric of places to dine and spend the night. Uncle Charlie soaks up the atmosphere, saying: 'It is not often I fancy that one can smoke the pipe of peace under a floor which creaked four hundred years ago to the unequal strides of a hunchbacked and irritable king. I thought I heard Richard's voice myself ... and the beautiful moulding in the oriel window of the Angel smoking-room gave life to illusion.'

The ByngAdvisor, on the other hand, suffers something of an existential crisis at the Angel: he begins to doubt the value of his travel journals: 'As I proceed in tour writing, I get bold and vain, believing that all diaries become valuable ...' as is the case with many an obsessive contemporary *TripAdvisor* reviewer.

Still, Byng also sees the funny side of these doubts, and goes on to tell a pretty good joke: '...tho' I often revert to some sad diaries I have read, or heard of, as one of a punctual woman, who wrote: "Friday. Buried my poor dear husband. Saturday. Turned my ass to grass."'

I had been planning to turn *my* ass to bed, but it's a pleasant evening, the sun a soft pink as it sets, so I slip out for a stroll around the quiet town. Not everyone likes Grantham. Certainly, after Stamford, you might agree with those who say it is merely a pretty ugly, pretty large Victorian town. I think that's harsh.

I head for St Wulfram's and navigate to it from the Angel simply by looking up at its 282ft tall spire. On arrival I decide that Grantham is not as bad as some make out. The church really does soar, like a streamlined cathedral, and it stands in the heart of medieval Grantham, in an area of grass between two ancient streets, Swinegate and Castlegate, that is not unlike a cathedral close.

This was the tallest building in England when completed in the fourteenth century. Above the south porch is The Chained Library, established in 1598 and quite possibly the oldest public library in England. Perhaps it will also become one of the last, given how fast other, later libraries are being closed down.

Also on Castlegate is a most unusual pub, the Beehive. As a building it's unremarkable: a two-storey, cream-rendered, cottagey little place. From the narrow pavement outside grows a pollarded lime tree. It's what is wedged high up between the stunted boughs of the tree that makes the pub unusual: a full-size beehive. Hanging beneath it is a notice that reads:

Stop Traveller! This wondrous sign explore
And say, when thou has viewed it o'er,
Now Grantham, now two rarities are thine:
A lofty steeple and a living sign.

A hive has been here since at least 1783, and is said to be the only living pub sign in the country. I can't say I saw any bees buzzing in or out during my visit, but then the pint or two of White Squall and USS Winston S Churchill from Grantham's Newby Wyke Brewery that I sampled may have blunted my powers of observation.

There is another theme to a visit to Grantham, and this stretch of the Great North Road. It concerns a politician who is one of the most divisive figures in British history. No, not Margaret Thatcher, our first female prime minister, who famously grew up in the town and who features in a group portrait of local notables at The Angel, alongside Nicholas Parsons and others I don't recognise. I'm thinking of Oliver Cromwell.

When Daniel Defoe passed through in the 1720s, on his *Journey through the Whole Island of Great Britain*, he wrote: 'About this time it was that we began to hear of the name of Oliver Cromwell, who, like a little cloud, rose out of the East, and spread first into the North, until it shed down a flood that overwhelmed the three kingdoms.'

Cromwell was here in 1643, after his victory in the first battle of the Civil War, at Gonerby Moor, which I will pass tomorrow, just to the north of town. Having taken Grantham and destroyed its fortifications, Cromwell settled down at The Angel, to write: 'God hath given us, this evening, a glorious victory over our enemies.'

Next morning, I travel through the site of that victory. The B1174 takes me out of town, the old road climbing to the village of Great Gonerby. It is 300ft above the town and a perfect vantage point from which to launch an attack. Here, in Pond Street, Cromwell's Cottage takes its name from the local tradition that Oliver stayed here while he planned that assault. A pub called the Recruiting Sergeant in the High Street recalls the story that he signed-up troops for his New Model Army there.

The old road drops gently down after the village and re-joins the A1 at Gonerby Moor, close to the site of the earlier battle. When Grantham North Services was developed in the 1970s, just before the roundabout that will take me onto the A1, bones and the remains of weapons were uncovered. I pull in, interested in a more recent piece of local history.

There was a Little Chef here until 2008, when it was replaced by a Costa. I pick up a coffee and pause for a minute's silence. It wasn't until I set out to drive the Great North Road that I learned Little Chefs, and their red gingham tied-back curtains, exposed brick walls and Formica-table-tops are a thing of the past.

They began life as a British take on the American diner; the old rail dining cars that, once their life on the rails was over, became roadside attractions. In 1958, Sam Alper, a Londoner who manufactured Sprite caravans, was in America on a sales trip along with Peter Merchant, who was looking for new ideas for his catering business. They loved the diners they stopped at as they travelled the country, in particular one called the Little Chef.

In Britain, as in America, the family car was becoming common, and road travel opening up to the masses. They brought the idea home, and opened what would be the first of many Little Chefs in an 11-seater caravan alongside the A4 in Reading. Others followed, but growth was slow until they joined forces with Trusthouse Forte in 1970, after which every major road got a string of Little Chefs along it: 174 by 1976.

As I learned when I drove past the site of another just after Alconbury Hill, they are no more. Costas's may be fine, but they don't offer anything like the famed Little Chef Olympic Breakfast with its two rashers of back bacon, pork sausage, two griddle-fried eggs, mushrooms, sauté potatoes, griddled half tomato, baked beans, and toast or fried bread.

I have to take the A1's nine miles of dual carriageway through the dead-flat corn fields until I can turn off and follow the Great North Road, as the B6326, to Newark-on-Trent. It's Newark's Market Place that I've come to see. A market has been held here since the twelfth century, and the square is lined with grand and historic buildings, including a number of former coaching inns. Ranks of stalls sporting red and white striped awnings fill the square, which proudly bears the title Newark Royal Market. Beyond the Moot Hall – once a courthouse, now a Starbucks – rises the cathedral-sized church of St Mary Magdalene, its soaring spire surveying the town as St Wilfrum's does Grantham.

I take an amble around the market's perimeter and find the former Saracen's Head, eighteenth century in its present incarnation. Today a Barclays Bank squats beneath the bust of a Saracen, who looks rather like Laurence Llewelyn-Bowen in his later, portly period, when he was applying his considerable skills to flogging bathrooms for Victorian Plumbing. There had been an inn here from the fourteenth century, and the very similar-looking former Clinton Arms, its near neighbour, is just as old.

The Clinton – aka the Cardinal's Hat or King's Arms – is also a bank, a Santander, with offices above, and has a coach entrance leading to a string of shops.

John Byng was happy neither with his stay at the Clinton Arms, nor the quality of the sightseeing. He reported: 'My sheets of last night I fancied damp, and so in my old custom I drew them on the floor, and slept betwixt the blankets.' At St Mary Magdalene: 'I order'd forth the clerk, and an odd dog he was, so drunk, so deaf, and so conceited: he swore, and brag'd about his church, which is certainly a grand building, but... has nothing for an antiquary, except some stain'd glass in one window.'

I'm on the hunt for lunch, so seek out Newark's one surviving coaching inn, The Prince Rupert. It's tucked away down a narrow side road, Stodman Street, that runs between the Market Place and the River Trent. The inn is a handsome but relatively modest building.

Time-weathered brick clads the ground floor, above which timber-framed plaster panels curve out elegantly beneath a tile roof. The pub is painted a conservation shade of dark matt green and looks very inviting. So I go in, to find an appealing row of hand pumps on the bar. I'm reminded of Celia Fiennes, who liked her beer, and said of Newark: 'At this we enter Nottinghamshire and here I met with the strongest and best Nottingham ale that looked very pale but exceeding clear.'

I have a pint of Acorn IPA which, while brewed in Barnsley, is every bit as good as what she had. Inside, the Prince Rupert is all green leather benches, stout pine tables and wainscoting, just the sort of classic but comfortable pub that you can lose an afternoon in.

It is named in honour of Prince Rupert of the Rhine, a Royalist cavalry commander during the English Civil War and Charles I's nephew. Newark, a Royalist stronghold, was besieged by Cromwell three times, but relieved by Prince Rupert, and held until near the end of the war. For which he gets a pub. Actually, it hasn't always been the Prince Rupert. It used to be the Woolpack.

Charles I ended his desperate journey through enemy territory, which had taken him through Stamford, just to the west of Newark. Here he reached Scottish Royalist forces, but the war was lost.

Some four centuries before, in 1216, King John died on this spot, in what was then a merchant's house, either from dysentery brought on by a surfeit of peaches, or from poisoning. Today the catering is above suspicion. I go for the '14 hour braised beef and ale pie'.

Forcing myself to move on, a little further down Stodman Street I come out by Newark Castle, which stands high above the Trent, a position that shows immediately why Newark was of such strategic importance that it was called 'The Key to the North'. Take the castle and your way was clear.

Approaching from the south, you come up behind the north curtain wall which, together with a gatehouse, is all that remains of the great fortress. What's left stands like a pattern, cut out and held up against the sky: a stretch of wall 12 feet thick, 100ft high and 50 yards in length. High above my head a run of stone has fallen from the wall, revealing a spiral of stone staircase exposed like decay in a tooth. I look down through a Gothic arch at the river, far below.

I get an even more impressive view of the castle from north of the river, as I am leaving Newark. I pull in just after crossing it on the B6326 and look back. From here the castle looks twice as tall as it did from the town, with the river as a mighty moat.

15. Scrooby Dooby Do
– Newark-on-Trent to Doncaster –

Six miles north of Newark I come to a very little place with a very big name: Cromwell.

My route has taken me across a long, low causeway, built in 1770, over the flood plain of the River Trent, the landscape dotted with lakes and bisected by dykes. Approaching South Muskham, I passed the remnants of Civil War earthworks and batteries, reminders of Cromwell's assault on Newark.

It's a surprise to find a village bearing the name Cromwell. After all, Oliver Cromwell's personal origins lie far south, at Huntingdon. As I head towards it I'm wondering: could village and Lord Protector be in any way related?

I have endured three miles on the A1 before, at Cromwell, the Great North Road peels off behind a BP garage. I think at first I've taken a wrong turning. Solid rows of trucks line both verges, and the road is so rutted and crumbling that I fear I've misread the sign and ended up in a lorry park. But no, I can squeeze on through.

I roll to a stop and take a look around. And as I do, I wonder.

If this is the ancient seat of the Cromwell family, why is there nothing in the village, or its church, to tell me so?

Cromwell is a one-street place, with old single-storey red-brick cottages that remind me of backroads France. The church of St Giles is a modest looking thing, with a tower that, despite being of stone and dating from the fourteenth century, somehow looks like a factory chimney made from breeze-blocks. I wander the churchyard in search of Cromwell graves, but draw a blank. There is a museum next door, but its subject turns out to be 'Dolls and Bygone Childhood', not the Big O.C.

Nevertheless, Uncle Charlie concludes that Cromwell was 'probably the original seat of that family many centuries before Oliver came into the world', so I probe further. The Nottinghamshire History website has this: 'The village of Cromwell gave its name to a famous family. One of them, Ralph, Lord Treasurer under Henry VI, was intimately associated with the county. This was not the case with Thomas Cromwell, chief minister of Henry VIII, and Oliver Cromwell, both of whom were distinguished members of that family.' So, it would seem there is a connection.

I drive on through the village, the Great North Road crossing the A1 from west to east. It's the start of a great drive. From here, for the nine miles to Tuxford, the old road – bypassed in the 1960s – snakes to east and west of the new. It is broad and smooth, running in sweeping curves along the valley of the Trent through handsome villages such as Carlton-on-Trent and Sutton-on-Trent.

As I drive, the many stationary lorries I pass tell me the Great North Road is now one elongated lorry lay-by all the way to Carlton. The overlooked old road now provides truck drivers with many places for overnight stops, meal breaks or just a good honest shit in the woods. Not that I blame them. It's not their fault there are so few facilities for long distance drivers to use when the tachograph tells them no more driving today.

Mostly they are parked up in spots with no facilities, but there is one surviving long-established truck stop, the Bypass Cafe, on the first loop after Cromwell. Until recently it was in a corrugated iron shack with a red roof on which CAFE was painted in giant letters. It's in a less historic Portakabin now.

For me, with no load at my back or delivery deadline to hit, this is a wonderful stretch of road. Off to the east, the Trent traces a loop rather like the Thames does on the credits to *EastEnders*, only sideways on. I'm reminded, as I drive, of the early days of motoring, when the Great North Road could be used as a race track on which to pit cars against each other. The most famous was the 1911 Rolls vs Napier Endurance Race from London to Edinburgh and back.

The cars used mainly the Great North Road to reach Edinburgh, travelling via Grantham, Doncaster, Newcastle and Alnwick, before returning down the west of the country. A close encounter with a donkey and cart at Archway nearly scuppered the whole race.

Napier is a forgotten marque these days, but in the Edwardian era it was Rolls-Royce's deadly rival, renowned for its highly engineered luxury automobiles. Napier threw down the challenge, pitching its Silver Bullet against Rolls's Silver Cloud. The cars had to complete the race using only top gear, carrying four passengers and their luggage, and under RAC observation.

They could be driven all the way in top gear thanks to their massive 7.5 litre engines, which allowed their drivers to slip the clutch in order to move smoothly from a standing start. Fuel consumption and fastest speed achieved were taken into account in determining the winner.

The Napier managed an average of 19.3 mpg and top speed of 76.42. The Rolls trounced it, with 24.3mpg and a top speed of 78.26mph. The result sealed the Silver Cloud's reputation as the best car in the world.

I stop in Sutton-on-Trent because of another long-lost practice. In coaching days villagers, who relied on travellers for their livelihood, had a unique way of showing their appreciation. Each spring they mounted a week of festivities during which every coach was greeted, and each traveller, coachman and guard was offered food and drink.

Uncle Charlie enthused: 'Half a dozen damsels, all enchanting young people, neatly clad, rather shy but courteously importunate, plied the passengers [with] exquisite home-made bread and biscuits, ale, currant and gooseberry wines, cherry-brandy, and sometimes spirits... Such ale! such currant-wine! such cherry-brandy!'

Today they put on a very good spread at The Deli in Sutton but, at least when I passed through, they weren't handing it out for free to travellers. Nevertheless, the special of the day was Jane's Beef Stew with Buttered Cob and the butchery offered Barnsley lamb chops and home-made Lincolnshire sausages. I settled for a coffee.

A mile or so before Tuxford I'm on the lookout for a curious roadside marker called the Rebel Stone. I find it, on the grass verge beside a yard where yellow-painted cranes are sticking their long necks in the air. Despite being a grimy 6ft tall block of Ashlar shaped like a stubby carpenter's pencil, it is Grade II listed.

This 300-year-old monument bears the inscription, crudely scratched into one sloping face:

HERE
LYETH
A REBEL
1746

Someone has recently decided it needed sprucing up and scratched afresh the word HERE, revealing the stone to be a soft pink under the grime and lichen. But then the scratcher must have got bored, because the rest is semi-indecipherable.

The stone is said to mark the burial place of a Scotsman who fell in the Jacobite Rebellion of 1745-6. Despite being firmly in the English Midlands, Tuxford took the Jacobite cause, supporting the attempt to place James II's Catholic grandson, Charles Stuart (Bonnie Prince Charlie) on the throne in place of Protestant William and Mary, who had been crowned in 1689.

The Rebellion ended in 1746, following Charles's defeat at the Battle of Culloden the year before.

The story told locally is that a group of Jacobite prisoners were being taken south for trial in London when one leapt from the cart in an attempt to escape. He caught his foot and fell heavily, breaking his neck, and was buried here, where he dropped. That's unlikely, because only commanders would get the luxury of a trial. Mere foot soldiers were summarily executed, or shipped via Scottish ports to Tilbury, for onward transportation to America.

Even if the story is true, why would someone in Tuxford stump up for an expensive memorial to an unknown Scottish rebel? However, it is known that Jacobite sympathisers held regular meetings at the house of Tuxford's postmaster. Perhaps they had a whip-round.

To get to Tuxford, the old road has to climb back over the A1 from east to west, replacing the old easy ascent with an awkward knot as the road doglegs west, climbs into the village, then drops down and swings back north again after it has passed the clutch of inns and houses that make up the place.

Facing me as I come up the hill is the former Newcastle Arms Hotel, unmistakably an old coaching inn with its grand eighteenth-century frontage stretching right along one side of Market Place, and running back for half a block to the former stables. It was boarded up for some years, but is now home to a mix of businesses: The Museum of the Horse, Sally Mitchell's

Gallery, and Euphoria Beauty among them. It's good to see it occupied, freshly painted and cared for once again.

This inn has had a long history, and several names. It was the Crown when, on 11 July 1503 Margaret Tudor, sister of Henry VIII, stayed while on her journey to Edinburgh and marriage to James IV of Scotland. According to Uncle Charlie:

> She was met by the vicar and churchmen near where the rebel stone is now standing, the bells rang merrily till midnight, and large fires kept burning in the market-place. The Virgin Queen slept in the room over the south-east angle, and proceeded on her journey on the early morning of 12 July, 1503. All the neighbours of the place came in on horseback, and a great train of persons on foot to see the queen at her departure from the town. These all fell into the procession and the minstrels commenced their avocations and played right merrily.

Charles I ate and drank here in 1645, another stop on his doomed zig-zag journey. It was the White Hart then.

Like Margaret Tudor I press on, the road rising steadily through the corn fields, for the two-and-a-half-miles to Markham Moor. In her day there were just a few cottages here, but from the coaching age it became an important travellers' hub. It still is, the A638 to Retford and the A57 to Lincoln converging here on the A1, with the old Great North Road passing via a flyover and a couple of roundabouts, as the B1164. Markham Moor Services has a truckstop, an old coaching inn, and a Travelodge. Once, it also had a Little Chef, on the southbound carriageway of the A1, now a Starbucks.

I can't reach it from here, but I can peer down at it, and I do stop off on a later trip back south. The building's curled-up white concrete form goes by the technical term of a hyperbolic paraboloid, and originally formed a canopy above the pumps of a futuristic 1960s petrol station.

Something called the National Transport Trust gave it an award, because 'it is a dramatic piece of concrete design which displays the hyperbolic paraboloid form in a daring manner... reflecting as it does the new dynamism of the 1960s and the enthusiasm for all things "road".' Its Grade II listing came partly because it 'harks back to the time when driving was still an adventure'. The pumps were removed, and a Happy Eater built beneath the famous roof, in the 1980s. Then came rebranding as a Little Chef, in 1995, and Starbuckification in 2012.

From Markham Moor the Great North Road proceeds as the A638, and will take me all the way via Retford to Doncaster, the A1 way off to the west somewhere. Retford fits the mould of the handsome old Midlands market towns the Great North Road has been taking me through. Like Grantham and Newark, it has a church towering over it, in this case St Swithun's. It also has a market square as fine as Newark's, its many stalls favouring blue stripes with the white, rather than Newark's red, and mirrors that town's shortage of surviving coaching inns.

Retford did have the Crown Inn – which became a branch of the Halifax Building Society and then the Litten Tree pub – and the White Hart. That's was the corner of the square, and has on its wall an old painted sign declaring: London 144 1/2 miles York 55 miles. The White Hart was most recently the Clockwork Molly's Presents Steamology cocktail bar. A name which I felt needed explanation. So I went on their Facebook page and learned... actually, I learned nothing but I did read this:

The word 'Steamology' refers to the science and art of steampunk mixology. Steamology is a hidden gem hosting an exciting take on the steampunk genre with our dry ice cocktail bar & beer garden, just off the square of the famous market town of Retford.

Right. That's OK then.

It's not just the inns that have closed down in Retford town centre. Almost everything old is now either disused, or pressed into a new use. The Court House is a dance centre, the Post Office is empty. Judging from the original terracotta sign above the door of the ornately decorated Victorian building which declares it to be The Old Bank, they must have anticipated it morphing into something like the council offices it is now.

There is something unique in the market square, however: a stone column on which sits what looks at first like a large bowl.

This curious object is a relic of the days, in the seventeenth century, when travellers might carry the plague with them. It's called the Broad Stone, and I read that it has a hollow in it that was filled with vinegar in which those travellers' coins could be disinfected.

It's since been mounted on a plinth, raising the top above my eye level, so I have to hold my phone up to take a picture over the rim to see that hollow. But I discover that the top is actually flat, and covered in moss. Still, far be it from me to diss local folklore, so I'll just leave it there.

Five miles further on along the A638, at Barnby Moor, I do find a surviving coaching inn. In fact the seventeenth-century Olde Bell is thriving, its car park lined with a bank of new accommodation. Lady Jane Grey is said to haunt the place. The wood panelling in the Bradgate Suite comes from Bradgate House in Leicestershire, home of Lady Jane, who was queen for just nine days, in 1554, before being executed.

The ByngAdvisor was satisfied for once, rating The Bell for having a 'civil landlord, a good parlour ... and a good bed in a good bed chamber.' Byng had a sore chest, and was given snail tea for breakfast. Ostensibly as a cure, possibly to give him something to complain about in his review.

In 1932, scenes were shot at the hotel for a film version of JB Priestley's *The Good Companions*, a book that celebrated the romance of the Great North Road. In the story, run-away husband Jesse Oakroyd goes in search of fame and fortune in the South, and is spell-bound by driving at night down the famous highway:

> Then there came a great moment... Oakroyd read the words painted in large black letters on a whitewashed wall. The Great North Road. They were actually going down the Great North Road. He could have shouted. He didn't care what happened after this... Here was another town, and the road was cutting through it like a knife through cheese, Doncaster, it was. No trams now; everybody gone to bed, except the lucky ones going down South on the Great North Road.

Four miles on, there is one more place to explore before Doncaster: Scrooby.

Scrooby is a seemingly insignificant place which, remarkably, played a key role in the creation of America. From here came one of that nation's founders, William Brewster, who sailed with the Pilgrim Fathers aboard the *Mayflower* in 1620 to establish the Plymouth Colony in present-day Massachusetts. These days the village inn is called the Pilgrim Fathers, and has a sign bearing the portrait of a man who looks a lot like the comedian Bill Bailey, in a leprechaun's hat.

To mark the 400th anniversary of that voyage, a multi-armed direction post was installed in the pub car park, topped with a roundel depicting the ship the Pilgrim Fathers sailed to the New World in, and surrounded with the inscription: Mayflower 1620-2020. The many arms point to various locations in England and America that are relevant to this search for a new life of religious freedom. Clearly lots of descendants of those pioneers come to the village, and there are information boards dotted all around it.

Brewster lived at the Manor House, which is on the eastern fringe of the village towards the River Idle, named after Eric, of

Monty Python fame. Brewster, and his father – also William – before him, were the postmasters, responsible for providing post boys and horses to carry the mail along the Great North Road.

The Brewsters were Nonconformists, and established the Church of Scrooby, a Puritan Separatist congregation, at the Manor House. They, and those who attended services, were breaking the law in failing to attend St Wilfrid's, the CofE church in the village. I pop into that church, where Brewster was baptised, and accidentally interrupt a meeting of the parish council. I tiptoe around them, to take a look at items commemorating the pilgrims. There is a cobblestone given by the city of Plymouth, and a plaque made in 1955 by descendants of the *Mayflower* pioneers. There is also a cabinet containing pilgrim mugs and candles.

Those Nonconformists, now lauded, were hunted and persecuted. Some were imprisoned, others had their houses watched day and night. Several fled.

I also want to see the Manor House, scene of that rebellious worship. On one of the information boards I read that, while the house itself is off limits, if I go to a particular spot down Station Road, by its junction with Mayflower Avenue, I will get a view of it. Unfortunately, it seems that the hedge has grown since that sign was made, because all I see are glimpses, through leaves, of a couple of distant, and indistinct, buildings.

No matter. Brewster, Bradford and John Carver of Doncaster led the foundation of the first American colony and Brewster, as religious elder, held the first Thanksgiving celebration in 1621. It is down to the beliefs of this colony that the first amendment to the Constitution of the United States, the right to religious freedom, was established.

From Scrooby it's just 10 miles on through Bawtry, yet another pleasant market town, to Doncaster, tonight's destination.

IV

GREAT NORTH ROAD
Doncaster
to Darlington

Darlington

The Great
North Road

Doncaster to
Darlington

Scotch
Corner

Catterick

Leeming
Bar

Londonderry

Boroughbridge

Ferrybridge

Wetherby

Wentbridge

Robin
Hoods
Well

Doncaster

From Doncaster to Darlington, the Great North Road is truly the wonderful drivers' road of old. A mere eight out of 84 miles are on the current A1, less than 10 per cent of the total, and the last 30-mile stretch from Boroughbridge doesn't encounter the modern road at all.

Which means I can enjoy several sustained stretches where the old road forges a way across high moorland, with the occasional dip to valley and village or town. Among the highlights are the 17 miles over Hook Moor and Bramham Moor from Ferrybridge to Wetherby, the 10 miles from Wetherby to Boroughbridge, and the 24 miles along Roman Dere Street, darting arrow-straight between the Pennines and Cleveland Hills, from Boroughbridge to Catterick.

For most of that mileage, the old route runs in the shadow of the new, occasionally flipping from one side to the other, allowing me to contrast the joy of the empty old road with the heavy traffic on the new, and pace myself against it. In theory the A1 should be the faster route, but in practice it often isn't.

This section also features a parting of the ways.

At Doncaster, the Great North Road is the high road to Darlington, and the York Road the low. Their division is rooted in coaching history. In the early days, most services from London ended at York. Once through services were established to Newcastle and Edinburgh, most coaches chose the more direct, but hillier route, which bypassed York. Both get to Darlington, but in their own sweet way. I'll take the low road to York Road later. For now, it's the high road for me.

16. Don Roaming

– Doncaster to Ferrybridge –

There is a human jukebox sitting among the smattering of afternoon drinkers in the Red Lion, Doncaster. He has his volume turned down low, so from a table away I can only just make out what he's singing. It's obscure stuff, and I only vaguely recognise some of what he is crooning to himself.

One song I do recognise is the Julio Iglesias Eighties hit 'Begin the Beguine'. But, the way our man sings it, 'beguine' sounds like 'bag in'. As in, if you want a strong cuppa, you ask for 'builders, bag in'.

Next up is the Herman's Hermits Sixties hit 'No Milk Today'. So he's made the tea, now he's putting the milk in. What's going to be next? A biscuit to dunk? Maybe 'Wagon Wheel' by Lou Reed? Or, with dieting in mind, The Killers' 'Leave The Bourbon On The Shelf'. That would be Bourbon as in Chocolate Bourbon.

I shouldn't really be sitting here. I ought to be out exploring Doncaster, but the rain is coming down and the wind is up and, I tell myself, with the history of this now-Wetherspoons inn and the town in a series of framed posters on the walls, this is as good a place as any to get acquainted with the town.

So I'm actually doing my research while having a drink. Which makes it tax-deductable. I'll do the leg work later. I scouted out one famous place on my drive in. The A638, true to the course of the Great North Road, took me past Doncaster racecourse, home of the St Leger, then on to Bennetthorpe and South Parade.

It was the founding of the St Leger, in 1776, that established Doncaster's status as a fashionable racing town, and the many listed three-storey, bay-fronted stucco terraces I admired as the traffic crawled on towards Hall Gate were built as a result of the prosperity and expansion that the race brought to the town. The old route continues straight on via Hall Gate to High Street and French Gate, crossing the River Don via North Bridge Road. But High Street is one-way only, and against me, and French Gate is pedestrianised, which means I've come as far as I can on wheels.

So I turn right, park in Laith Gate and walk to the Market Place, where the Red Lion has stood since 1742.

The race's name was settled upon at a dinner held in the Duke of York Room at this very inn, and honours Anthony St Leger, the Doncaster Army officer and politician who devised it. There's a brass plaque recording the connection in the pub, and other memorabilia associated with the race, its greatest horses, and jockeys including Lester Piggott.

The St Leger Stakes, held every September for the past 250-odd years, is the oldest of Britain's five Classic races. The Classics are for three-year olds and are contested by the very finest racehorses. To win one of the Classics denotes a horse that is among the greatest of its generation. To win two or three shows it is truly exceptional.

I haven't recognised the last couple of songs from the human jukebox, but then comes 'Cinderella Rockefella', a novelty hit for Esther and Abi Ofarim. I'm beginning to feel like all my past *Top of the Pops* are flashing before me, like your life is supposed to do just before you die.

When the jukebox goes outside for a fag, all sorts of long-forgotten songs start coming to mind, one by one. It's like when someone mentions 'The Birdy Song' and then, for the rest of the day, you can't stop humming the bloody thing. To stop myself doing just that, I can only try to replace it with another. Except, each song I think of is even more irritating than the last. I mean, 'The Macarena'? 'Son of My Father', by Chicory Tip? No!

I wonder if the human jukebox comes in here every afternoon. Maybe he is a Wetherspoons version of an artist in residence: a piss artist in residence.

I get up to go to the loo, and the very fact of getting up makes me think of the lyric 'git on up' from 'Get Up (I Feel Like Being A) Sex Machine' by James Brown, who also became known as *the* Sex Machine. Was he though? Or, what with all that grunting, just really, really constipated?

On the way up to the loo I pass a portrait of Doncaster-born plumber Thomas Crapper, who invented the ballcock system for flushing lavatories. It was a breakthrough akin to when Steve Jobs had Apple perfect the touch screen on a phone. Thanks to Crapper, everyone wanted a chain to pull.

There's no sign of the rain letting up, but I really can't put off having a look around Doncaster any longer, so I pull my hood up and slouch out into the Market Place.

Of all the fine market towns the Great North Road has taken me through, this is the grandest. Ever since the Romans started trading here in 43AD, this market has been the big, beating heart of Doncaster. In past centuries 60,000 fleeces passed through the wool market every Saturday in summer, and its corn market was among the most important in the North.

The Victorians added extensive market buildings, plus the very grand red sandstone Corn Exchange and Concert Hall, which stands in splendid isolation at the centre of the broad expanse. Today, there's a thriving three-day-a-week market boasting 400 shops and stalls. It's actually several markets in one. Some, such as the meat and fish market, under cover, others spread out across the square, which is fringed by a string of boozers extensive enough to offer a challenging pub crawl.

I do a circuit without going into any of them, and pass beneath the modern processional arch at the Sunny Bar Gateway, where ornately patterned, deep-pink brick columns support a 20-foot-high steel arch. Atop one column stands a bronze statue of a sheep, on the other a pig. Both have their snouts raised as if uttering trumpeting oinks and bleats. Or maybe just singing along to the human jukebox.

Charles Dickens and Wilkie Collins came for the St Leger in 1857, staying at The Angel and Royal. The trip wasn't entirely successful. The pair encountered: 'a gathering of blackguards from all parts of the racing earth. Every bad face that had ever caught wickedness from an innocent horse had its representation in the streets.' Next morning they found these hung-over revellers crowding into chemists' shops, pleading: 'Give us soom sal-volatile or soom damned thing o' that soort, in wather – my head's bad!'

The night after the race, Dickens and Collins were kept awake by a 'groaning phantom' who lay in the doorway to one of the rooms and howled all night. The landlord told them the man had lost £1,500 or £2,000 by backing 'a wrong 'un' and had drunk himself senseless.

The Angel and Royal was knocked down to make way for the Frenchgate Centre in 1962, and the pub of that name in Cleveland Street has no connection with it. That building started life as a Yates's Wine Lodge in 1997.

Maybe one day the history of Yates's will be celebrated. I remember the Yates's of thirty years ago. The barmaids: older ladies in carpet slippers and pinnies; the champagne and port served on draught; the string quartets that sawed away – ignored – and the bouncers employed to keep drinkers in the upstairs balcony bar away from the edge, to prevent them gobbing on the punters below. Happy days.

The ByngAdvisor reviewed the original Angel as 'nasty, insolent and with city stabling'. He didn't rate the food either. I wonder what he'd make of the new Angel and Royal, which describes itself as a: 'Spacious boozer, with a mezzanine level, for a range of hand-pulled beers and simple comfort food.'

You know what? I think it's time to say goodbye to the Byngster. He's not at all happy this far from home, and needs to get back there. I've another travelling companion about to join me.

The rain defeats me and I head back to the Red Lion, to experience the rest of Doncaster's history out of the wet. The town didn't cease to be a transport hub when the railways killed the coach roads, because it became a great rail town.

As another of the framed posters tells me, the Great Northern Railway set up their carriage building works here in 1853, going on to build the first 100-miles-per hour locomotive – the Flying Scotsman – in 1923, and Mallard, which has held the world speed record for a steam locomotive since 1938, when it reached 126 mph.

Another poster tells me that, among the employees at the Doncaster works was an apprentice railway engineer called Walter Owen Bentley, who later went on to found the Bentley Motor Car Company.

Next morning, it is still raining as I pick up the continuation of the Great North Road at North Bridge Road and, at the roundabout just over the river, reach an historic parting of the ways. Here, I have the choice of two routes north. If I go straight ahead I am on the Great North Road, which will take me to Darlington, via Wetherby, as the A638. Take the next exit off that roundabout and I will still get to Darlington, but via York and Selby. This route, now the A19, was known as the York Road.

There are those who claim the former is the true historic route, and others who favour the latter. Both are right. The latter road was the key route in the days when York was the limit for coach services from London. But, when north-bound coaches ran on to Newcastle and Edinburgh, they favoured the hilly, but more direct route, largely along Ermine Street, via Wetherby.

I am going to explore both routes, starting with the Great North Road. And, having sent the ByngAdvisor on his way, I want to introduce a new travelling companion: Yorkshireman JS Fletcher: Fletch. Joseph Smith Fletcher, who lived from 1863 to 1935, was a journalist and author, among whose books is 1901's *Nooks and Corners of Yorkshire*.

Fletch was born and brought up in the village of Darrington, which I'm on my way to, and his love of the Great North Road through Yorkshire is as strong as John Byng's was for the old road through his native Bedfordshire.

This is Fletch bigging up the route in his book:

> The motorist, the cyclist, or the pedestrian, who wishes to form a good impression of the heart of Yorkshire and incidentally to see much of the country which is not usually visited by the average tourist who seeks out the famous show places, cannot do better than traverse its entire length from the south to north by way of the Great North Road.

He likes it because it:

> ...passes through scenery which is essentially middle-Yorkshire, and therefore most characteristic of the Yorkshire of long ago... the entire country on either side of the Great North Road is pastoral and agricultural, as Yorkshire was in the main before manufacturers and steam and railways came into being. Nowhere are seen the black vapours of Sheffield, the greyness of Leeds, the gloom of Barnsley – the wide belt of land which runs from south to north in Yorkshire... is an expanse of corn-land and meadow-land, deep woods and quiet villages, old manor houses and ancient churches.

Now, I should say that Fletch has a few quirks when it comes to the route of the old road. He favours a route that, further north, jumps in a couple of places between the Great North Road and the York Road, but we can't get bogged down in that.

He's a knowledgeable guide, and *Nooks and Corners* still gives many reliable pointers to interesting places for me to seek out today.

Fletch also has wise words about the pace at which the old road should be explored:

Naturally such a journey along the Great North Road must be made in leisurely fashion. A swift motor could travel across the county... in a few hours, and a good cyclist would accomplish the journey in a day without discomfort, but neither would have time for turning aside from the old highway whose foundations were largely laid by the Romans. And to see the nooks and corners of the Great North Road it is necessary to turn aside very often – sometimes for a hundred yards, sometimes for a mile, sometimes for a few miles, but never without profit.

Just north of Doncaster, at Scawsby, I hit one of those nooks. The road has run over a series of little viaducts to the junction where, before the Sun Inn, the Barnsley road runs left as the A635. This used to be a charming rural spot known as York Bar, today it's a nondescript suburban stretch of road lined with metal-box shopping outlets. But something momentous happened here in the sixteenth century, which stemmed from the fact that Henry VIII's Dissolution of the Monasteries was by no means universally popular.

Rebellions against the policy sprang up, the most serious occurring in Doncaster, and posed a challenge to Tudor rule. In 1536, a 40,000-strong throng of Yorkshire folk of all classes, led by Robert Aske, a London-based barrister whose family was from Selby, marched in protest on what was known as the Pilgrimage of Grace. They called on Henry, and Thomas Cromwell, to reverse the break with Rome and halt the plundering and destruction of the monasteries.

The uprising was considered so serious that here, at Scawsby Leys, the marchers were met by emissaries of the king including the Duke of Norfolk, with a force of 7,000 troops. Norfolk, seeing he was severely outnumbered and unable to put the rebellion down by force, promised that a parliament would be held at York within a year, and that no more abbeys would be seized before it sat, plus a pardon for all those who had joined the march.

Believing Norfolk spoke in good faith, Aske had the pilgrims disperse. His trust proved to be misplaced. Henry had not authorised Norfolk to make such promises. Aske and other leaders were tried for treason and executed. His body was suspended in chains at York.

A couple of miles on, at the Red House roundabout, named after an old inn, the A368 veers off to the west, and I am on the A1 again, for the first time since Cromwell, 48 miles back. But only for seven miles, which is just as well.

I need to pay attention, because another nook is fast approaching, just after Skellow: a blink-and-you'll miss it little place called Robin Hood's Well. But I can't actually get to it from the north-bound carriageway. All I can see above the crash barriers is a squat limestone shelter supported on four arches. So I have to loop back to it. Coming south it is even harder to spot. I almost miss the unsignposted, rutted layby that runs off behind a belt of scrubby trees.

It's another of those truckers' rests, the road rutted, the hedges behind a line of black and yellow striped poles, there to warn lorry drivers of the danger of toppling off into the fields. Today it's marked on the map in the tiny olde worlde lettering the Ordnance Survey reserves for ancient monuments, but this was once a hamlet with farms, cottages and two inns serving 30 coaches a day. One, the Robin Hood, had stabling for 60 horses.

In 1960, with the opening of the A1(M) Doncaster Bypass, the Great North Road was replaced by a dual carriageway along a new alignment. The Robin Hood Inn was demolished to make way for the south-bound lanes. The three-storey New Inn limped on for another decade, but is now a private house, just where I turned off.

I bounce 500 yards down the layby, which was once a kink in the old road, to the far end, and park by the stone dome I glimpsed heading north. This is a well house, which once covered a spring beside a stream called The Skell. That stream is actually just to the north of the point at which I left the road, and the well house was moved to its present spot at the time the Robin Hood Inn was bulldozed. In coaching days, travellers would drink from the well. One, in 1640, described a stone chair; and an iron ladle to drink out of, chained to the seat.

So where, given we are in Yorkshire rather than Nottinghamshire, does Robin Hood come in? This area was once covered by Barnsdale Forest, which has long-standing claims to be the original setting from Robin Hood's rob-from-the rich, give-to-the-poor enterprises. Records of Hood's association with this spot, and the well, date back to 1422.

The present well house is from 1710, commissioned by Charles Howard, 3rd Earl of Carlisle, and designed by Sir John Vanburgh, in an attempt to cement Robin Hood's connections with the spot. Vanburgh also designed Castle Howard for the earl, at Henderskelfe, 15 miles north of York. Among those Robin Hood practised his distributive policy on here was the Bishop of Hereford who, it is said, was made to dance around a tree in return for safe passage along the Great North Road.

The well head is a sorry looking thing, despite having been Grade II listed in 1968. It seems to have lost something in height when it was moved, judging by old photographs, and now stands on a concrete base. Still, it makes a handy trap for the litter that whirls around in the draught from passing vehicles.

Even in the 1970s this was a grim stretch of road. Norman Webster wrote that: 'Traffic, heavy in volume and in weight, sweeps past, noisy and polluting, careless of the interest and attractions of the surroundings, mindful only of its objective.'

I'm glad, once I get back on the north-bound carriageway, that I'm only on it for a handful of miles, before I can turn off for the village of Wentbridge, another nook with a Robin Hood connection.

This is an exposed stretch of the A1, high on the hills, whipped by wind and rain. I pass an artic trailer in a field: 'Prepare to meet thy God' on the side, 'Jesus is Lord' on the front. On a clear day, there are fine views east from this high ground stretching from Selby Abbey to the Humber Estuary and the distant Wolds away to the east. But this is not a clear day.

The old road, now the B6474, peels off to the west to drop down to Wentbridge, with trucks parked up on well-churned unofficial lay-bys. The Blue Bell Inn, once a coaching house, now a lovely village pub, is on the right as I drop down through the village.

Bearing in mind Fletch's warning not to rush blindly through Yorkshire, I stop beside the little bridge over the River Went, and go for a walk. This peaceful valley is quite a contrast to life on the A1. I feel like I'm back in the real world. Crows are the noisiest thing around.

A blue plaque on the old bridge commemorates the fact that Wentbridge is one of the only place names that can be identified in accounts of Robin Hood's life. The steep drop into the valley here, and the rough climb up the other side, made this one of the most arduous stretches in coaching days, and became a bottleneck for twentieth-century motor traffic.

That changed in 1961, when the village was bypassed and the valley spanned by the great 100 yard-long concrete viaduct which I can see off to my right, striding across on 100ft-long scissor legs.

Coming down such a steep valley I had expected to find a torrent raging through under the bridge. I find a trickle. The River Went needs to get its prostate checked. But, downriver, it passes through quite a wide flood plain, so maybe it does get a real power-wazz on at times.

That trickle is very suggestive, and I have to find a discreet spot for a pee. It's not the first time I've been caught short lately. It happens more and more often, something I had been putting down to age, but the thought occurs to me: maybe it's not that at all. Perhaps, as I age, I'm becoming more dog. In which case, it wouldn't be peeing, it would be marking my territory. If so, with the many hundreds of miles up the old road to cover, there'll be a lot more stops like this to come.

Fletch says this spot is 'little known except to travellers along the road' and calls it 'one of the prettiest villages and most charming scenes in Yorkshire'. Here, 'beauty bursts upon one' and it has 'a view which is Alpine in its characteristics'.

I take a stroll north along the old road, past the Wentworth House Hotel, and a decommissioned bus stop like a garden shed with a 'Stop Not In Use' sign. As the road begins to climb, an even older route runs up on its right-hand flank. Today it's a pleasant woodland walk but, until 1830, it was the main road and so steep that, to spare the horses, coach passengers had to get out and walk. In that year an easier route was hacked with great labour out of the sandstone but, as I see when I drive up it later, it's still quite a climb.

The woodland track takes me past twin modern mansions, one recently competed to the left of the road, the one on the right still under construction, no doubt built here to take advantage of the views along the valley. The climb brings me out to a cabbage field, on the far side of which, right on the horizon, trucks shuffle left and right on the A1.

The next and last of Fletch's nooks on this stretch is Darrington, his home village. As there is a back road to it, I can avoid going back on the A1.

Fletch loved Darrington as much as John Byng loved Southill. In his book *Darrington: A Yorkshire Parish* he described the heart of the place, where church, school, dovecote and tithe barn clustered beside an apple orchard 'unique in England, all being in one tight group in the heart of the village'.

In the 1930s, one of the earliest stretches of A1 dual carriageway split Darrington in two, but a flyover reunited them again in 1970. It strides, high and mighty, over the village. Fletch's little cluster of buildings survives intact, all but the tithe barn. I walk up to them, entering St Luke's church where a twelfth-century sandstone crucifix, part of a unique double cross discovered in a garden wall, is displayed.

Across the churchyard is the turret-like former dovecote, now a house, and bearing a stone plaque reading: 'Darrington Jubilee Church House AD 1887'. The tithe barn survives as just a shoulder-high, right-angled stretch of wall, and the former school is just beyond it, across a lane. I can see what Fletch meant: this really is a very special spot.

Within the triangle formed by church, dovecote and school is Church Orchard, the few trees now aged and scrawny. But a sign in the glass-fronted noticeboard says: 'The vicar and PCC are looking for sculptors to donate modern art sculptures for installation in this orchard which belongs to the church council'.

I have to join the A1 for a split second at the flyover, but almost immediately turn off onto the A162, which performs a complicated bit of acrobatics to take the old road swinging up and over the A1, then vaulting the M62, and on to Ferrybridge. And Ferrybridge, as I am about to discover, offers a stark contrast to the rural pleasures I have enjoyed on the 12 miles since Doncaster.

17. Bridge to Bridge
– Ferrybridge to Boroughbridge –

You know Fletch said this route was pastoral and agricultural, avoiding the steam, vapours, greyness and gloom that blight other stretches of Yorkshire? Well, I think he was being a little light with the truth when it came to Ferrybridge.

It is an awkward turn off the A162 and descent on the B6136, where I find a lay-by alongside the River Aire, and pull in. This is very clearly a post-industrial town, and must have been a grimy place when Fletch came through around 1900. Something he turned a blind eye to.

It was also a substantial transport interchange; the point at which the Great North Road crossed the east-west route from Hull to Huddersfield. Today, the trans-Pennine M62 sweeps cross-country traffic to the south of the town, where it links with the A1(M).

Here, also, the River Aire connects – at a lock – with the Aire and Calder Navigation, a canalised offshoot of those two rivers that links Leeds with Doncaster and Goole. It dates from 1704, and at its peak carried 1.5 million tons of coal a year. Goods would be transferred from barges to carts for onward travel via the Great North Road. It was finally abandoned in 1986.

From my parking place on the riverbank, I have the old, 1804 Great North Road bridge to my left, the new A162 bridge to my right. The new bridges spanning Wentbridge and Darrington had the grace to sail high above the towns they bypassed. Not here. This one has almost taken the town off at the hairline. Ferrybridge cowers beneath it.

The old bridge crosses the Aire in three elegant, arching strides. For over 150 years it carried the north road. I walk over what is now a pedestrian path, to find that the course of the old road butts up against the embankment supporting the new one.

I look back to Ferrybridge. To my right are the cooling towers, chimneys and big boxy things with wires coming out of them (sorry to get so technical) of Ferrybridge Power Station. In an attempt to humanise it, a stretch of wall on the perimeter has been painted with a mural, featuring a kingfisher among other more industrial imagery of a train and a man in an orange hi-viz jerkin and hard hat. In the background another figure is running away. I don't blame him.

This was by no means the first bridge on the spot. The ferry was replaced in 1461, after the Bishop of Durham offered a 40-day indulgence (that's a discount on your soul's time in purgatory) for those who contributed to building and maintaining it. Meaning the town really ought to have shortened its name to Bridge over 500 years ago.

As I walk back I pass the former toll house, and what must be an old mile-stone, a head-high limestone cylinder like a stone post box, but with no identifying signs on it.

I walk beneath the new bridge to a former coaching inn, The Golden Lion, just beyond. Its walls are painted a sort of pale gold and, when I get closer, I see the building has been stuccoed, with the sort of mad slap you see in ersatz Greek tavernas.

I had heard that, during lockdown, it was looking pretty sad, a forlorn banner offering 'Accommodation available, contractors welcome', and I feared finding it had gone out of business, like too many other former coaching inns. So I'm pleased to see it has a fresh banner: 'New owners, new ideas'.

According to Uncle Charlie, the Golden Lion used to be a favourite with drovers. He writes:

Drovers were a great feature of the road, and their flocks and herds an unmitigated nuisance to all other travellers. Uncouth creatures from Scotland, they footed it all the way to London with their beasts, making their 20 miles a day; their sheep and cattle often numerous enough to occupy a whole mile of road, and raising dust-clouds dense enough to choke a whole district. It was, at the pace they went, a three weeks' journey from the far north to London and the fat cattle that started on the four hundred miles walk must, with these efforts, have become the leanest... on arrival at Smithfield.

On the quay beside the pub, bollards are reminders of the days huge barges docked here. Just beyond is the lock guarding the entrance to the navigation.

The Golden Lion is in one corner of The Square, once the transport hub of the town, now reduced to a triangle, thanks to the embankment supporting the new road stomping on it like the big boot at the start of *Monty Python's Flying Circus*. There were several other major coaching inns nearby: The Bay Horse, The Greyhound, The Angel, and the Swan, none of which survive.

Fletch says the end, for what was 'a station of the highest importance in coaching days' came 'with startling suddenness. The coaches – there were at least fifty used to pass through a day – stopped running; nobody used post chaises anymore; nothing to do; grass grew in the stable-yards and in the square. Few places have more ghosts than this, or witnessed more diverse scenes'.

I drive the winding way back up to the A162 and over the Aire. It takes me minutes to fly over the river today, but the causeway spanning the Aire and the marshy land on its north bank was once prey to the huge force of the river in full spate. By way of illustration, Fletch says: 'Here William the Conqueror fumed and fretted for three weeks because the River Aire was in flood and barred his progress on his grim mission of burning and devastating York.'

Just across the river, the A1246 bears left to follow the route of the Great North Road. It diverts around the villages of Brotherton and Fairburn, but I stick to the old road, passing the Thaal Indian restaurant, once another drovers' house called The Fox, and on alongside an almost sheer drop to the glittering, marshy valley of the Aire.

A combination of the A1246 and A63 keep me on the old road. I feel very smug when the A1(M) swings in close from the west, clogged with cars and trucks moving only slightly faster than I am on my empty road.

I wind through the former mining village of Micklefield, which Uncle Charlie saw when coal was still king, and called 'an abject coal-mining village.' In 1896, an explosion sent a fireball surging through the Peckfield Colliery here, killing 63 of the 105 men and boys down the pit, plus 19 of 23 pit ponies. The mine closed in 1980, and the village is now spruced up. I had half expected to find a community ravaged, but in fact it is a pleasant enough place, with a railway station that makes Leeds – 12 miles away – accessible for work.

A steady rise takes the road up on to Hook Moor, where coal's successor, the giant wind turbines at Hook Moor Wind Farm, conjure clean energy from the air. Uncle Charlie rated this one of the finest stretches of the old road. My route takes me – feeling very smug once again – over the junction of the A1M with the M1, swarming with traffic, and on to a die-straight descent on the course of the Roman Ridge road into Aberford.

Here, the way opens up. There are wide grass verges on either side of the road, lined with neat stone and brick walls, an approach similar to that of many a village in the Yorkshire Dales. I pass the very grand Gascoigne Almshouses which, with a central stone tower and twin chapels at either end, is more stately home than refuge for the poor.

This is sandstone country, and there is a softer, more honeyed look to the houses in Main Street as I drop down to the point where the road crosses Cock Beck, now much diminished from when it was the Cock River, and occupied all three of the arched passages beneath the bridge at the centre of the village. Today, one arch is enough. Aberford staked a claim to being the midpoint between London and Edinburgh, before bypasses and motorway section altered the equation, but there were a couple of rival claims at Wetherby.

Remembering Fletch's advice to seek out nooks, I park and take a look around. Aberford is hunkered down, secure in its hollow, a refuge tucked between the starkly beautiful, wind-swept uplands of Hook Moor to the south and Bramham Moor to the north. The Swan Hotel, once a fine coaching inn, had its white-painted render removed in 2017 and scrubbed up nicely as two handsome homes, the arched entrance to its stable yard revealing its former role. The Arabian Horse, its one-time rival, lives on.

Uncle Charlie gives this account of the two hostelries:

The picturesque old settles and yawning fireplaces of the Swan, and of that oddly-named inn, the Arabian Horse, eloquent of the habits of generations ago, survive to show us what was the accommodation those old inns provided. If more primitive, it was heartier, and a great deal more comfortable than that of modern hotels.

I seek out St Ricarius, a nineteenth-century flower of a church on twelfth-century roots. It's the only church in England dedicated to Richarius, a seventh century French hermit and monk. He travelled England on a donkey, preaching and curing the sick, and visited Aberford in 630.

By the churchyard wall stands part of the old market cross, which was discovered by the roadside and placed here in 1911, together with a plague stone, a more modest version of the one I saw at Retford, in whose vinegar-filled hollow money could be sterilised as it passed between shopper and trader. It is well-preserved, unlike some of the sandstone graves, which centuries of wind have whittled away at, turning them slowly into lace doilies.

Norman Webster summed up Aberford's charms in the 1970s, and what he said then holds true today: 'Aberford was one of those many delightful places on the northern road which contributed much to the romantic atmosphere of the highway and which was regarded with affection; its removal from the modern alignment has brought forthrightness to the new road at the expense of lost charm.' Which is why it is worth leaving the new road for the old.

Heading on, I find the A1(M) pacing itself against me as I climb up onto Bramham Moor. Then, at the junction with the east-west A64, I flip from left to right of the new road and follow the discreet side road, aptly named Paradise Way, on to Bramham.

From there I enjoy another fast, quiet, vastly superior alternative to the new road as I follow the long gentle descent to Wetherby, joining the A168 for the final approach over the wonderful old bridge on the River Wharfe.

Wetherby is one of the loveliest spots on the old Great North Road. I use the car park down a steep lane immediately downriver of the bridge, and head up to the Wetherby Whaler for fish and chips, then take my parcel to a bench from which I can look up at the bridge and admire it as it soars overhead. There has been a bridge here since the thirteenth century, built thanks to those who took up the same offer the Archbishop of York made at Ferrybridge.

It was rebuilt after being damaged in a flood in the seventeenth century, and widened twice, as traffic on the Great North Road grew, in 1773 and in 1826.

The town, and the bridge, were bypassed first in 1959, by what is now the A168, then in 2005 by the A1(M) which loops round to the east of town, leaving Wetherby in peace.

Just upriver from the bridge, the Wharfe thunders down a weir, over which Uncle Charlie watched the salmon leap as they fought their way to their spawning grounds. He had this to say about Wetherby:

This is a hard-featured, stony town; still, as of old, chiefly concerned with cattle-raising and cattle-dealing, and crowded on market-days with farmers and drovers driving bargains or swearing at the terrified efforts of beasts and sheep to find their way into the shops and inns.

Today Wetherby is an altogether gentler place with, still at its heart, the handsome Market Place, with its galleried run of former butchers' shops on The Shambles. The High Street, course of the Great North Road, runs just to the east of the market, and here I find the two old coaching inns. First is the Angel or, as it is now, Sant' Angelo Ristorante Pizzeria, and then the seventeenth century Swan and Talbot.

The Angel was the pre-eminent coaching inn from 1760 until 1840, when the trade died, with stabling for 100 horses. The Angel also claimed to be the half-way point between London and Edinburgh, as did a milestone a mile or so north of Wetherby. I pass that spot, just past the point where the Great North Road, having left Wetherby as the B6164, joins the A168. Alongside it was an inn, the Old Fox.

The Fox offered neither horses, food nor accommodation, just beer, relying on its location to bring in trade. Drovers in particular made a point of marking the half-way point in their journey with a drink at this modest, two-storey thatched inn whose sign swung from a tree, but there is nothing to mark the spot today.

In the twentieth century the Fox became the Alpine Lodge, a Samuel Smith pub, but closed in the 1990s. It was demolished in 2007 after being badly damaged by fire.

The A168 takes me swiftly through the three miles to Walshford, where the original course was abandoned in favour of the present A road, shortly after crossing the River Nidd. Here, between the course of old and new roads, is what was once the modest Walshford Inn, a posting house that, unusually, is far grander now than it was in coaching days. Today this is the much expanded, four-star Bridge Hotel and Spa.

This was always one of the quietest stretches of the Great North Road, and still is. If it weren't such a joy to drive, I might turn off it onto an even older route just before the hotel, and then off again along a track that leads to stately, seventeenth century

Ribston Hall. Fletch has this to say about it: 'At Ribston Hall, once a preceptory of the Knights Templars [and hence a pilgrim and traveller's hostelry], is the famous original Ribston Pippin tree, which was raised from seed brought over from Normandy two [now three] centuries ago.'

I do think about seeking out this further nook for a second, but the pull of the road, which leaps the A1(M) and flies on for another 10 glorious, uninterrupted miles to Boroughbridge, is just too strong to resist.

18. Dere Street

– Boroughbridge to Darlington –

There is a lovely, pervasive smell of baking hovering over Boroughbridge, as if the whole town has just been taken out of the oven.

Down the High Street and around the Market Square there are not just bakers' but pie makers', butchers' and cake makers'. Dotted around Boroughbridge are those other constituents of a proper town: an old-fashioned ironmonger; a bike shop; and a newsagents' with a window full of toys to make any child dream pocket-money-busting dreams. There are fresh veg and bedding plants outside Fink 'the face of fine food'; a vintner and, of course, a surviving coaching inn.

In the centre of Market Square is the most elaborate well you are ever likely to come across. As wide as a family-size hot tub, it has a gabled, tiled, circular roof supported on stone columns, and is topped with a cupola and a weathervane. It supplied water to almost everyone in town until the 1930s.

Fletch called Boroughbridge 'an old-world, quiet-streeted place, by which one flashes on the way by road north or south' and suggested his readers have a good old poke around, because 'the hunter of curiosities will find some rare things in the old parlours and in the quaint glass-fronted cupboards and on the high mantleshelves'. Which sounds just a little too intrusive to me.

I have turned off the A168 to come into town along Wetherby Road, and park in Horsefair, where the Great North Road meets Fishergate. This is another once-important junction: a route to York heading south-east, the Great North Road forging on over the River Ure as the B6265. Coaches for Carlisle, Edinburgh, Glasgow, Durham and Newcastle passed through daily, as did 2,000 cattle. The River Ure, linking Ripon upstream with York down, was also a busy transport route.

Two coaching inns once stood at this junction: The Three Greyhounds on the west side of Horsefair, staring across at the Crown, on the corner with Fishergate. Only the Crown, which once had stabling for 100 horses, is still in the hospitality business, but the three-storey cream stucco frontage of the Greyhounds is instantly identifiable from the trio of galloping dogs bearing the numbers 1, 2 and 3 on their colours, running in a semi-circle beneath the round window high on the gable.

According to Uncle Charlie, 'ruin, stark, staring, and complete fell upon it when railways came' but, in the motoring age, Boroughbridge became a popular resting place for long-distance drivers, until bypassed by the now A168 in 1963, ending 800 years as a travellers' town, and by the A1(M) early this century.

Today it certainly has its equilibrium back, and is a major nook to be explored. Not just for the town as it is today, but for two remarkable historic sites on its perimeter: the location of the Roman town of Isurium Brigantum; and the Devil's Arrows, three great spears of rock standing stark in a line alongside the A168 and A1(M).

As Fletch says: 'No other place in England possesses quite the same archaeological curiosity as the three monoliths known from time immemorial as the Devil's Arrows.' I walk out to them up Roecliffe Lane and read that among the previous names they were known by is The Three Greyhounds, which suggests that whoever decided to put those dogs on the front of the old inn was barking up the wrong tree.

The arrows date from between 5000 and 3000BC, the same period as Stonehenge, but surpass that monument in one respect: the tallest of the three dwarfs anything there. It reaches 22.6ft, with an additional 6ft underground. These millstone grit monoliths run in a line from north-north-west to south-south-east, and there may once have been four or even five of them.

They were probably quarried nine miles away, but what purpose or significance they served is unknown. In the eighteenth century it was believed that the Devil, angered at something done by the villagers of nearby Aldborough, hurled the stone arrows in retribution, only for them to fall short. Shit shot, the Devil.

I walk to Aldborough along the river. It is just on the outer edge of Boroughbridge, tucked down on the water meadows beside the Ure, and makes a pleasant destination for an afternoon stroll.

Isurium Brigantum, upon whose sandal-print the modern village stands, was perhaps built as a pleasure resort for the rich Romans of York. Placed where Watling and Dere Streets crossed the Ure, it was the capital of the Romanised Brigantes, the largest tribe in Britain. The river crossing was then shifted east to Boroughbridge by the Normans, after which, bypassed Aldborough fell into decline. If that hadn't happened, the Great North Road would probably have run through it.

Uncle Charlie has a theory that the Normans shifted the town because they were spooked by 'the ruined and deserted city of Isurium. Afraid of the bogies and evil spirits with which their dark superstitions peopled the ruins, they dared not live there.'

The village's fourteenth-century church, St Andrew's, stands on the site of a temple dedicated to Mercury, and a relief-carving of the god, discovered in the foundations during rebuilding works, is set into a wall.

The village is said to retain part of the Roman street plan, although it feels entirely English to me as I stroll around, gathered as it is around a green that sports a tall red-, white- and blue- striped Maypole surmounted with a crown. It has a lovely pub, the Ship Inn, with ornately carved, dark-oak panelling on the bar and walls.

A sign at a crossroads, standing beside a very tall, very slender fifteenth-century village cross, points the way to the remnants of the Roman town, on Front Street. Two mosaics and a section of the town wall survive there.

Back in Boroughbridge, I wander down Horsefair to lean against the eighteenth-century bridge that takes the Great North Road over the Ure, and ponder just how important a place this quiet backwater once was.

As well as the daily torrent of travellers, there were three fairs held here a year, granted by Edward II in 1310. The biggest, Barnaby Fair, was held in June, close to St Barnabus' Day, and drew people from across the north. It began with 14 days of horse-trading – hence the name of the street I am standing on – followed by three days for cattle sales and general revelry.

Everyone in town took the opportunity to make a few bob out of the visitors. Anyone could turn their house into a pub during Barnaby Fair, so long as they hung a green bush over the door. Barnaby Fair only died out in the 1980s.

Celia Fiennes rated the beer here, reporting that 'I drank small beer four years old – not too stale very clear good beer well brewed'. She also liked the fish, reporting that the river flowing beneath my feet: 'affords very good fish salmon and codfish and plenty of crawfish.' Cod from a river? I think Celia's confusing locally caught fish with that brought in from the North Sea.

Anyway, the prices were good: '...we had a very large codfish there, above a yard long and more than half a yard in compass very fresh and good and cost but 8 pence; I saw as big a one bought for 6 pence, and six crabs as big as my two hands – the least was bigger than one of my fists – all cost but 3 pence.'

Uncle Charlie was less impressed: '...the streets are dull, the bridge... spans the weedy stream in a useful but highly unornamental manner'.

From here, the B6265 takes me back to the A168, Leeming Lane, running alongside the A1(M) on top of the course of Roman Dere Street. After Dishforth I have to join the motorway briefly, but am soon off again on the A6055, still surfing along Dere Street, with the motorway alongside me, for a total of 24 fast, traffic-free miles, all the way to Catterick.

It is a lonely and impressive road, straight and level, with the Pennines to my left and the distant Cleveland Hills to my right. This is truly the real Great North Road I have come looking for, minus the heavy traffic that made the motorway necessary.

The A6055 temporarily leaves the Roman line to bypass Londonderry and Leeming Bar, but I stick to the Great North Road, taking the unclassified route to Leeming. I divert south, briefly, in Londonderry – named after the Marquesses of Londonderry, who owned collieries locally – where the old road forms a cul-de-sac through the village and is blocked off at the southern tip. Londonderry is one of those places that really do feel abandoned. The Londonderry Lodge, a roadhouse since the mid-eighteenth century, became a truck stop in the twentieth, but the business moved three miles north to Leeming Bar in 2014.

Too small to sustain itself once bypassed, Londonderry has sunk into a quiet retirement. There is still – shades of Route 66 – an old McEwen's Export sign high on the flaking whitewashed front wall of the shuttered Londonderry Lodge, and the just-discernible word 'Garage' painted in giant white letters on the slate roof, but it is no more.

The Londonderry Lodge offered the undemanding traveller the basics: bed and breakfast, a transport and tourist cafeteria, TV room, lounge and bar, and was rated old fashioned but good value. Today, lorry drivers use the Coneygarth Truck Stop at Leeming Bar. The homely, individual attractions of the Londonderry Lodge are replaced here with identikit Costa, Subway and Londis.

Headed north once more, I rejoin the A6055 for a further six miles of fast, quiet road alongside the motorway to Catterick, where I turn off to continue on the old road, along the High Street. Catterick is a pleasant place, the Great North Road gliding through, wide and clear, as it does in so many former transport stops.

I cross Borough Beck, a shallow stream that snakes through the village, bordered with wide grassy banks dotted with trees beyond which, keeping a respectful distance, run lanes lined with stone houses. Fifteenth century St Anne's church watches over Catterick from a grassy mound at Church Green.

In the churchyard, a stern notice of probably Victorian vintage warns: 'Suffer none to play here. Do not pluck the flowers. Tread not on the graves.' You know when someone tells you not to do something that you actually had no intention of doing until they mentioned it... but I resist the urge. I play not, I pluck not, and I tread not.

Maybe the sign is not so over-the-top when you consider who is buried here. His name was Richard Braithwaite, but he achieved notoriety as Drunken Barnaby, the nom de plume under which he published, in 1638, *Barnaby's Travels*, a rhyming itinerary in Latin of his journeys along the Great North Road and elsewhere in the North, and which made him famous.

This odd and mysterious character was a Royalist captain during the Civil War, and travelled from town to village, inn to inn, cadging food, drink and accommodation. A bit like a dipsomaniac ByngAdvisor, he gave his verdict on how he was treated in each place he tried it on, in verse that was crude, witty and often caustic. He is buried under the chancel at St Anne's, and a plaque on the wall memorialises him.

He drank, gorged, fornicated and swindled his way up the Great North Road, his journey mirroring mine. In Doncaster, he poured 'spritely wine' down his throat, and had an amorous encounter with an older woman.

His verse loses something in the translation, but here's his comment on that:

> For when youthful Venus ageth,
> She my fleshly force asswageth.

On the road north, hung over and with a mouth like the floor of a parrot's cage, he reaches Robin Hood's Well and makes use of the cup that used to be chained there for thirsty travellers:

> Thirst knows neither mean nor measure,
> Robin Hood's well was my treasure;
> In a common dish enchained,
> I my furious thirst restrained:
> And because I drank the deeper,
> I paid two farthings to the keeper.

That's a rare example of Drunken Barnaby paying for a drink. By the time he got to Ferrybridge he was exhausted, but recovered sufficiently to guzzle some wine he judged inferior, and tuck in to a plate of wild boar:

> Thence to Ferrybrig, sore wearied,
> Surfoot, but in spirit cheered:
> I no sooner the grape tasted
> But my melancholy wasted:
> Never was wild boar more fellish,
> Tho' the wine did smally relish.

Barnaby was often on the York Road, and I'll join up with him again there.

Dere Street takes me on past Catterick Racecourse to Catterick Bridge and the crossing over the Swale, beside which is the enormous Catterick Bridge Hotel. It is closed and swathed in scaffolding when I pass, so it's hard to see whether it lives up to the billing Uncle Charlie gave it as 'one of the oldest and quaintest posting houses' on the old road.

Fletch called it 'a typical specimen of the wayside tavern of the coaching days – a long, low-roofed building with quaint gables and windows, vast stables, and great, echoing rooms.' He reckons that it was the contrast between the long, desolate stretches of the Great North Road that travellers endured between rests that made the inns such havens of warmth and comfort.

Charles Dickens doesn't mention the Catterick Bridge Hotel in his account, in *Nicholas Nickleby*, of the journey north to Dotheboys Hall with the sadistic master Squeers and a clutch of cowering, miserable pupils. But, says Fletch, 'they would certainly stop at it to change horses and Squeers would just as certainly get down to stretch his legs at the bar.'

Once across the Swale, the A6055 swings me back over to the western flank of the A1(M) for another glide, this time to one of the most famous spots on the Great North Road: Scotch Corner.

Dickens modelled Dotheboys Hall on a notorious establishment at Greta Bridge, which is off to the west near Barnard Castle, so his characters would have left the Great North Road here, along what is now the A66.

Today the great orange brick frontage of what is currently the Holiday Inn Darlington dominates the junction, but a forerunner was called the Three Tuns, and stood from 1820 to the east of the present hotel. The Three Tuns is no more, or rather it's here no more. But it hasn't been lost. It was dismantled and taken to the open-air museum at Beamish, near Chester-le-Street, further up the Great North Road. There it is used to demonstrate how a coaching inn worked. What's more, you can check in.

The present Scotch Corner hotel dates from 1939, when the Roman road became a dual carriageway, and brought a new level of modern luxury to accommodation along the Great North Road. Among the innovations was hot water in every bedroom, and an American-style bar. But, during the Second World War, it was a hospital for convalescing RAF men and women, and only opened in 1945.

It's a pleasant place today, with an elegant central staircase in the well of which dangles a very long chandelier. The view from my window it of a great oval roundabout, created in 1971, to ease the flow of traffic at what has been a vital junction since Roman times, and is now where the A1(M) leans right for the North East and Edinburgh, and the A66 leans left for the North West and Glasgow. But it's no coaching inn, and, once checked in, I decide to head on and cover the final miles into Darlington.

Today the A1(M) swings to the west of Darlington, but when the A1 was created one hundred years ago, it ran along the now unclassified route through the villages of Barton and Stapleton. Here I say goodbye to Dere Street, which I have followed since Boroughbridge.

The old road is even more of a joy to drive without the distraction of the new motorway at my shoulder. I drop down to Barton, past the Half Moon, an old coaching inn now with an ominous 'Pub to Let' sign nailed to it, and on towards Stapleton. A mile and a half before it is a rare survivor from the days when this was the A1. At first I think Willow Bridge Service Station is abandoned. A 'For Sale' notice stands at the roadside, the sign that once listed fuel prices is blank, and three of the four pumps lined up before the two-storey station appear to be out of commission. Nevertheless, a mangled sign propped up with a lump of concrete reads OPEN, and there is a light on in the shop. But they only sell diesel, which is no use to me.

Willow Bridge was built in 1936, and Campbell Dawson, who has lived in the station since 1954 remembers the glory days. He told the *Northern Echo*: 'My father had eight staff on the pumps all day every day, and it was heaving from seven in the morning until 11 at night, but when the motorway opened in the 1960s, it flattened everything.'

Now its days are numbered. With planning permission for two detached houses on the site, it is for sale at £695,000, and I doubt it will be there when I next drive this way.

At Stapleton I come up against the end of the A66(M) and turn right to cross the River Tees by Blackwell Bridge, leaving Yorkshire for County Durham, following the route of the Great North Road as first the A66, and then the A167, into Darlington.

V

THE YORK ROAD
Doncaster
to Darlington

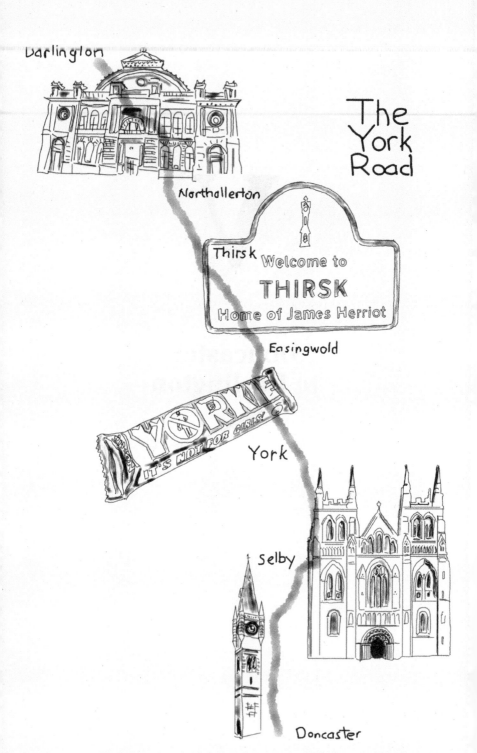

Darlington

The York Road

Northallerton

Thirsk Welcome to
THIRSK
Home of James Herriot

Easingwold

YORKIE
IT'S NOT FOR GIRLS!

York

Selby

Doncaster

The York Road has always divided opinion. To some, it, rather than the path I drove via Wetherby in the last section, is the real route of the Great North Road. To others it is an inferior branch line running over dull country. As Uncle Charlie says: '...both claim to be the true Great North Road'.

In the sixteenth century, when York was as far as most London coaches reached, there was no question over which was the true route. From the late seventeenth century, when coaches from the capital travelled on to Newcastle and Edinburgh, they had a choice of paths between Doncaster and Darlington: either, keep serving York, or travel on a more westerly path via Wetherby.

As Norman Webster writes in *The Great North Road*: 'The main line of posting was through Doncaster, Wetherby and Northallerton and on the whole coaches adhered to this as far as possible before branching [off to their final destinations]; in this way they gained all the advantages of the main road with its fine surface, improved line and chain of well-equipped posting houses.'

The coming of the A1, choosing the route via Wetherby, made the debate redundant. It also meant that the road via York has seen far less improvement. It did not have the makeover the A1 gave to the Great North Road, so there are few sections of old, bypassed road for me to seek out.

So will it be boring, identikit A-road all the way? I'll find out. But I have high hopes, as the road takes me to Selby, with its abbey, and to York itself, which has a rich coaching history to delve into. It also passes through Thirsk, a fine market town with a handsome coaching inn.

175

19. Hunky and Chunky

– Doncaster to York –

York, and the York Road, can mean only one thing to a man of a certain age: the Yorkie Bar.

The big n' chunky Yorkie Bar was invented by Rowntree of York in 1976 to appeal to men. TV ads featured lorry drivers tucking in, with the sexist copy line 'It's not for girls', an ad parodied by the BBC sketch comedy show *Not the Nine O'Clock News* in their 1981 single 'I like Trucking'. Corgi made toy lorries bearing the logo, to give boys (not girls) something to aspire to.

One TV ad featured a billboard on York railway station reading: 'Welcome to York', and beneath: 'Where the men are hunky and the chocolate's chunky'. That's a big claim, York.

Time has not been kind to the Yorkie Bar.

Rowntree has been absorbed into Nestlé (which in my day was pronounced 'Nessells', rather than the affected, acute-accented 'Nes-lay' of today). Its six chunks have been reduced to five, its weight cut from 2.5oz to 1.5oz. Which means it will take two bars, rather than one, to get me from Doncaster to York.

It's been a while since I last drove north out of Doncaster. Then, it was summer. Now, winter is drawing in and, in the meantime, I've driven right up to Berwick on the Great North Road. Last time, after following North Bridge Road out of the town centre and over the River Don, I took the second exit off St Mary's roundabout onto the A638, which soon acquires the name Great North Road. This time, I go one exit further round and leave the roundabout on the A19, Bentley Road.

My hopes are not high as I set out. Uncle Charlie warns that the route is 'as flat and uninteresting a road, so far as the cathedral city [of York], as it is possible to imagine'. Norman Webster writes: 'The Selby road is a dull highway on the whole and lacks the attentions devoted to the A1... As the modern A19 follows the York Road's line almost exactly, it does not offer the same opportunities for exploring backroads and alternative routes, but it could be included for those who want to visit York.'

Well, I do want to visit York, so I suspend judgement. But only for a mile or two. The climb out of Doncaster via Bentley and Toll Bar offers dowdy suburbs and post-war housing estates, followed by a run over flat and featureless farmland where even the sheep look too bored to graze.

Uncle Charlie found it very quiet. He writes of 'passing through lonely woods and past pools and lakes, with a stray grouse or so, and astonished hares and rabbits, as the sole witnesses of the explorer's progress in these deserted ways.' It's a sweeping two-lane highway these days, but not unduly troubled by traffic.

Road-side Thornhurst Manor boasts of its wedding and conference venue plus golf course, Owston Hall chips in with another golf course and, between the two at Little Owston, I see a sign for a very handily placed natural burial ground. Should you die of excitement playing all that golf you can end your days beneath a wild flower meadow, literally pushing up the daisies.

The Toddle Inn perks my interest until I realise that, while it sounds like it might be a pub, it's actually a day-care nursery.

Then comes Askern, which has had its ups and downs. In the eighteenth and nineteenth centuries Askern was a fashionable spa town, with a railway run in to bring guests from Manchester and Liverpool, who drank and bathed in its sulphurous waters at the Spa Hydropathic Establishment, the Hydro, and five other bath houses clustered alongside Askern Lake. The waters of the five springs that fed the lake were said to rival those at Harrogate and to be effective in treating rheumatism.

Then came coal. In 1911 a seam was discovered, a pit sunk to exploit it, and a new village built to house the miners who –

by the First World War – had driven out the well-to-do spa visitors. The Hydro became the miners' welfare, but later succumbed to mining subsidence.

Writing of that time in *Nooks and Corners of Yorkshire*, my companion Fletch (Joseph Fletcher) records how Askern 'has been, like most Yorkshire villages, made hideous by its houses and cottages, inconceivably ugly to those who have not seen what abominable places Yorkshire folk are capable of building and living in.'

But some visitors were still coming: 'its old pump-room and its lake are the resorts of York and Doncaster's trippers in summer-time, and those holiday-makers derive just as much health from rowing in pleasure-boats on the lake as did their forefathers, who, a hundred years ago, quaffed its evil-tasting sulphurous waters.'

At its height in 1975, Askern colliery produced 750,000 tonnes, but closed in 1992. I see reminders of both spa and coal as I drive through: boats on the lake to my right, a row of coal trucks converted into planters on my left. Askern's still got its greyhound stadium, which has stood to the north of town since 1939, after which I follow a 13-mile stretch of pretty featureless road to Selby.

Fletch describes:

A flat, watery, treeless, featureless plain, its negative qualities tempered by the frankly mean and ugly villages on the way, and criss-crossed by railways, sluggish rivers, and unlovely canals. So utterly without interest is the road, that a crude girder-bridge or a gaunt and forbidding flour-mill remain vividly impressed upon the mental retina for lack of any other outstanding objects.

I pass over the M62 and the wide waters of the Knottingley and Goole Canal, part of the Aire and Calder navigation, and through Whitley Bridge and Eggborough with its great, gaunt power station. I've passed from South to North Yorkshire, but the landscape remains the same, the road elevated on a causeway over the floodplain of the meandering River Aire. On the approach to Selby, the A63 bypass urges me to skirt east around town, but I stick to the A19 through Brayton into the centre, where the old road runs right past the wonderful abbey.

Selby perks me up, dominated as it is by the triple towers of that Norman masterpiece. Two of those towers, twinned on the abbey's west front, face the cobbled market place, which is flanked by The George, a fifteenth-century coaching inn. The light is fading this November afternoon, and the abbey is closing shortly, so I hurry on in.

If you led me here blindfold and let me open my eyes in the nave, I'd say I was in Durham Cathedral. Well, almost. It has a lot in common with Durham, in terms of scale and sombre grandeur, with great Norman pillars etched with chevron designs, and dark stone that seems to absorb the light. The abbey suffered a calamitous fire in 1906, in which the bells melted and poured molten metal down into the church, but you wouldn't know it. The great oak roof above my head, studded with gold bosses like a double row of shiny buttons is not medieval, as it appears, but a twentieth-century replacement.

Simon Jenkins, in *England's Thousand Best Churches*, gives the abbey five stars, describing it as 'a stately old lady, retired to the country with her dignity and memories intact'. I don't know about that. The abbey's as chunky as a stone Yorkie to my mind.

The original timber abbey was founded here by Benedict of Auxerre in 1069. Today's stone one was begun in 1100 by Abbot Hugh, a master builder who rolled up his sleeves to get things done. Despite that, it took 800 years to complete, major building continuing until 1935, interrupted by that fire.

To the north of the choir a series of pillars against the outer wall have, at head height, capitals fashioned as lattices of stone, a couple of which are hollow. One has a chunk knocked from its outer wall, revealing the carved face of a man peering out. I look closely at the others, to see if there are more hidden faces. I only find one, the stone lattice around it still intact. By shining the torch on my phone in I can make out a finely carved little head in what appears to be white marble rather than the rougher stone of the other. I see a gentleman with a distinctly Edwardian appearance and droopy moustache.

This, it turns out, is a bust of King Edward VII, who was on the throne at the time of the post-fire restoration. It is one of the Strudwick Carvings, the work of Thomas Strudwick, who worked on the abbey's restoration following the fire. But why give the king this secret tribute? He was one of the main benefactors of the abbey, contributing generously to the restoration fund.

The fourteenth-century East Window is a treasure much easier to spot. Also known as the Jesse Window, and dating from 1330, it depicts the Kings of Israel from Jesse of Bethlehem to Jesus and Mary. It is reckoned to be second only in magnificence to the West Window at York Minster, and was only saved from the fire when the wind changed direction.

I walk out and round to the Market Square, at the far end of which stands a much-weathered market cross, now a shank or spindle of stone tapering to a crumbly point. Alongside it, the George looks tempting. I give it a miss, but only because I plan a coaching inn pub crawl in York tonight.

The abbey became the parish church at the Dissolution, and the extensive monastery buildings – cloister, abbot's lodgings, chapter house and other ancillaries that covered the market square – were destroyed.

However, one medieval element survives. I walk from the Market Square down Finkle Street and Micklegate to the mill buildings on the banks of the River Ouse – the waterway that leads from the North Sea to York – and a point where ancient and modern collide.

As I approach, the twin columns of the Westmill flour mill loom above me like the ugly sisters to the abbey's elegant towers. One column is of orange brick bearing the scuffed lettering IDEAL FLOUR. The white concrete one alongside it bristles with mobile phone masts.

I cross Water Lane and walk into the yard, where an artic is being loaded with great bags of flour, and turn right to find the Abbot's Staithe, the monastery's fifteenth-century warehouse where its goods were stored before or after trips on the river.

I'm finding Selby a place of unexpected interest but Fletch, inevitably, was underwhelmed by it. He concedes that the abbey is beautiful, 'but the rest is an effect of meanness. Mean old houses of no great age; mean new ones; mean and threadbare waterside industries; second-hand clothes-shops, coal-grit, muddy waters and foreshores of the slimy Ouse, shabby rope-walks, and dirty alleys: these are Selby.'

Today that's no longer the case. It's a place that, disfigured during the industrial age, holds on to its history, and offers up delights to those who work at it.

I head on for York. The Crescent takes me through town to what my map calls the Old Toll Bridge, which takes the York Road over the Ouse. Actually it's not old, nor is it still a toll bridge, but the name has persisted. Until 2004 when the A63 Selby bypass opened, the toll bridge was the only crossing in the area. It had stood since 1791, replacing a ferry that was here from 1260. The eighteenth-century wooden swing bridge was replaced in 1970 with a steel and timber replica.

This was a bottleneck on the York Road. Traffic queuing to pay the tolls often snarled up the whole town, before charges were dropped in 1991.

Fletch is more impressed with the countryside north of Selby. One of his bugbears is no longer a problem: the railway level crossings which 'have their wicked will of the road, and are indeed its principal features, through Barlby and Riccall'. He urges Selby folk to rise up and tear away the barriers, as their forebears did in 1753 when they smashed the hated toll gates on the road.

Today the A19 bypasses Barlby and Riccall, and the lane that took Fletch and Uncle Charlie north has been straightened out. I take the old route through the villages, but I can't say it adds much to the joy of the journey, unlike the many sweeping stretches of the old-route alternatives to the modern A1 that I have enjoyed.

Riccall is worth travelling through for its key role in the Norman Conquest. This was once a seaport. The wide waters of the Ouse, now constrained in a channel away from the village, enabled ships to sail upriver from the North Sea, via the Humber.

In 1066, two weeks before William the Conqueror's triumph at the Battle of Hastings, a Norman invasion force anchored at Riccall to blockade the waterway to York. From here they advanced on, and took, the city. They were routed, but William's southern invasion force prevailed, an early example of the South letting the North down. But the Normans would be back, three years later, as I'll discover in Chapter 21.

Fletch found nothing in Riccall to conjure up anything of those days, and nor do I as I follow the old route of the York Road along Main Street. It's a pleasant, unremarkable little place today, but Fletch reported: 'The village itself bears nothing on its face telling of great events, and is of a placid dullness, a character shared by Escrick and Deighton, on the way to York; the road itself gradually becoming an abomination of desolate fields until the village of Gate Fulford is reached.'

It's dark as I drive the last stretch on the A19, Fulford Rd, entering York at Fishergate. Here, the ancient city opens up before me. The Yorkie bars, my stomach is now telling me with some insistence, sustained me only as far as Selby, so it's time to take on something even chunkier. A pie would be nice.

20. I'll Drink to That

Uncle Charlie talks of the sense of achievement and occasion that should accompany an arrival in York. OK, so the modern traveller from London won't feel the need to give thanks at York Minister for their safe deliverance from the perils of highway robbery, flood, and calamity on treacherous roads, as a seventeenth or eighteenth-century coach-passenger might, but reaching York is still a significant milestone.

Like Charlie, I feel a sense of occasion. He wrote, a century ago: 'One comes to York as the capital of a country, rather than of a county, for it is a city that seems in more than one sense Metropolitan. Indeed, you cannot travel close upon two hundred miles, even in England and in these days of swift communication, without feeling the need of some dominating city.'

The same is true today. York still offers a truly significant half-way house: a capital of the North to hold the balance between London and Edinburgh. The alternative route via Wetherby has nothing like it. It does, however, offer what was generally considered a finer approach to this city than the one I have followed. Some coaches would take the Great North Road out of Doncaster, before peeling off it at Wetherby, to travel via Tadcaster and enter York from the east, through Micklegate.

Fletch contrasts the two approaches like this: 'By that route York is most romantically entered, across Knavesmire, where York's martyrs, felons, and traitors were done to death in the old days, and where the racecourse now runs; coming to the walled city through Micklegate, the finest of all the medieval defensible gateways which are York's especial glory.'

By the Selby route, in contrast, 'we seem to slink in by the back door through Gate Fulford and along Fishergate.' Fletch adds: 'York Minster, although so huge and imposing a pile when reached, is not glimpsed by the traveller approaching the city from the Selby route until well within the streets.'

OK, so York's greatest glory does not reveal itself to Selby travellers as it does to Tadcaster's. But they reach the same still-walled city, and walk the same medieval streets. However you get here, you should arrive thirsty. Because a wide range of coaching inns survive in these narrow, cobbled streets. They offer the perfect excuse for a pub crawl.

Not that you need an excuse, but there is an historic precedent for a booze cruise around York.

In Chapter 18, on my way from Boroughbridge to Darlington, I came upon a chap with a prodigious thirst. You may recall I visited his grave in Catterick. He was Richard Braithwaite, but achieved notoriety as Drunken Barnaby, the name under which he published, in 1638, *Barnaby's Travels*, a rhyming itinerary in Latin of his travels through the North, and which made him famous.

I bump into him again in York, where his philandering, boozing and gorging take on even more gargantuan dimensions.

In *Barnaby's Travels* he writes of an encounter with a willing and unfaithful wife, and of besting her cuckolded husband:

Thence to York, fresh youth enjoying,
With a wanton weaver toying:
Husband suddenly appears too...
Who as he fumed, fret, and frowned,
With a chamber-pot was crowned:
Wisely silent, he ne'er grudged
That his Betty with me lodged.

Not that I intend to have anything more debauched than a few pints in a few pubs, but I do hope something of York's atmospheric past has seeped down through the centuries. At the end of the nineteenth, its coaching history was certainly intact. As Tom Bradley wrote in *The Old Coaching Days* in 1889: 'There are few places, if any, in Yorkshire where the ancient landmarks have suffered so little from the eradicating march of progress as in the old city of York, where a number of the old coaching inns still remain practically intact.'

But what about today? Would I feel an affinity with past travellers as I drank at their old inns? I parked close to my lodgings alongside Micklegate and walked back to the southern entrance to the city, at Fishergate. This, the modern A1036, took traffic from the south along Tower Street and then Coney Street, where the most famous coaching inns stood. But I'm getting ahead of myself.

I walk through Fishergate Bar, a gateway not available to coaching traffic because it was bricked up after a riot in 1489, and not opened again until 1827. The reason for coming this now-pedestrianised way is to visit the grave of Dick Turpin. I haven't mentioned this Biggus Dickus among highwaymen since I stopped at the Ram Jam Inn, north of Stamford. But, read some accounts of travel on the Great North Road and you can't get away from the flashy little crook.

Turpin achieved folk-heroic status partly thanks to a monumental ride he supposedly made in 1735 from London to York after a robbery, covering the 200 miles overnight on his mare Black Bess, an unheard of feat, and winning himself an alibi that stood up in court.

However, arrested for horse theft three years later – he was in the habit of nicking and discarding a string of horses as he travelled, a sort of taking-and-riding-away, or joy-riding – he was sent for trial at York, and convicted. Turpin was hanged on the gallows at Knavesmire, the Tyburn of the North.

His grave lies in a small forgotten cemetery of St George's church (which is no more), where Fishergate becomes George Street, at the junction with Lead Mill Lane. There aren't many gravestones left in what is now more of a park, but Turpin's low, chalk-white stone survives. The inscription reads: 'Richard Palmer alias Richard Turpin, notorious highwayman and horse stealer. Executed at Tyburn [Knavesmire], April 7th 1739.'

His rest was rudely interrupted by grave diggers, who had him away in the night, but robbers and remains were tracked down, and Turpin's bones returned. They're big on ghosts in York, and there are stories of a ghostly figure on horseback galloping up and down the narrow streets around the grave.

A great crowd came out to witness Turpin's death. Once his body was cut down, it was taken to an inn called the Blue Boar, and I'm headed there next. This is one of a clutch of old inns that I'm going to visit on my historic pub crawl. All were coaching inns but, unlike at most points along the road, they are not clustered along one street. Rather, as I found in London, they are spread around, which means any weaving about that I display this evening is due not to inebriation but a desire to hit all the historic spots.

To get to the Blue Boar I walk west to Tower Street, crossing the River Foss just before it joins the Ouse, and then turn right up Friargate to Castlegate. There are a lot of gates in York.

Turpin's body was left hanging at Knavesmire from morning until late afternoon, before being taken down and brought to this inn. It lay here overnight, before his burial next morning. Which to me makes this a pretty significant place, especially in the context of the old road and its perils.

Inevitably, Turpin is said to haunt the place, and an A-board beside the old coaching entrance, leading to a courtyard I'd happily sit in on a warmer night, challenges: 'Dare you drink in his haunted cellar?'

I stick to the main bar, where another sign suggests: 'Always do sober what you said you'd do drunk'. I buy a pint of Black Sheep Pale Ale and ponder that thought. Would it mean, say, all politicians governing like Boris Johnson? It's early on a Monday night, but I can see this is a lively little local. It has live music and a quiz night, offers three Becks for a tenner and a menu of stone-baked pizza. A good start to my pub crawl. In fact, I learn that locals saved it. The pub closed in 2011, but a campaign brought it back to life two years later.

Castlegate leads to Coney Street, known as 'York's Golden Half Mile', where a couple of the most famous coaching inns were, but are no more. They were the Black Swan, at No. 44, and the George, at No. 52.

Uncle Charlie says: 'From the purely coaching point of view, the Black Swan is the most interesting of York's hostelries' and did the bulk of the stage-coach business 'from the beginning of it in 1698 until the end, in 1842... It was here that the old "York in Four Days" coaching bill of 1706 was discovered some years ago.'

That bill announced that the service would begin on 12 April, leaving the Black Swan at 5am every Monday, Wednesday and Friday 'if God permits', en route to the inn of the same name in London's Holborn.

For passengers merely passing through York, their stop here was a rushed one. Uncle Charlie, in *Stage-coach and Mail in Days of Yore*, writes: 'Half an hour is allowed for dining, and, unlike the majority of houses down the road, the table-cloth and the knives and forks and glasses are not the only things in readiness.' Hot roast beef or lamb, cold chicken, peas and boiled potatoes are ready to be whipped in front of the hungry traveller, with apple tart to finish. The coachman would have a steak and a beer in the bar.

The Black Swan survived until the 1930s or 40s, when it was demolished to make way for a British Home Stores, before being split to house a Sports Direct and a USC clothes store.

The American novelist Nathaniel Hawthorne stayed here in 1857, by which time travellers came to York by train. In *The English Note-books* he writes that the bill announcing the four-day stage was on the wall, and marvels that 'still, after 150 years, the Black Swan receives travellers in Coney Street.'

He says of it: 'The Black Swan is a good specimen of the old English inn, sombre, quiet, with dark staircases, dingy rooms, curtained beds, all the possibilities of a comfortable life and good English fare, in a fashion which cannot have been much altered for half a century. It is very home-like when one has one's family about him, but must be prodigiously stupid for a solitary man.'

A century ago, Uncle Charlie reported: 'The house remained one of the very few unaltered inns of coaching days, the stableyard the same as it was a hundred years or more since, even to the weather-beaten old painted oval sign of the Black Swan, removed from the front and nailed over one of the stable-doors.'

The George Hotel was another grand inn replaced by a shop, in this case the Leak and Thorp department store, in 1869. That was later split to become a Next, Monsoon, and River Island.

At the far end of Coney Street, in St Helen's Square, was the York Tavern, which was alongside the post office, and from which the mail coaches departed.

To find my next surviving coaching inn I turn right up Coppergate to No. 16 The Pavement, and the Golden Fleece, which dates from 1503. It's been squeezed, a shop colonising the section alongside the entrance to the stable yard, so that the inn itself has been rebuilt in that yard, a wall slotted into the arch that led to it. Hanging from a bracket above the entrance is the model of a golden sheep, suspended from a strap around its belly.

This is the symbol of the Merchant Adventurers' Guild, wool dealers who grew as fat as that sheep on the fleeces they traded, and whose members drank here.

The first bar I come to is underwhelming. No one behind the counter, the tables empty, but continue down the sloping corridor to the bottom bar and all is different. It's busy, the staff dressed and made up as if for Halloween, although we're well past October 31. Monday is open mic night, and a battered upright piano awaits nimble fingers in an alcove at the back of the room.

Every pub in York has to have at least one ghost, and this has five, itemised on a notice beside the front door, which adds: 'as seen on TV's *Most Haunted*'. There's a skeleton sitting at the bar, dressed in a red coat covered in snowmen, and sporting a red hat topped by a white pom pom. Or possibly this is a regular, still living but well kippered.

Beside him is a Tupperware box half filled with water in which lemons are floating. There's a challenge: Place a coin on a lemon and if it doesn't slip off for five seconds, you win... to be honest I can't remember what you win, possibly a snog with the skeleton. But I had a go, using the change from my pint of Timothy Taylor's Landlord.

The coin slips off. I ask the barmaid whether she's ever seen a coin not slip off. She says she has, once. So with my next pint I try again. And then again, with the next. But no joy. The bar is filling up with musicians lugging instrument cases. I have reached that point where, sunk in my seat, feeling pleasantly warm and mellow, I could stay all night. But I don't. In the interest of research I force myself to get up and walk out, and up The Shambles.

I can't make up my mind about The Shambles. It's as quaint as you could imagine, a narrow cobbled way with medieval houses almost touching as they lean in above the shops on either side. It's such a perfect representation of a medieval city street that it feels fake. It's full of shops selling Lord of the Rings and Harry Potter merchandise. Yet it has genuine history and powerful stories, one of them attached to the house of a saint, at No. 35. Margaret Clitherow became a Catholic at a time when to do so was an act of treason.

She attended Mass at this, her husband's butcher's shop, and ran a small school where children were taught the Catholic faith. For which she was martyred, crushed to death between two doors, on Good Friday 1586. To be fair, a walking-tour guide is telling a group the story outside the shop as I pass, but he's dwelling too much on the gruesome nature of her death, rather than her role as a heroine, for my liking.

The Shambles also houses one of my favourite food shops: The Sausage and Pie Company. It's closed, but the taste memory of their pork pies, made piquant with smoked ham, gives me the rumbles. Or maybe that's the beer sloshing about. I hurry on to Kings Square, and Low Petergate, for the Old White Swan, at No. 80 Goodramgate, an inn that is as big and lively as it ever was in coaching days. Tom Bradley was able to write, in 1889, in *The Old Coaching Days in Yorkshire* that: 'A visit to the yard of the White Swan on a market day will carry one back by easy transition to the bustle and turmoil of the coaching days'.

It's just as busy today. This is the first place I've visited in York that still has the scope of a grand coaching inn. It's a rambling, sixteenth-century place with several bars leading off the courtyard to choose from. I opt for the Stagecoach Bar and a pint of Nicholson's house pale ale. The White Swan is a cluster of nine buildings, the oldest timber framed and medieval, Georgian wings flanking the courtyard.

Stamford and The George may have had their 52-stone giant, Daniel Lambert, but the Old White Swan had the world's tallest man: Patrick Cotter O'Brien. O'Brien was minding his own business, which was bricklaying, in his native County Cork when a passing freak show proprietor told him he could make far more money making a spectacle of himself. The reason being, Patrick was 8ft tall. He was exhibited here in 1781, the landlord charging a shilling a look.

According to the *Irish Post*, when he travelled: 'The floor of Cotter O'Brien's stagecoach had to be modified specifically to fit his height. One particularly unlucky highwayman had the shock of his life when he stopped the wrong stagecoach. The outlaw fled at the sight of the eight-foot Irishman inside.'

Like Daniel Lambert, Patrick died young. His excessive growth – gigantism – killed him at the age of 46. He left £2,000 in his will, £350,000 today, but people insisted on looking at him even after his death. His body was exhumed to satisfy medical curiosity in 1906, 1972 and finally in 1986. After that he was cremated.

I decide to try one last inn, and head on up Low Petergate. Just before York Minster I turn left into Stonegate for Ye Olde Starre Inn. You reach it not via a coach entrance but down a narrow alley, or 'snickelway' to Yorkies. The approach promises little, but opens out to a courtyard and a very classy inn. First things first, I look at the menu and order a steak and ale pie with triple-fried chips. For my fruit course I go for a pint of Old Rosie cider.

The Olde Starre dates from 1664, a significant year, and not because Kronenberg named a lager after it. This was the year Cromwell laid siege to York. The royalist landlord is said to have named it the Olde Starre in reference to the deposed king, Charles I. Parliamentary forces commandeered the pub, using its cellars as a hospital and mortuary which means, inevitably, that it's got its ghosts.

I end the night at the Starre, before completing the route through York by walking on up High Petergate and past York Minister to Bootham Bar.

On the far side is the point at which I'll start my drive to Darlington tomorrow, back on the A19. This was the north-western entrance to the Roman city, and the present gateway, which was rebuilt in the fourteenth and nineteenth centuries, retains some stone from the eleventh.

Drunken Barnaby came this way, but apparently transformed into an older, wiser and possibly more sober man. He seems to have come to regret his dalliance with the weaver's wife, writing:

The York Road

Farewell York, I must forsake thee,
Weaver's shuttle shall not take me:
Hoary hairs are come upon me,
Youthful pranks will not become me.

Winter has now behoard my hairs,
Benumb'd my joints and sinews too...
Leave city then, to th' country go.
Poets, when they have writ of love their fill,
Grown old, are scorn'd, tho' fancy crown their quill.

I have a feeling, as I try to navigate my way to my lodgings at Micklegate, that my indulgence in the boozy delights of York might bring on similar regrets in the morning.

21. All Features Great and Small

– York to Darlington –

Once, to pass through Bootham Bar was to enter not the comfortable suburbs of Bootham and Clifton, but to plunge into the wilds. The Forest of Galtres came right up to the city walls, haunt of wolves and highwaymen, and guards were stationed here to escort passengers the 13 miles through the forest to Easingwold.

This morning, I swing in from the west, having driven round the city walls from Micklegate to where the A19 departs north from Bootham Bar. I join the early morning crawl out through the suburbs.

Uncle Charlie said of this stretch of road: 'Today, outside the walls we come at once into the district of Clifton, after Knavesmire the finest suburb of York; the wide road lined with old mansions that almost reek of prebendal appointments [a prebend is a canon at a cathedral], justices of the peace, incomes of over two thousand a year, and butlers.' It's still very smart; an affluent suburb with Georgian and Victorian terraces and hotels, most of which contain the words boutique or apartment in their names. The many long pauses in my progress give me plenty of time to look around. I crawl past St Peter's School, where a master who looks exactly like a young Gordon Brown is hurrying along beside two lanky boys in grey suits. If I were a messenger from the future, and this were the real young Gordon Brown, I could yell out a warning to him: 'Gordon! Don't trust Tony! He'll never step aside until it's too late!'

I drive on past The Burton Stone. This inn (even the thought of a pub causes me to wince this morning) is named after a medieval plague stone pierced with three sockets that stands on the corner of Burton Stone Lane.

The story locally is that it was once the base for three medieval crosses. When they were removed at the Reformation, the sockets that supported them were filled with vinegar, in which coins held by travellers, potential plague carriers, could be dipped and disinfected. I came across similar things at the market in Newark, and beside the churchyard in Catterick. The Burton Stone, which is protected behind iron railings, may not be in its original position, but the fact that a chapel dedicated to St Mary once stood here suggests it might have been a point at which travellers prayed for protection from plague.

At the village of Skelton I leave the main road, on Uncle Charlie's advice, for a look at St Giles' church. It is said to have been built in 1227 with stone left over from the south transept at York Minster, and to a similar design, though on a much more modest scale. Certainly the minster's treasurer, Roger Haget, funded this church, and mason's marks on the stones suggest that they were carved by the same craftsmen.

I look out for its bell-cote over the rooftops on a rise to the north of the village. It's a lovely, simple place, with fine stonework, some beautiful triple lancet windows and a handsome porch beneath a grey-green slate roof. It was restored in 1814 by nineteen-year-old Henry Graham, son of a York rector, and the church – according to the guidebook – became 'a source of inspiration to the architects of the nineteenth century Gothic Revival'.

There's another piece of – contemporary – reinvention in the village: I see a sign for York FootGolf, 'York's premier foot golf centre'. I check its website later and find that, yes, its like golf only you kick a football around the course, aiming for football-sized holes. Genius.

As I drive I reflect that the Forest of Galtres, established by the Normans, stretched many miles further, making villages such as Skelton mere clearings in the woods. Today the A19 runs straight and flat over open fields. For Uncle Charlie:

> This country is dullness personified. The main road is flat and featureless, and the branch roads instilled with a melancholy emptiness that lives in every ditch and commonplace hedgerow. A deadly sameness, a paralysing negation, closes the horizon of this sparsely settled district, depopulated in that visitation of fire and sword when William the Conqueror came, in 1069, and massacred a hundred thousand of those who had dared to withstand him.
>
> They had surrendered on promise of their lives and property being respected, but the fierce Norman utterly destroyed the city of York and laid waste the whole of the country between York and Durham. Those who were not slain perished miserably of cold and famine. Their pale ghosts still haunt the route of the Great North Road [he means the York Road] and afflict it, though more than eight hundred years have flown.

I can't say I'm as attuned to such past suffering as Charlie, but it's certainly flat and empty out here, as I sail past Shipton and Tollerton. At Tollerton, Drunken Barnaby raises his throbbing head once again. In the 1600s there was a race-course here. Barnaby writes:

Thence to Towlerton [Tollerton], where those stagers,
Or horses courses run for wagers;
Near to the highway the course is,
Where they ride and run their horses;
But still on our journey went we,
First or last did like content me.

By which I take it that he was still forsaking the temptations he renounced on his way out of York, and didn't care which horse won.

It's a relief to reach Easingwold, at last to find a recognisable coaching town whose wide main thoroughfare – Long Street – is catching some weak winter sun. I have to leave the A19, which has bypassed Easingwold since 1994, to get to it, and I'm glad I do. Oven-ready geese are for sale at the roadside, and the bright, white New Inn looks every bit the eighteenth-century coaching inn, with its stable-yard archway.

Easingwold was a natural first stop for coaches coming north from York, and in 1780 there were 26 inns serving travellers.

Charlie, travelling seventy-odd years after the death of the coach trade, was unimpressed. He found: 'a grimly bare and gritty wide street, with narrow pavements... a roadway filled, not with traffic, but with children at noisy play. Shabby houses lining this street, houses little better than cottages, and ugly at that; grey, hard-featured, forbidding. Imagine half a mile of this... and you have Easingwold.'

What he saw was the poverty caused in so many little towns by the loss of road trade at the opening of the railways. Since then Easingwold has scrubbed up nicely and, with its cobbled market place and tree-lined streets, is a very pleasant little Georgian market town.

Another Long Street coaching inn, the Rose and Crown, which Charlie singled out as the only interesting building in the place, has not survived. It, says Charlie, was once the principal coaching establishment, stabling 20 horses and serving coaches on the stage coaches from here to Thirsk. The surviving New Inn, 'an inferior house' says Charlie, served the Royal Mail coaches for London, Newcastle and Edinburgh, and the Highflyer for Newcastle.

Out on the A19 again, I pass a succession of loops of old road to left and right of the new, climb up to Thormanby and on through Birdforth. I resist the temptation to divert for roadside attractions such as Flamingo Land, or the kangaroos at Monk Park Farm as I approach Thirsk, the road running parallel with what to Uncle Charlie were the 'sullen' Hambleton Hills.

Thirsk was the next staging post, and is the third highlight for me on the York Road after Selby and York itself. Charlie, again, hit it at a low point, writing: 'There have been those who have called it "picturesque." Let us pity them, for those to whom Thirsk shows a picturesque side must needs have acquaintance with only the sorriest and most commonplace of towns.'

Today, those who think Thirsk picturesque number the many millions who know it from the tales – in book, film and televised form – of the town's one-time vet, James Herriott. Again, the A19 bypasses the town, and I turn off, to follow the original York Road along Finkle Street to the Market Place. It's not market day, so the square is a car park, but a highly decorated one. It is just before Remembrance Sunday, and the town's power knitters have been busy transforming the square in honour of the dead.

They've draped the long neck of the clock tower in a net covered with knitted poppies. All the bollards in the square wear poppy hats, and the post box has a scarlet poppy bonnet. There are poppies in the window of the White Horse Cafe – proud boast '72 seater fish and chip restaurant' – on railings and on any other surface where a poppy might flower. They make a heart-lifting display of bright red on a grey November day.

I take a stroll, and drink the place in: its Ritz Cinema, a period-piece of a picture house; the butchers' lorry from which pig carcasses are being lifted off their hooks and shoulder-carried into the shop; the heady aroma of manure from the piled-high poppy-red trailer being towed by tractor past the posh boutiques; and the Golden Fleece, a mellow-brick former coaching inn which sports the same fat sheep suspended above the door as its namesake in York.

I have a half hour to wait before the World of James Herriott, housed in the former veterinary surgery in Kirkgate, opens. I could spend it in The Three Tuns, a second former coaching inn now under the custodianship of Wetherspoons, but I choose the Golden Fleece, because it is owned by the same group as the Bell at Stilton, and offers the same affluent but cosy comfort.

The Fleece dates from the 1500s, and was one of the north's foremost coaching inns. The Royal Mails for London, Edinburgh and Newcastle stopped here every evening, as did the Highflyer for Newcastle 'and all points north'. It also serviced The Wellington, for London via Doncaster, Grantham, Stamford and Huntingdon; and The Expedition, for Boroughbridge, Wetherby and Leeds.

Its fame persisted in the motoring age. In 1911 The Fleece served up a grand lunch for a selection of Europe's rich and famous as they competed in a stage of The Prince Henry of Prussia Cup, one of the world's first international motor rallies. The Prince, brother of the German Kaiser Wilhelm II and cousin of George V, saw the race as a way of cooling the heating enmity between the two countries.

The race started in Hamburg, the cars were shipped to Southampton, then drove on to Edinburgh. Lunch at Thirsk came on a stage from Harrogate to Newcastle. Among the competitors was Sir Arthur Conan Doyle, creator of Sherlock

Holmes. I take my coffee into the Writing Room and ponder the enduring appeal of James Herriott.

It's striking how durable his stories have proven to be. These are simple tales, and all the more effective for it, with the triple appeal of well-rounded, clearly-drawn characters, Yorkshire country life, and animals. They present life-and-death drama against the comforting, reassuring backdrop of the characters' minor setbacks, adversities, and successes. I love them and, I am about to discover, I love the house where they were written.

There are three signs on the front wall, one a blue plaque: 'James Alfred Wight 1916-1995 veterinary surgeon and author of the James Herriott books lived and worked here', the other two are what look like the original name plates for Alf Wight and Mr DV Sinclair, model for the crusty, sometimes bombastic but ultimately sympathetic character of Siegfried.

Inside, the ground floor is a lovingly detailed recreation of the house as it was. I peer into the dining room and office – which also served as a waiting room. Next comes the sitting room with chintzy sofas sporting antimacassars, an open fire, upright piano, well-stocked bookshelves and French doors onto the garden. In a little side-parlour the BBC's *All Creatures Great and Small* flickers on a tiny round-screened TV. I walk through the kitchen and scullery, heart of the house, where washing is drying, a baby is in its pram, and the table is set with a sort of brunch-and-tunch (tea and lunch) mix of boiled eggs, toast, cupcakes and apples. There are jars of pickles and preserves on the shelves, the onions and peaches looking decided post-mortem, as if they might be mis-labelled samples awaiting analysis.

So seductive is this re-creation that I feel I could easily slip into the life lived here, and in Thirsk generally. A pint at the Golden Fleece, a visit to the flicks at the Ritz, pick up a cut of prime Yorkshire lamb on the way home, where I put my feet up before a roaring fire, nose in a book.

Of course, I'd have to learn this vetting lark first, but the books in the dispensary – *Introduction to Pathology, Early Embryology of the Chick,* and *The Dairy Farmer's Veterinary Book* among them – would quickly tell me what to do with all the medicines in little white boxes labelled Cleansing Drink for Cows, Hoose Mixture for Calves, Warble Fly Powder, and Waterproof Harness Paste. I mean, how hard can it be?

Upstairs I come across the highlight for any schoolboy: the chance to stick your hand up a (prosthetic) cow and see how hard you have to tug to deliver a reluctant calf. The answer is, quite hard. But I did it, so I'm half-qualified already.

I walk on through a recreation of sets from the BBC adaptation of the books – ninety-one episode and two specials – and a room dedicated to the new version on Channel 5. On my way out they ask if I've enjoyed my visit. I have.

I'm in a mellow mood as I take the A168 the seven miles to Northallerton, running through blink-and-you'll miss it Thornton-le-Street and dodging between its twin brothers Thorton-le-Moor and Thorton-le-Beans.

Northallerton is an altogether more down-to-earth town than Thirsk. Uncle Charlie called it 'a mile-long dullness'. You might say the same today, if you wanted to be mean. I drive up High Street, the B1333, past the usual chain stores and park close to the Golden Lion, a former coaching inn today hosting a bed sale out the back. Charlie's verdict on the inn: 'large but not lovely'. I know a few people like that.

There are some posh spots in the town. Across the road from the Golden Lion is a Betty's Cafe and Tea Rooms. Nearby is Barkers, a family department store that has been here since 1882. Northallerton's got a Lakeland and a Seasalt.

I choose a late lunch at Betty's over the Golden Lion. The trouble is, so has everyone else. Two o'-clock on a November Tuesday and the place is packed. I queue first on the pavement to be let in to the lobby, then progress to standing just inside the restaurant, before being invited to perch on a green banquette with a copy of the menu. There is still one couple ahead of me, but I feel the anticipation I also get when I'm hanging on the line to a call centre and they tell me I am (finally) number two in the queue.

While I read the menu a string of waitresses in white blouses and black skirts, and waiters in white shirt and black trousers, whizz past me and in and out of the automatic sliding door into the kitchen. The trouble is, they all move faster than the doors, which almost clip them at every approach.

The cafe is packed with ladies who dress up for lunch, and who seem to consider cream cakes a square meal. I read through the menu and look up to see if anyone looks like moving. No one is, so I pop upstairs to the loo. Back down again, I'm still number two in the queue. So I read the menu again, more slowly this time. My rumbling stomach has forced me to upgrade my intended order from a sandwich to either the Betty's Burger or fish and chips. Wait much longer and I'll have to order both.

Finally I think, sod it, and go down to Greggs and take my steak bake and chicken roll back to the car, where I think about how Northallerton got robbed of a place on the A1, and was turned from transport hub to backwater overnight.

Once, the two rival courses of the Great North Road converged here. The decision to run the A1 via Scotch Corner – made late and after some cartographers had taken a punt and included Northallerton on maps of the new route – established the supremacy of the western path once and for all.

Back on the York Road, sprucely whitewashed milestones tick off the distance to Darlington: 14, 13, 12. It's a good fast road with little traffic to Great Smeaton, on a rise, where one of four coaching inns – the Black Bull – survives, then a gentle descent followed by a swift drop to Croft-on-Tees, where I pass from North Yorkshire into County Durham.

Tucked in just before the bridge is the Croft Spa Hotel, once a posting house, transformed into a far grander place in 1808. It drew visitors from across the country to take the waters which, Uncle Charlie reports, are 'as nasty as those of Harrogate, with that flavour of rotten eggs so highly approved by the medical profession, and only the vagaries of fashion can be held accountable for the comparative neglect of the one and the favouring of the other.'

Now, Charlie says, 'a gentle melancholy marks the spot where the mouldy-looking Croft Spa Hotel fronts the road, its closed assembly rooms, where once the merry crowds foregathered, given over to damp and mildew.'

It looks quite fit and healthy today, but I prefer an attraction on the far bank of the river. I walk across the bridge which, with its seven elegant gothic arches, dates from 1356 and – since restored a couple of times – is one of the finest in the North. I cross the wide, shallow river running around islets masked in willow scrub to a long, low church where Lewis Carroll's father was rector.

St Peter's, built from red sandstone cut from the river bed, looks as if it's missing its roof, but isn't. It's just hunkered down below the crenellations. Beyond it is the rectory, where the author born Charles Dodgson came, age 11, in 1834. It was the family home until 1868, when his father died, which was after *Alice in Wonderland* was published, but before *Through the Looking Glass*.

Carroll is said to have written *Alice* under the acacia tree in the garden. On the website *Story of Our Village* Edith Lumley writes that, while Alice Liddell, the girl on whom the title character was modelled, never visited, 'Alice Raikes, a young cousin of Lewis Carroll, did. She was one of the inspirers of *Through the Looking Glass.*'

When the rectory was being converted into flats, Edith continues, 'the floor boards of Lewis Carroll's room were removed and treasures were discovered illustrating his many poems; an embroidered hanky, a glove reminiscent of those worn by the White Rabbit in Wonderland, a small well-worn shoe of the type Alice might have worn, remnants of a child's china tea service and a thimble.' They are kept in the church.

Carroll is said to have drawn on features in the twelfth-century church. The Cheshire Cat was inspired by a grinning cat (or maybe lion) carved into the sedilia, the set of stone seats provided for clergy alongside the altar. The grin disappears when you stand up from the pews, as it eventually does in *Alice in Wonderland*.

The first verse of the poem *Jabberwocky* was written at Croft, and this fearsome creature with 'The jaws that bite, the claws that catch' may be based on the legend of the Sockburn Worm, according to which a ferocious winged dragon ravaged the village of Sockburn, five miles downriver from here.

The sword said to have killed the Sockburn Worm is presented to each newly-consecrated Bishop of Durham on the bridge outside the church. I wonder what the past Bishop of Durham who famously thought the Resurrection was a conjuring trick with bones thought of that little ceremony?

I have just over three miles to drive before Darlington, joining the Great North Road that I followed in Section IV at Blackwell, and it's time to compare the two routes of the Great North Road. It's no contest really. Apart from York, Selby and Thirsk, this road has nothing like the wealth of interest on the western route. It's not a bad drive though.

VI

GREAT NORTH ROAD
Darlington
to Morpeth

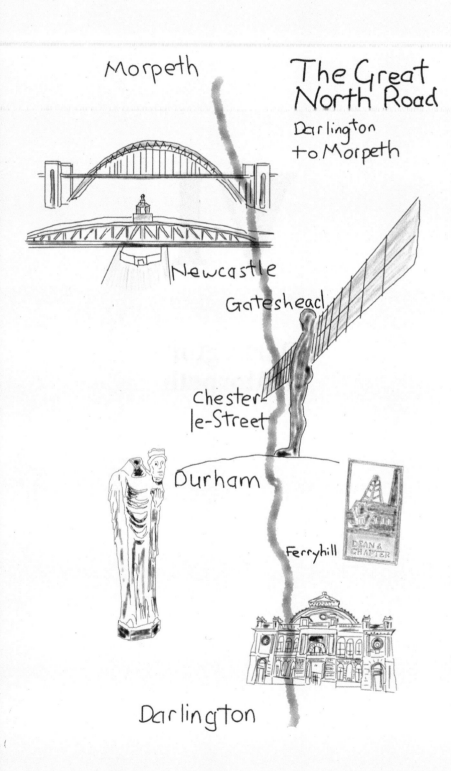

Morpeth

The Great North Road

Darlington to Morpeth

Newcastle

Gateshead

Chester-le-Street

Durham

Ferryhill

DEAN & CHAPTER

Darlington

From Darlington, the railway town where the seeds of the Great North Road's destruction were sown, I drive on to a northern powerhouse that serves as a second capital of the North: Newcastle-upon-Tyne.

That great Northern Saint, Cuthbert, is among my historic companions on this stage, albeit he journeyed this way post-mortem. In the seventh century, Cuthbert had been abbot of Lindisfarne Abbey on Holy Island, off the Northumbrian coast. He was buried there, but his remains were exhumed two centuries later when Danish invaders threatened the island. Monks fled with his remains and, for a further century, carried Cuthbert around the North East.

His remains rested for a while at Darlington, and at Chester-le-Street, before his final resting place at Durham, all places I will visit on this stage of the Great North Road.

Also on the route is the giant iron sculpture of the Angel of the North. I had thought it a purely secular creation, but the string of little improvised shrines I find alongside it make me realise that there is more than I had imagined to link this angel, and people's sense of its power, to the medieval pilgrims who followed St Cuthbert on the Great North Road.

I barely drive on the A1 at all on this section. There are just two short stretches, totalling a mere 2 miles, 4 per cent, on the final approach to Morpeth, out of the 48-mile total.

22. Darling Town

'Darling town, Darlington'. Said nobody. Ever.

In 1617, James I of England (James VI of Scotland), called it not Darlington but 'Darneton' and said: 'I think it's Darneton th' Dirt'. Fifty years later, Daniel Defoe said 'it has nothing remarkable in it but dirt, and a high bridge over little or no water'.

Uncle Charlie Harper, in his *The Great North Road*, also gives Darlington a good twentieth-century kicking. First softening his opponent up by acknowledging it is 'very busy, very prosperous,' then going in with a series of catty killer punches, saying it demonstrated 'a sub-Metropolitan swagger of architectural pretension in its chief streets. There is a distinctly Holloway Road – plus Whitechapel Road – and Kennington Lane air about Darlington which does but add to the piquancy of those streets.' In a word, he's calling it provincial, or maybe suburban.

Charlie hates the way:

> Tumbledown houses of no great age and no conceivable interest are shouldered by flaunting "stores" and "emporia"; these alternating with glittering public-houses and restaurants.
>
> The effect can be paralleled only by imagining a typical general servant dressed in a skirt and train for a Queen's Drawing Room, with ploughboy's boots, a cloth jacket, and ostrich-feathered hat to complete the costume.

I suspect that what Charlie is really hopping mad about, as a lover of the old road, is not the fact that Darlington got rich quick, but how it got rich. That was down to the railways, and the invention here of the steam locomotive. And, of course, the railways killed the Great North Road, at least for a century or so. But I'm going to try to keep an open mind.

Old Darlington is pretty much hidden away, wrapped in new roads. I follow the route of the Great North Road in on the A167 inner ring road and get to the Grange Road roundabout, where the road system tries to force me east to skirt the town on a horseshoe-shaped 1960s dual carriageway. But I'm able to turn left on the course of the old road and find a place to park in a brave new bit of the town centre called Feethams.

It's an odd spot. There's a square, which I bet is called a piazza, and a great curtain wall of concrete, monolithic enough to make the Pink Floyd *The Wall* album cover, blocking off any view of the town centre. The wall is blank, other than for a sign, fashioned in what looks like astroturf, in its centre. It reads: 'DL1 Film. Food. Fun.'

Which, as far as I can see from here, translates as 'Vue. Hungry Horse. Erm...'

Beyond the Great Wall of Darlington I can just make out the tip of the Clock Tower, one of three town pinnacles that I want a closer look at, and set off on a tour of them.

I first head east, away from the centre. I navigate the rampart of the ring road, beneath which the River Skerne is squeezed into a concrete culvert, and climb towards the first of those three peaks: the tower, as imposing as any on a grand, Victorian Gothic Revival parish church, that rises above the railway station.

I get to it up Victoria Road, passing a red-brick church, now Bathroom World; the Book and Film Exchange, its windows supporting leaning towers of paperbacks; and a terrace of houses and a big pub called Hogans, which have their windows screened with metal security shutters.

The railway spire towers above, as befits what could be considered the most important station in the country. In 1887 the North Eastern Railway shelled out £9m in today's money to build this station at Bank Top, having been stung by a comment from Queen Victoria that the old one was unworthy of a town that had invented the railway system.

I imagine striding beneath that clock tower to reach the platforms, but find I have instead to duck into a cream-brick tunnel like a Victorian gents to get to them. However, emerging into the long tube of glass and cast-iron ribs that span the rails is like stepping from the wings onto a dazzlingly bright stage.

The overall impression is of a beautifully simple, functional, and elegant space. I sit on a bench and look around, taking in the thought, care and local pride that has gone into the detail of the design. There are the coats of arms of Darlington, Durham and Newcastle, and shields of the old railway companies that linked them, in the roof support arch spandrels. I admire the great owl-faced station clock suspended high above the platforms, and the ornate capitals on the cast iron columns supporting the roof.

I'm beginning to think Darlington deserves more respect than it has been given by the travellers I've quoted. That thought is strengthened once I head back into town and cross the Skerne via Stonebridge to reach the second pinnacle: the spire on the church of St Cuthbert and St Mary. The present church, known as the Lady of the North, is twelfth century, but has Saxon antecedents, and houses crosses and a sundial from that period. St Cuthbert's remains rested here in 995, as Lindisfarne monks fleeing Viking raiders took them from Ripon to Durham. There is a statue of St Cuthbert, holding the head of St Oswald, high on an external wall. I'll learn more about that image when I get to Durham.

It's not all good. I puzzle over the purpose of a great square brick chimney rising among the gravestones before walking on, and encountering the brutalist sixties town hall. It resembles a vast, concrete kitchen table with, hung beneath it, and suspended above an empty layer of car park, a glass screen which no doubt houses offices.

I imagine it as some vast recycling plant, with trucks pulling in beneath that glass curtain to be filled with used bureaucracy. Meanwhile, a staunch symbol of the independence of the old North lies empty. It is the former offices of the *Northern Echo*, on the corner of Crown Street and Priestgate. It is about to become apartments, which is a bit of a miss. It would make a mega-Wetherspoons.

I get back on the track of the Great North Road through town, walking up pedestrianised High Row, where the since-demolished coaching inns once stood, to the third eminence.

Darlington Clock Tower rises like a mini Big Ben, with extra rocket boosters in each corner, above the Covered Market. I take the steps up to the market, and enter a place that embodies the best of Darlington. Butchers, fishmongers, and greengrocers, in khaki or green cotton work coats, are selling the finest local meat, fish and veg.

Outside, three days a week, there is a general market, which proved very handy for one of my travelling companions, Celia Fiennes, when she had a clothing crisis. Treking south from Durham 'by the way I lost some of my nightclothes and little things in a bundle that the guide I hired carried; this is a little market town, the market day was on Monday which was the day I pass'd through it.' So she was able to replace the lost items.

Another companion – Braithwaite's Drunken Barnaby – made merry, and managed to persuade some poor woman to marry him, in Darlington. Naturally, that didn't stop him boozing, fornicating and swindling:

Thence to Darlington, where I housed
Til at last I was espoused:
Marriage feast and all prepared,
Not a fig for th' world I cared;
All night long by t'pot I tarry'd,
As if I had ne'er been marry'd.

So, not much of a wedding night for his poor bride then.

The Great North Road made a dog-leg turn past the market, swinging right into Tubwell Row, where the Binns department store has reopened after Lockdown and is bobbing along with a 50 per cent summer sale. Then it's a left into Northgate, and on via High Northgate. From here I can drive the route, so I head back to pick up my car. I reflect as I do that Darlington's not a bad place at all, and there are several ambitious regeneration schemes underway, including the one I encountered walking up to Bank Top. But it is struggling – like so many other towns – with what to do with its town centre.

I drive around town on the A167 to meet the Great North Road, and follow it into High Northgate. A little way along, and just off to the west, is the place where the seeds of destruction were sown for the Great North Road, and every other highway.

The former North Road Station, in Station Road, is the Queen Victoria-disparaged predecessor of the station I visited on High Bank. It was one of the stops on the world's first steam-powered passenger railway, the Darlington and Stockton, and is now the Head of Steam railway museum. Until recently, the museum's prize exhibit was George and Robert Stevenson's Locomotion No 1, which sounds like a song popular on the 1970s Northern Soul circuit, but was in fact the first steam locomotive to haul a passenger-carrying train on a public railway. 'In', as Jeremy Clarkson would say, 'the woorrld'.

For 163 years, since going out of service, the engine was on display in Darlington, but lately got shifted nine miles to another museum, at Shildon. Darlington is still sore about it.

Eight thousand signed a petition to keep it in the town, resulting in a time-share deal. Locomotion No 1: a barrel on a trolley with a tall chimney, that looks like a mobile kipper-smoking oven, will return here for six months in 2025, to mark the two-hundredth anniversary of railway travel.

It was 23 years after the Darlington debut of the railway before the rail link between London and Edinburgh was completed with the bridging of the River Tweed at Berwick, in 1848. After which, it was all downhill for the Great North Road. But, for a couple of decades, road and rail as the future of travel were in the balance. It looked for a while as if steam-power would be applied to road vehicles rather than track-bound trains.

In the 1820s and 30s, many good steam-driven motor-cars were being developed, but with railways being rolled out across the land at a phenomenal rate, and legislation forbidding locomotive carriages on highways, rail won out. Not until the invention of the internal combustion engine would the pendulum swing away from rail and back to road, cutting off the source of Darlington's wealth.

Thomas De Quincey, author of *Confessions of an English Opium Eater*, couldn't get his head around the switch from horse-drawn coach to rail. In *The English Mail Coach*, he says that moving at fifty miles per hour rather than ten was not something the senses could grasp. OK, he concedes, if he finds himself in York four hours after leaving London then he must accept that he has been racing along, but such speed was not something he could feel as a personal experience. It was 'lifeless knowledge, resting upon alien evidence'.

He writes that trains:

...cannot compare with the old mail-coach system in grandeur and power... I myself am little aware of the pace. But, seated on the old mail-coach, we needed no evidence out of ourselves to indicate the velocity. We heard our speed, we saw it, we felt it as a thrilling; and this speed was not the product of blind, insensate agencies, that had no sympathy to give, but was incarnated in the fiery eyeballs of the noblest amongst brutes, in his dilated nostrils, spasmodic muscles, and thunder-beating hoofs.

Mind you, given what De Quincy was probably on, he was already speeding faster than any train could take him, so obviously it felt slow in comparison.

The Great North Road runs, as the A167 Durham Road, out through the suburb of Harrowgate Hill, undulating on through Beaumont Hill to crest and then descend to the hamlet of Coatham Mundeville. Here, with rail and the River Skerne to the east, I cross the modern A1(M). That'll be my last encounter with the modern road for 30 miles, when I pass over it alongside the Angel of the North, south of Gateshead, and I won't actually drive along it until Stannington Bridge, just south of Morpeth, 46 miles onward.

In the village of Aycliffe I turn off for a short bounce up a rutted track to a very old church, and another encounter with the theme of saints. Today, St Andrews is just a twelfth-century parish church, but there has been a place of Christian worship here for 1,200 years and, in Saxon times, it was of great religious significance. In the eighth century, when this church was dedicated to St Acca, a Northumbrian saint and Bishop of Hexham, two synods were held here, in 782 and 789. Synods, then and now, are church council meetings at which matters of doctrine or administration are decided.

The *Anglo Saxon Chronicle* records that the synods held here related to the deaths of 'Werburh, Coelred's Queen and Cynewulf, Bishop of Lindisfarne' and will have concerned the question of succession.

The old name for Aycliffe was Aclea, meaning clearing in the oaks, but there is no forest here now. It was felled by Cromwell, during the Civil War, when he was on his way to subjugate Royalists in the North. He turned the trees into logs to strengthen the Great North Road, and give his troops and ordinance a solid path onward.

Two Saxon crosses in the church, both restored from

fragments, are thought to be relics of the synods. One depicts the Lamb of God (Agnus Dei) with a mythical, spear-bearing character riding upon its back.

There are other remnants of Saxon crosses incorporated in the present church, including part of a cross-shaft re-cut to form a window lintel and, built into the churchyard wall facing the car park, an unusual triangular panel showing an early Christian cross. The Normans, who rebuilt this and virtually every other church in their conquered land, really didn't rate Saxon religious artifacts, and used them like bits of rubble.

The descent from the village once led across a lonely marsh, but now a belt of light industry joins Aycliffe and its new-town twin, Newton Aycliffe, where the curiously named Gretna Green Wedding Inn welcomed travellers on the Great North Road. Curious because Gretna Green is way over on the west of the country, just over the border when travelling from Carlisle to Scotland. Curious also because the lax rules that allowed eloping couples to marry at the Scottish Gretna Green did not apply here, just north of Darlington.

The Gretna Green Wedding Inn stood across the road from the Bay Horse, and the spot was known as Travellers' Rest. Both these inns were post houses, but the Bay Horse is gone, and the other is now called simply the Gretna Green Hotel, and serves as a pub to the Premier Inn behind it.

Uncle Charlie wrote of this spot: 'An indescribable air of romance dignifies these two solitary inns that confront one another across the highway, and form all there is of Traveller's Rest.' It's clear from his account that the owner of the Wedding Inn intended to heighten the romance of the spot through the allusion to its Scottish counterpart. Charlie writes: 'The Wedding Inn... has for its sign the picture of a marriage ceremony in that famous Border smithy.'

I turn off right into Ricknall Lane and pull into the car park to have a nose around. I can confirm that there is absolutely nothing romantic about the Gretna Green Hotel today. The present building dates from the 1930s, but I peer across the road in hope of seeing some remnant of the Bay Horse, of which Uncle Charlie paints a vivid picture.

He wrote, a hundred years ago: 'Dating back far into the old coaching and posting times, its stables of that era still remain; but what renders the old house particularly notable is its sign, the odd figure of a horse within an oval, seen on its wall, with the word "Liberty" in company with the name of "Traveller's Rest".'

The sign referred to the legend of a prisoner being escorted to Durham jail who took advantage of his guard being thrown from his horse by jumping on it and making his escape. The horse was called Liberty.

During the Second World War there was a vast munitions factory to the west of this spot, the marshy location and attendant fogs providing cover from Luftwaffe bombers. After the war Newton Aycliffe was built there, a modern industrial village intended to be a model for the new Welfare State.

With demobbed soldiers returning to an area in which coal, steel and shipbuilding were in decline, Lord Beveridge envisaged Newton Aycliffe as a classless town, with manager and mechanic living side by side in council houses that were grouped around greens on which children could play safely.

It may not have lived up to those soaring expectations, but it does have the distinction of lying in the Sedgefield constituency once represented by Tony Blair, the only living, elected, former Labour Prime Minister. I spot no statues to the great man on my drive through, but I bet there are loads tucked away. Maybe some of his former constituents have little shrines to Tone on their mantle-pieces. Or maybe not. It's gone Tory, at least for now.

The road drops on down to Rushyford where, just before a roundabout that takes the east-west A689 Bishop Auckland to

Hartlepool road across my path, I want to check on another old coaching inn. Uncle Charlie writes of 'a pretty scene, where a little tributary of the Skerne prattles over its stony bed and disappears under the road beside that old-time posting-house and inn, the Wheatsheaf... black poplars overhang the scene and shade the little hamlet that straggles down a lane to the left hand.'

I'm in for another disappointment. What since Charlie's day has become the Bay Eden Arms Hotel has concrete barriers blocking the entrance to its car park, and is not currently in business. It's vast, looking like a long terrace of cream stuccoed houses, and faces north, at right angles to the Great North Road. The 'weddings conference banqueting' promised on its sign are things of the past, at least for now.

The Wheatsheaf was once the regular holiday destination of Lord Eldon, who performed two stints as Lord High Chancellor between 1801 and 1827. Charlie records that the landlord, a Mr Holt, was a boon companion of the lawyer and politician, who kept his own cellar at the inn, stocked mainly with a fearsome-sounding brew called Carbonell's Fine Old Military Blackstrap Newcastle Port. I picture it as a sort of Newcastle Brown Ale (Newkie Brown) with added brimstone. I'm surprised Drunken Barnaby never mentions it.

Apparently, Holt and Eldon would share seven bottles a day, moving up to eight on a Saturday to fortify them for the church service they would have to endure on Sunday.

The road climbs from here to one of the highest points on the Great North Road, at 450ft above sea level, where the former pit village of Ferryhill stands on the horizon. I turn off the A167 for the final approach, following the old route up Darlington Road, the B6287, and park in the market square.

The climb here was a slog for horses and, in the early nineteenth century, a cutting was begun into the crest of the ridge, a task abandoned when the railway killed the coaching business, but finally completed in the 1920s when road traffic was resurgent once again.

After the disappointments encountered over the past few miles, I'm delighted to find this is a lovely little town, old-fashioned in a homely way: the sort of place I can imagine living a pleasant life.

Alongside the little wriggle that the old road follows through the village is a pub called The Post Boy, the name a reminder of coaching days. There is a little one-shop-wide former cinema, with PAVILION in flaking maroon lettering on its stucco front, now offering prize bingo and amusements, and tucked between Tasty House and Pizza HOT. Up the road is a newsagents' called Spendwise. Sound advice.

Ferryhill has a library on the market square, and public loos, in front of which the railings support window boxes bright with yellow, orange and red marigolds, and petunias in mauve and pale green: evidence of a strong sense of local pride.

In a place so spick and span it would be easy to pass through oblivious to the grim human toll exacted during its industrial past. Easy, if it were not for a pub called the Dean and Chapter, named after the pit that once dominated the village. Painted right across the front is a sign reading: 'This pub is dedicated to the 73 miners who lost their lives at the colliery from 1904 when production began until 1929. The colliery closed in 1966.'

From the car park beside the working men's club I can look north from the lip of the ridge, along the ribbon of the old road, which runs through pale green and gold fields reaching, at the horizon, the red and white slab of a big KFC.

This chickens' graveyard is on a rise where another east-west route, the A688, crosses my path, and beside a site with a ghoulish story recounted by past travellers on the Great North Road. The spot was known as the Thinford Inn roundabout, and a photo from 1950 which I am looking at now shows a scene that would have been common on the Great North Road at the time:

a big wayside inn on one side of the worn tarmac, a corrugated iron petrol station on the other, and a string of Morris Minors and boxy Fords ambling through on a road without clear margins and no markings.

Go way back to 1685 and a traveller would have seen a gibbet standing beside the inn, with a wretched criminal swinging from it.

Andrew Mills, a servant of the Brass family, who farmed the land here, had murdered their three young children. Mills was 18, and claimed a demon drove him on with commands that he 'kill, kill'. Mills was hanged, but cut down while still alive and forced into a cage, hung from the gibbet, in which he survived for several days. I'll let Uncle Charlie continue the story:

> His sweetheart brought him food, but he could not eat, for every movement of his jaw caused it to be pierced with an iron spike. So she brought milk instead, and so sustained the wretched creature for some time. Legends still recount how he lingered here in agony, his cries by day and night scaring the neighbouring cottagers from their homes, until the shrieks and groans at length ceased, and death came to put an end to his sufferings.

The gibbet became known as Andrew Mills' Stob, and the wood from it was believed to cure toothache, rheumatism and heartburn. Which meant that slivers were chipped off it, until nothing was left. After which, Uncle Charlie wonders 'what the warty, scrofulous, ulcerous, and rheumaticky inhabitants did then' for medicine.

The Thinford Inn closed in 2012, became the victim of vandalism and arson, and was demolished in 2015. Today as I pass through the site is being reborn as a drive-through coffee shop and bakery, part of the new DurhamGate development of shops, homes and offices.

In addition to KFC, I have the choice of Starbucks, McDonalds and Burger King as I swing through the roundabout and on towards Durham: a prime selection of four brands serving nothing I want to eat.

Never mind, I'm about to reach one of the pleasantest spots on this stretch of the old road as I drop down through Croxdale and reach Sunderland Bridge, a now-superseded point at which the old road crossed the River Wear. Croxdale gets its name from 'the Cross in the Dale', and marks a spot, where the road dipped through a dark hollow, at which a cross was erected to ward off the fiends medieval travellers believed lurked there.

The road to the old bridge peels off to my left as I descend, behind barriers and a sign appealing: 'Wanted, dead or alive, Caravans and Motorhomes'.

I have to loop around on the B6300 to reach the far end of the old bridge, but can then park and walk back over it. There are lovely views downriver to the green-steel new bridge, and up to the elegant wide arches of the pink-brick railway viaduct. A footpath sign tells me I am on one of the Northern Saints Trails, a reminder of the inescapable saintly theme of this stage of my journey. But there were perils here in coaching days.

Norman Webster, in *The Great North Road*, says of this spot: 'It was the very charm of this combination of woodland and river valley which distracted the attention of coachmen when negotiating Sunderland Bridge and which resulted in a series of accidents.' In one incident, in 1821, the Edinburgh to London mail came to grief when 'the coach struck one side of the bridge at the approach, causing the vehicle to overturn. Two passengers were thrown over the parapet to their deaths, the driver, guard and three passengers fortunately escaping without serious injury.'

As a result, the bridge was first widened and the parapet raised before, in the 1930s, the new bridge was built.

Durham is almost in sight now, and as I cross Browney

Bridge and climb the approach to the city I have a choice of routes. At Farewell Hall I could stick to the A167, which would take me looping around to the west, a route that was popular with coaches and, later, motorists who wanted to avoid the sharp descent to the city centre, and the tortuous climb, descent and climb through it.

Instead, I bear right onto the A177, which takes me via Church Street and the loveliest approach to any city that I know of. Glimpsed to my left, beyond the oxbow of the River Wear that almost encircles the city centre, stand the great, solid twin towers of Durham Cathedral. I follow the old route into New Elvet, then go right into Old Elvet, and park.

23. City of Saints

– Durham to Newcastle –

In theory, I could drive right through Durham on the route of the Great North Road.

But, if I did motor on over the old Elvet Bridge, I'd be herding before me, snow-plough-like, the crowds choosing a lunch place on Sadler Street, listening to the busker in the Market Place, or window shopping on Silver Street. So, by the time I got to Framwellgate Bridge and left the heart of the city, I'd have half a dozen tourists on my bonnet. And that would be rude.

So instead I walk down Old Elvet, where former coaching inns such as the County Hotel have been joined by new hotels that have colonised grand old buildings, such as the Indigo in the Shire Hall, and spend a minute gazing over the parapet of Elvet Bridge.

Deep below me the River Wharfe flows between the rock cliffs and wooded banks that guard the high tongue of land on which cathedral and castle sit, and make Durham such a strong natural fortress. There are rowers on the water, and walkers on the riverside paths, enjoying what feels like a country stroll in the heart of the city. Over Elvet Bridge, Sadler Street climbs narrow and new-stone flagged to Market Place. Here people are sitting around the enormous statue of a soldier and diplomat who, in the nineteenth century, developed coal mines across County Durham.

He is Charles William Vane Stewart, 3rd Marquess of Londonderry, the one who has a former truck stop near Catterick named after him. Vane? He should spell it Vain. He's on his horse, which looks feisty but which he is manfully controlling. He has a Flashheart-style cloak and a great big plume on the front of his helmet.

At the other end of the square is a more modest statue, of Neptune sticking his trident into a sea monster, signifying the pacification of the ocean. It references the scheme to link Durham to the sea by improving navigation on the River Wear, and reminds me of how often on my journey up the Great North Road, river and road have interconnected.

The busker outside the entrance to the Market Hall tells me it's too late, baby, but I press on beneath a sign declaring that this is 'More than just a market, Durham's independent department store'. Which it is. Why, I could buy a vinyl LP, a ball of wool, a paper bag of old-fashioned boiled sweets shaken from a jar, a shotgun and a bottle of Lindisfarne Mead, all under the same roof.

From here the old road swings left on Silver Street, and descends steeply once more to cross Framwellgate Bridge. I walk on up Milburngate to the point where it crosses the A690 and where, later, I will be able to drive on along the Great North Road, now the B6532, without posing a hazard to pedestrians.

This rollercoaster ride through Durham – descending to cross the River Wear twice, with a climb up the ridge to the Market Place and winding descent down the other side between the two – proved intolerable in the motoring age. Any traveller who didn't need to go into Durham favoured the western route through Neville's Cross – once designated A1 but now the A167 – or, from 1969, the A1(M) that runs three miles to the east.

For those who did need to go into Durham, the New Elvet Bridge was built in 1975, just downstream of the old bridge, and it is that road I'll take later as I head north.

But first I want to enjoy Durham, and pick up the saintly thread I first touched upon in Darlington. So I walk back to the town centre, re-cross Framwellgate Bridge, and turn right down the steps to the riverside. I'm in search of the first of three holy wells, one dedicated to St Cuthbert, one to St Oswald and the third emerging from beneath the tomb of St Bede.

St Cuthbert's Well, I've been told, is hidden away on the steep bank between the cathedral and the Wear. I approach along the riverbank path and finally see, almost completely hidden in the trees, a scrabble path going up, on the wrong side of a handrail beyond which is a much neglected set of concrete steps. I scramble up to the well head.

It looks impressive at a distance, a stone wall into which is set a Norman arch. Above the arch is an illegible inscription which I'm told reads 'Fons Cuthberti 1660'. I see the lip of a spout and beneath it a stone trough. But when I look in, it's been used as a litter bin for plastic bottles and Haribo wrappers.

You know how, if football fans misbehave, their clubs can ban them from the terraces? How about, if the purchasers of a product dump the wrapping rather than binning it, they get banned from buying? Sounds like a vote-winner to me.

Just a sad trickle of water dribbles onto the litter, but I put my cupped hand beneath it and take a sip anyway. Bad idea? Well, I lived to write this, so I guess I got away with it.

I scramble on up, and vault a couple of strands of barbed wire and red-and-white tape that make the well look like a crime scene, to gain a path that runs beneath the towering walls of the cathedral. At the foot of the wall is a grating. This is the Galilee Well, which runs out beneath the Galilee Chapel, which holds St Bede's tomb.

This well is even less impressive than St Cuthbert's. I peer through the grill where, several feet down, a grey plastic drain pipe runs across a damp, earthy pit.

For St Oswald's well I continue downstream, cross the Wear by Prebend Bridge, and take the path angling up the bank to St Oswald's church, which I passed on my drive into the city. Oswald, the seventh century warrior, king and saint who allowed Aidan to Christianise the North, deserves better than this. His well is a mere indentation in the sandstone bank to my right, from which water trickles beneath the path to dampen a patch of leaves before seeping into the Wear. Once, apparently, there was a stone well-head here, destroyed by nineteenth century vandals. I slide down to wet my hand in its waters.

Then I head to the cathedral for a more meaningful encounter with the saints. Durham Cathedral never ceases to impress me. The sheer girth of the great pillars that line the nave, with their check and and chevron patterns: so formidable, so solid. A muscular church for muscular Northern saints: Oswald the warrior, Cuthbert the Lindisfarne prior-turned-hermit, and Bede whose *Ecclesiastical History of the English People* records the conversion of the Anglo-Saxons to Christianity.

Then there is the cathedral clock, like a giant golden carriage clock crowned with a set of pinnacles like the spires I shall see later on Newcastle's cathedral. And the baptismal font, with a 40ft, ornately carved, seventeenth-century oak cover. Celia Fiennes thought it resembled pictures she had seen of the Tower of Babel.

Beyond the high altar is the shrine of St Cuthbert, a simple marble slab bearing the name Cuthbertus replacing the elaborate, bejewelled one destroyed at the Reformation. Alongside it is a headless statue of Cuthbert carrying the head of St Oswald. It reflects the tradition that, when the tomb was opened, a second skull was discovered within it. I realise the statue I saw high in a niche at Darlington is a copy of this one.

Cuthbert's remains arrived here in 995, and first a church, then this cathedral, were built around them.

St Bede's tomb is at the other end of the cathedral, in the aforementioned Galilee chapel. Irritatingly, it is the setting for an art installation when I visit, and in almost complete darkness. I can barely make out Bede's tomb, nor read the words of Bede's prayer, which are alongside it.

An electronic gizmo sends red laser lights flitting around, sliding over the bodies of visitors. It's bloody irritating. I want to shout 'Armed Police!' Or taser! taser! taser!' I mean, I know other cathedrals have paid host to a helter skelter, and a full-size dinosaur but, come on, at least keep the bloody lights on, so that those who are actually interested in the cathedral for what it is can experience it properly.

It's time to drive on. I pick up the old road on the other side of the city centre, and take Framwellgate, the B6532, up Windy Hill and then, on the outskirts of Framwellgate Moor, turn right onto unclassified Front Street to pass through the village.

When Uncle Charlie came this way, it was a far grimier scene than the quiet suburban place it is today, post coal. He wrote:

> It is at Framwellgate Moor, a mile and a half from the city, that the presence of coal begins to make itself felt, in the rows of unlovely cottages, and in the odd figures of the pitmen, who may be seen returning from their work, with grimy faces and characteristic miner's dress. Adjoining this village, and indistinguishable from it by the stranger, is the roadside collection of cottages known as Pity Me, taking its name from the hunted fox in the sign of the Lambton Hounds Inn.

The pub is still there, on Front Street. Norman Webster has this to add:

> This is coal mining country ... with a character and culture of its own evolved from the days when the pitmen were a distinct race living jealously in their own villages, worshipping in churches of their own, and seldom intermarrying with their agricultural neighbours. They had what was effectively their own language, devised their own amusements and sang their own songs.

On the other side of Pity Me my route joins that of the alternative, western path around Durham, and I am on the A167 for a country stretch of dual carriageway to the outskirts of Chester-le-Street. Here, I leave the A road to follow the Great North Road, built on the line of the Roman highway, along Durham Road into the town centre. The town's name is an echo of the time when this was simply a military camp on that Roman street, a staging post on the road from York to Hadrian's Wall.

Chester-le-Street became a backwater when it was bypassed in the 1930s, and the town's narrow main street has survived much as it was. Most of that bypass out to the east was overlaid by the A1(M) in the 1960s.

The old road runs down to an area, once a market square, now lined with cafes, their tables outside. Chester is no longer the 'old dirty thoroughfare town' that Daniel Defoe described, but it doesn't have much to recommend it either.

St Cuthbert's remains were taken to the safety of the Roman fort, where they stayed from 883 to 995, before moving via a short stop at Ripon to Durham. A church was built to house the saint at Chester, on the spot where fourteenth-century St Cuthbert and St Mary now stands, its spire poking 156ft above the town. That spire guides me a block east from the Great North Road to find the church, but it's locked. So is the parish centre across the road.

This church's other claim to fame is the surviving anchorite's cell, a two-storey dwelling built against the north wall of the tower, so I skirt round to have a look at it. Here lived a solitary holy man, known as an anchorite to distinguish him from a mendicant, who travelled from place to place.

Anchorites were anchored to the place, and theirs was one of the earliest forms of Christian monasticism. Windows on the churchyard side allowed food and offerings to be passed through to the anchorite, who was also entrusted with the keys to the church's treasure chest. A squint on the church side allowed him to see through to the nave, and observe the altar when Mass was being said. So he was a bit like a captive caretaker cum security guard.

When, at the Reformation, the anchorite was kicked out and told to go and earn an honest living, the curate moved in to what was a very desirable little residence. This is said to be the finest surviving anchorage in the country. But, of course, it's also locked.

So I give up on Chester-le-Street, and head through town on Newcastle Road to re-join the A167, still on the course of the Roman road. It's undistinguished suburbs all the way to Gateshead now but, a century ago, Uncle Charlie found a grim industrial scene: 'The three miles between Chester-le-Street and Birtley afford a wide-spreading panorama of the Durham coal-field,' he writes. 'Pretty country before its mineral wealth began to be developed, its hills and dales reveal chimney-shafts and hoisting-gear in every direction, and smoke-wreaths, blown across country by the raging winds of the north, blacken everything.'

Charlie described Birtley as 'a typical pit village': 'The paths are black, the hedges and trees ragged and sooty, and tramways from the collieries cross the road itself, unfenced, the trucks dropping coal in the highway.'

Today it's just another bit of suburbia.

The A1 loses its (M) in Birtley, and swings west to skirt Gateshead and Newcastle. The original Great North Road followed its Roman fore-runner out the other side of Birtley, a route called Long Bank, but the modern A1 cuts that road in half. I could regain it by taking the B1296, Durham Road, which on the map is still the most direct route to Gateshead. But if I did that I would miss out a modern highlight of this section: the Angel of the North.

To get to it I go across the modern A1 at a roundabout, and take the A167, which was also once the Great North Road, and became the A1 in 1921. The Angel of the North is on my left, just after that roundabout. Antony Gormley's remarkable emblem of the North, its industrial past and its people, is the largest sculpture in Britain. It is truly impressive. People taking selfies are having to walk to the fringe of the grassy mound on which it stands, right over to the queue for Miami's ice cream van, to get its wing-tips in.

What I hadn't expected is the string of shrines that have grown up beneath the bushes on the fringe of the green. One, to a little girl, has flowers, votive candles and a teddy wearing a T-shirt on which is written '4 today'. A message reads 'Please take care of my little girl, the one with the big blue beautiful eyes and soft ginger curls, she was extra special, as you should know. I really didn't want to let her go.' I'm surprised to see that on this apparently secular site, the presence of a higher being, if not God himself, is being invoked. I walk along the row of shrines. There are hearts and teddies hanging from the bushes, with dedications to grandparents, grandchildren, sons, daughters, mums and dads. There are photographs, football shirts and scarves. At one, two teenage girls lay fresh flowers, which they then photograph.

It's a very unexpected and moving spectacle. That people come to this work of art rather than a place of organised religion, and incorporate the angel, an iconography of Christianity, with stars and unicorns makes me wonder why they prefer such a place to a church or cathedral. Maybe the light shows put them off. Or the helter skelters. Perhaps it's the dinosaurs. But then, you don't get such distractions in most churches.

If it were possible to double back at this point, I could take the route of the Roman road through Gateshead to the Tyne, but I don't get that option until I am well up the A167, so I press on, on the route through Low Fell. Meanwhile, the current A1 swings way out west, to cross the Tyne at Blaydon.

Slow-crawl traffic takes me through the suburbs until, after Shipcoat, the Roman alignment joins from the east and crosses to the west to become High West Street, running on to the river. I continue on the A167, making the sudden, steep descent to the Tyne, but turn off just before it crosses the Tyne Bridge for Bottle Bank, and my hotel overlooking the river.

24. The Grime on the Tyne
– Newcastle to Morpeth –

It isn't the fog on the Tyne that is obscuring my view of Newcastle, it's the grime on my hotel window.

Not that Gateshead is anything like the 'dirty lane leading to Newcastle,' that Dr Johnson encountered in 1773. Nor is it any longer 'a centre of work, noise, smoke and dirt; iron works, brass works, chain and cable works, glass works, bottle works, and chemical works.' That description comes from the Victorian artist Joseph Dodd, who came from here so was presumably unbiased.

So what is Newcastle today? From what I can see through my window, it's now a place of outdoor drinking.

At the Gateshead Hilton they tell me proudly that they have a river-view room for me. Except it is actually a view of a great city veiled in grime. If I peer hard enough I can see three bridges: the Swing Bridge right in front of me, the Tyne Bridge to my right and the High Level Bridge to my left. The Swing Bridge, built where the Roman and several subsequent bridges were, carried the Great North Road from 1876 and the A1 from 1921. The Tyne Bridge carried the A1 from 1928 until 1967, when the Tyne Tunnel was opened out to the east of the city centre.

Opinion differs about whether the High Level ever carried the Great North Road. It doesn't seem to have had the official designation, but Uncle Charlie is confident that, with the opening of the High Level, in 1849, the predecessor of the Swing Bridge 'lost its favour' because traffic could now avoid the steep descent to the river and climb on the other side. And Noman Webster insists: 'For nearly 80 years the High Level bridge carried the line of the Great North Road.' An assertion which makes things very confusing as, if he's right, then the Swing Bridge could never have carried the Great North Road.

Depending on which was the official route at the time, the approach roads took slightly different courses to reach their river crossings. I set out to walk them, starting with the Swing Bridge. The road to that went via High Street, Church Street and Bridge Street. The way I drove in is as close to that route as you can get today, and I could have driven on over the bridge, but I want to walk it.

Uncle Charlie speculates that Gateshead, which to the Saxons meant 'road's head', may have got its name because of the abrupt descent to the river, where 'the road would seem to be coming to a sudden end'.

Reaching The Swing Bridge is like walking on to a car ferry. The narrow roadway runs between red-and-white painted cast-iron arms which support a sort of command post – an octagonal cupola topped with a blue lighthouse – like the captain's bridge on a ship.

I pause halfway across. Up-river is the High Level Bridge, a lattice of sand-coloured cast-iron beams supporting a double-decker crossing: the railway on top, a road and pedestrian layer beneath. Down-river is the Tyne Bridge, an inverted semicircle of rusty iron, painted a green the shade of the patina on copper.

When the swing bridge was built, timbers were discovered from the original bridge that gave Newcastle its Roman name: Pons Aelius, or Bridge of Hadrian. So not only did Hadrian have a wall, he had a bridge to get to it, at the wall's original eastern end. Two Roman altars, to the water gods Oceanus and Neptune, were found in the river, and a slab recording the arrival, by boat, of Roman legionaries from Germany. There were timbers from a thirteenth-century bridge too.

The Roman bridge lasted a thousand years, replaced by a medieval one from 1248 until it wasdestroyed by floods in 1771. The next bridge, the one the mail coaches would have travelled across, lasted just 70 years, its narrow arches an impediment to shipping and the flow of the tides.

So the Swing Bridge has at least two millennia of history behind (or beneath) it. The first Roman settlement on the Gateshead side of the river was found alongside where the Hilton is now. It consisted of a row of roadside shops serving the soldiers and civilians, and followed the exact same route I have just followed to the bridge.

I walk on over, and notice that the seagulls which perch on every ledge have painted the town white. They've sprayed every surface they can get a foothold on, including the roof around the cupola on the Guildhall, and the pavements beneath every bridge and gutter. How is it that seagulls, with all the crap they eat, can shit whiter than white? And why can't we do that?

Uncle Charlie continues his tale of grime on the Newcastle side of the Tyne, where he finds a 'steep and smelly street, paved with vile granite setts and strewn with refuse'. Traffic headed north would turn sharp right off the Swing Bridge into Sandhill, which runs along the riverfront; cross the steep-sided Lorton Burn, a stream that ran into the Tyne; then sharp left for the punishing climb up The Side to Pilgrim Street. Later, Lorton

Burn was stuck in a pipe and the riverside levelled, with Dean Street and Grey Street offering an easier way up from the river.

Immediately up-river of the Swing Bridge was the Fish Market, which William Cobbett compared to London's fish market, Billingsgate, which was similarly placed alongside London Bridge. This market differed 'only with the fish a little fresher, and with fishwomen not quite so drunken nor quite so nasty'.

So that's something for Newcastle to boast about: 'our fishwives were never as foul as London's.

The traffic flying round the corner off the bridge forces me to walk downriver to find a crossing, which happens to be opposite a towering terrace of timber-framed Jacobean houses, one of which bears a reminder of the man who drank all that Fine Old Military Blackstrap Newcastle Port at the Wheatsheaf back in Rushyford.

A plaque on No. 41, Bessie Surtees House, reads: 'From the above window on Nov 18th 1772 Bessie Surtees descended and eloped with John Scott, later created 1st Earl of Eldon and Lord Chancellor of England.' I'm beginning to see this man as the Boris Johnson of his day.

Towering above this stretch of riverfront, and tangled in with the high viaduct of the main railway line to the north, is the Norman castle that gave Newcastle its name, and the Cathedral Church of St Nicholas. It is topped with a unique fifteenth-century lantern, its ribbed arches and cluster of thirteen pinnacles sitting like a stone crown on the head of the city. That lantern once contained a light, burning to guide shipping on the Tyne.

I avoid The Side for a steeper but quicker climb up a flight of stone steps to Castle Garth. Here, Uncle Charlie encountered 'shoemakers and cobblers of footgear of the most waterside and unfashionable character [who] still blink and cobble in their half-underground dens, the descendants, probably, of those whom a French traveller remarked here in the time of Charles II.'

I press on beneath the railway arches to reach what was the heart of old Newcastle, passing through the Black Gate and on to the cathedral. In 1644, when the city was being defended against a Scottish army, the besiegers threatened to blast the lantern to bits with their canon, a threat that was defused when the defenders stuck all their Scottish prisoners in the tower beneath it.

I pass through the old merchant heart of the city on my short walk downriver to the Tyne Bridge. The high, Newcastle Brown-coloured stone terraces where once trade, banking and all the attendant professions were practised still stand, but today they all seem to be vast student-focused bars and chain restaurants. The former Bank Chambers is the Miller and Carter steak house, British Provident House is home to Flares, which threatens to give you the 'funkiest grooviest big night out'.

The new Tyne Bridge brought traffic on the A1 sailing high above the river and directly on to Pilgrim Street. That street was so named for the devout who were headed to the holy well and chapel of St Mary at Jesmond – a name derived from Jesus Mount.

I use the honeycomb of passageways beneath the Swan House Roundabout to reach an old pilgrim hostelry, the Holy Jesus Hospital, which has been caring for travellers and townspeople for 700 years. Today, jammed beside a smelly armpit of roads and underpasses, it houses the National Trust's Inner Cities Project.

Several strata of development are piled on this north bank of the Tyne. The fourteenth-century hospital, eighteenth-century merchants houses and nineteenth-century railway viaducts are topped with a couple of great white tower blocks, like bright white molars implanted in these withered brown gums.

I walk above the rooftops to the Tyne Bridge and the view of the south bank, dominated by The Sage Gateshead concert venue, like a great bloated silver worm of a place, engorged as if it had devoured everything else that once stood here.

On the Gateshead bank, vast bars with outdoor tables lined up for hundreds of yards are just filling up with people out for an afternoon drink, an appetiser for the evening.

The river itself is empty, in contrast to 'the ships innumerable' that William Cobbett found, 'lying below the bridge as far as you can see down the river... It is impossible, by the use of any words, to give an adequate idea of the stir and bustle upon this river, of which there seems to be scarcely any square yard of water which experiences one half hour at a time without something or other being floating upon it.'

Cobbett, who visited in the 1820s, called it 'this fine, opulent, solid, beautiful, and important town.' Comparing it to the capital, he thought London could be the father and Newcastle the son or, as he put it, 'it would almost make one believe that the former place had bred, and that this was a young one.'

In all, Newcastle 'is a really solid fine town... but the most interesting and valuable product of this part of England is the people, of whom it is impossible to speak too much in praise.'

And that's still true today. Once over the bridge I take a seat at one of the riverside bars and listen to a cheery bunch of young Geordies discussing what they'll do this evening. There's a lot to be admired in the Tynesider's optimistic, fun-loving, easy-going attitude, and then there's that accent. It's one of my favourites, and it's easy to do.

With Geordie, as with other accents, I've found that there's a word or phrase that unlocks it. Say it and you're already speaking like a native. For Geordie it's 'Basmati rice'. It's impossible to say Basmati rice without sounding Geordie. The key to the Edinburgh accent, on the other hand, is 'Masarati'. Give it a try, say 'Ooooh, I see you have a Maseratiiii.' There you go. In Belfast it's 'Persil Automatic'. Canadian's the toughest. I know you're meant to say 'oat' instead of 'out' and 'a boat' instead of 'about', but I just can't string a sentence together.

Anyway, I've finished my beer, let's move on. I walk upriver to the double-decker High Level Bridge, designed by Robert Stephenson and opened in 1849. It formed a key link in the rail route between London and Scotland, which superseded the Great North Road for a century. The lower road-and-pedestrian crossing was slung beneath it to bring in revenue from tolls.

Even though it was never officially known as the Great North Road, I want to walk it out of curiosity. And it is a curiosity. For some reason its lattice of iron arches, struts and beams is painted in a sort of pale sandy yellow that might be called Desert Camouflage, and the pedestrian walkways are lined with mesh screens, which makes me feel like I'm looking out from a bird cage.

A train rattles, thumps and bangs overhead, but it's nothing to what Uncle Charlie experienced. He wrote: 'the smoke and rumble of its trains mingle with the clash of Newcastle's thousand anvils and the reek of her million chimneys.'

Halfway across I look downriver, lining up the low, convex lens of the red and white Swing Bridge with the pale green Tyne Bridge, stretched between its stately stone piers. The mesh at this point is covered in lovers' padlocks. Chained to the Tyne.

It's the Tyne Bridge that I choose when I leave Newcastle next morning. On the far side, Pilgrim Street heads straight on, on the line of the Great North Road, but then runs into pedestrianised Northumberland Street, so I allow myself to be deflected for a little way to arc east on the A167(M) before, at the far end of Northumberland Street, I can swing north and back on to the Great North Road, the B1318, and on over the eastern edge of Town Moor.

Once this was wild, exposed heathland but now, behind the laurel hedges that line the road, parks stretch out. I pass a patch of allotments, and rows of houses tucked in behind neat front gardens. Celia Fiennes, heading south here in the seventeenth century, when coal was a cottage industry, 'saw abundance of little carriages with a yoke of oxen and a pair of horses together, which is to convey the coals from the pits to the barges on the river... this country all about is full of the coal, the sulphur of it taints the air and it smells strongly to strangers; upon a high hill two mile from Newcastle I could see all about the country which was full of coal pits.'

A century ago, Town Moor was still pretty grim. Uncle Charlie describes 'a once wild waste of common, and even now a bleak and forbidding open space whose horizon on every side commands the gaunt Northumbrian hills, or is hidden with the reek of Newcastle town, or the collieries that render the way sordid and ugly.'

Things didn't get better as he pressed on through Gosforth and Wideopen. He progressed 'with sinking heart, appalled at the increasing wretchedness and desolation brought by the coal-mining industry upon the scene.'

At Seaton Burn I need my wits about me to avoid being shunted on to the modern A1. Instead of following the commands to take the first exit off the roundabout where the Great North Road meets the A19, I must keep my nerve and go further round, exiting on an unpromising lane that almost immediately rises to cross that dual carriageway and continues on its western flank.

Through gaps in the hedges alongside what is still known as the Old Great North Road I get glimpses of the current A1 to my right. It has swung in from the west, having avoided Newcastle entirely. I haven't encountered it since the Angel of the North, and haven't had to drive on it since a little way north of Boroughbridge, 70-odd miles ago.

I do have to join it, briefly, at Stannington Bridge, but a loop takes me off again almost immediately and through the village of Stannington. Then it's a mere 1.1 miles back on the A1 before, at Clifton, I escape onto the A197 and snake down, on what Uncle Charlie calls 'the long and tortuous descent into Morpeth, lying secluded in the gorge of the Wansbeck'.

VII

GREAT NORTH ROAD
Morpeth
to Edinburgh

Edinburgh

Dunbar

Welcome to Scotland
Failte gu Alba

The Great
North Road
Morpeth to
Edinburgh

Berwick-upon-Tweed

Belford

EDINBURGH
for
BERWICK
to
NEWCASTLE
and
YORK

The
Great North Road
Map

EDINBURGH TO YORK
BY H. R. G. INGLIS

with a large scale
Contour Plan of the Road

Scale: Half an Inch to a Mile

GALL & INGLIS
25 Paternoster Square London. E.C.

Alnwick

Morpeth

From Morpeth to Berwick is Border country. The Badlands. Fought over by the English and Scots through centuries of sieges, stormings, assaults, massacres and atrocities.

Morpeth also marks another parting of the ways.

From here there are two routes to Edinburgh. The A1, mainly following the route of the Great North Road, hugs the coast. Telford's Road of 1828 is a cross-country route through Wooler and Coldstream designed to supersede it. Why that never happened will be revealed along the journey.

In this section I follow the coastal route, and I'll begin my journey south via Telford's Road in Section VIII.

The Great North Road bounds across moors and plunges into valleys. The A1 has ironed out those sharp descents and steep climbs, but I will follow the old road into them, and discover now-overlooked towns and villages such as Morpeth and Felton, lying in valleys watered by rivers running from the North Pennines and Cheviots to the North Sea.

I'll take in the key border town of Alnwick, and the much-fought-over frontier town of Berwick-on-Tweed. From there the road hugs the clifftop as it crosses the border into Scotland, before looping west to the port of Dunbar and Portobello, Edinburgh's seaside, before entering the city itself.

I reckon that, between London and Morpeth, I have only used 57 miles of the current A1, out of a total of 321 miles travelled. That's about 18 per cent of the total journey on the new road, 82 per cent off it.

From Morpeth to Edinburgh is a further 106 miles, and the balance does shift a bit. I drive 45 miles (42 per cent) on the A1, 58 per cent off it.

My total drive from London to Edinburgh, including my 30-odd miles of wanderings off the route, is 429 miles, out of which I have driven 102 miles on the new road, 327 on the old. So that's 24 per cent on the A1, 76 per cent on the Great North Road.

25. Badlands

Morpeth bears all the hallmarks of a frontier town. The two castles guarding the crossing of the River Wansbeck reflect its strategic significance in this border territory: these Badlands. Morpeth endured centuries of conflict, skirmish, attack and counter attack between the English and the Scots.

I park outside a former coaching inn, the Waterford Lounge pub in Castle Square, and walk back, up through Carlisle Park to the castles, first to the site of the eleventh-century motte and bailey affair, now a denuded grassy mound forming a lump on the head of Ha' Hill, then beyond it to the surviving gatehouse of the thirteenth-century one, now a Landmark Trust holiday let.

From here, the little town laid out beneath me in its wooded valley, I can trace the old route of the Great North Road, which crosses the River Wansbeck, turns sharp left past the shops along Bridge Street and then, just past the market square, goes sharp right to climb out of town for its rendezvous, at Fair Moor, with the bypass that has been the modern A1 since 1970.

Morpeth gets its name from 'moor path', and from here it's clear why. The old road is just that. It runs on the moorland a few miles in from the Northumbrian coast, bounding like a triple-jump champion in a great loping hop, skip and jump over the moors and planting a foot in the dips at Morpeth, Felton and Alnwick as it goes.

These places have grown up in valleys created by the rivers running off the North Pennines and Cheviots as they make their way east to the sea. For past travellers on the Great North Road, that meant a series of steep descents and sharp climbs, before bypasses smoothed out the wrinkles. Sticking to the old route into Morpeth gives me another four miles off the busy modern A1, but that road is going to become harder to avoid as I push closer to my final destination. From up here, I can see that two bridges cross the Wansbeck: a road-traffic one dating from 1831, alongside its thirteenth-century predecessor, now just a footbridge. I walk back down to town and over the old bridge, which runs across to the Chantry, once home to a hermit who maintained the bridge and begged alms from travellers.

I have dropped in on a lovely town. From the footbridge I can look down-river to the 'new' bridge and, up-river, to a weir, on which a heron squats patiently, keeping a beady eye out for fish that tumble over.

The Chantry has been put to multiple uses. From the thirteenth to nineteenth centuries there was a school at one end, a church at the other. Since then it has been a theatre, council offices, a cabinet maker's workshop, cigar shop, butcher's, rod and gun shop, tearoom and ladies' loo. It was restored in the 1980s and now houses the tourist office and a bagpipe museum, a reminder that it's not just the Scots who can make bladders squawk.

The new bridge was built because, according to John Hodgeson's 1830s *History of Morpeth*, the old one was 'inconvenient and dangerous' for coaches: 'the Mail and Wonder coaches having each, within the last three years, once carried away the south end of its west battlements, and been thrown with their passengers and horses into the river – fortunately without loss of life.'

It was a condition of building the new that the old be destroyed, and the arches were blown up in 1835. Bad idea. The new bridge was not pedestrian-friendly. In 1869, the old bridge got its present pedestrian walkway, which tiptoes daintily across the huge surviving stone stumps of those arches.

I pass the Chantry to reach Bridge Street where there was a string of old coaching inns. The Black Bull survives, with its curious round bay forming a turret up the front. I walk to the market place through a pleasantly busy, affluent and stylish town that demonstrates a strong hold on its past, and a knack of incorporating that past into its present.

The handsome John Smail and Son, Ironmongers, has retained its bold gold sign but been re-purposed as the Lollo Rosso restaurant. There is a dinky little department store, Rutherford and Co; opposite which are the cream ceramic tiles of a building that proudly bears the name 'Sanderson House 1939'. It has been transformed into Sanderson Arcade, a row of posh clothes shops and jewellers. One, Renaissance, has a quote on the wall from Carrie Bradshaw of *Sex in the City*: 'I like my money right where I can see it. Hanging in my closet'.

Once, the money came into Morpeth on four legs, and mooed. The square I reach at the end of Bridge Street once held the second largest livestock market in England. That history is reflected at the other end of Sanderson Arcade, where a sculpture of a great bull, Black Prince, stands above the entrance. Livestock got here along the Great North Road.

The coming of the railway ate into that trade but, even in the 1920s, according to Uncle Charlie: 'Market-day brings crowds of drovers and endless droves of sheep and cattle to this spot, to say nothing of the pigs, singularly plentiful in these parts. "He's driving his swine to Morpeth market," is an expression still used of a snoring man in the neighbourhood.' A useful phrase, I'm sure you'll agree, and one that deserves to be revived.

Just beyond the market place, a curious stone tower stands in the middle of Oldgate. This is Morpeth's seventeenth-century Clock Tower, and looks like a church tower in search of a nave. It was built from stone filched from a town abbey at the Dissolution, and the six bells in its belfry were tolled each night to mark the curfew.

Morpeth was once a vulnerable outpost in border territory and, during the Civil War in the seventeenth century, the castle was occupied by 500 Scottish soldiers who held out against the Royalist forces for 20 days. In 1715 Morpeth took the side of the

Scots in the first Jacobite Rising, supporting the attempt to put the Catholic James Stuart, the Old Pretender, on the English throne in place of George I. It seems this issue may have been the Brexit of its day, with strong feelings on both sides.

Down the centuries, travellers on the Great North Road have reported strong anti-Scottish feeling. Tobias Smollett, whose novel *The Expedition of Humphry Clinker* features a trek south on the road in around 1766, says that, right down to Doncaster, the windows of every inn were scrawled with abusive rhymes about the Scots.

William Cobbett travelled with trepidation to Edinburgh in 1832 because of his attacks on Scotland and its people. He was urged not to go, and wrote that he had been warned his journey would prove 'not only mortifying and disgraceful, but even personally perilous'.

Cobbett, a nationalist who believed countries including Scoland should not 'swagger about and be saucy to England', had been involved in vitriolic exchanges about the relative intellectual merits of the two peoples. At the time, an outpouring of intellectual and scientific accomplishments was occurring north of the border, known as the Scottish Enlightenment. When he got to about this point in his journey he wrote, ridiculing the idea that Scots might be brighter and more cultured than the English:

To-morrow morning I start for "Modern Athens"! [Edinburgh]. My readers will, I dare say, perceive how much my "antalluct" [intellect] has been improved since I crossed the Tyne. What it will get to when I shall have crossed the Tweed, [on the border] God only knows. I wish very much that I could stop a day at Berwick, in order to find some feelosofer [philosopher] to ascertain, by some chemical process, the exact degree of the improvement of the "antalluct." I am afraid, however, that I shall not be able to manage this; for I must get along; beginning to feel devilishly home-sick since I have left Newcastle.

Now there's a man asking for a kicking. I'll be interested to see what sort of welcome he gets in Edinburgh. I decline to make him a companion, though. We may be going in the same direction, but he's definitely not with me.

A hundred years ago, Uncle Charlie found evidence of surviving anti-Scottish feeling in 'certain proverbs and sayings reflecting discreditably upon the Scottish people.' He saw that as natural: 'That Morpeth folk still cherish old anti-Scottish sayings is not at all remarkable; for old manners, old sayings, and ancient hatreds die slowly in such places as this, and moreover, the Morpeth of old suffered terribly from Scottish raiders.'

He goes on: 'Later times saw a more peaceful irruption [sudden change], when Scottish youths came afoot down the great road in quest of fame and fortune in the south. People looked askance upon them as Scots, while innkeepers hated them for their poverty and their canniness.'

I leave Morpeth on Newgate Street, following the old road. It is now the A192 and looks rather careworn, a previous layer of red tarmac showing through the black as if the road is rusting away. A short stretch on the Morpeth North Bypass, the A197, brings me back to the A1, where I have to elbow my way into a solid line of traffic.

Half a mile onward comes a parting of the ways. Thomas Telford's new road to Edinburgh, now the A697, peels off north-west to reach Edinburgh, via Wooler and Coldstream, on what was intended to be a replacement for the Great North Road, but never caught on. I'll explore that route later.

For now, I grind on, in more traffic than I have encountered at any point on my journey north. There are those who see joining the largely single carriageway A1 north of Morpeth as a sort of halleluiah moment: the point after which they are mainly on the course of the old Great North Road.

I find it a slog, and feel like I am holding my breath, waiting for the next point at which the A1 bypasses a town, where I can run off onto the old road and breathe again. It shows that all those new motorway sections and bypasses further south have done the old Great North Road a huge favour. Without them it would be a nightmare to drive. Here, with fewer diversions from the original route, there are fewer safety valves. But I come to relish those that do exist.

Only when I turn off for the steady descent to Felton – bypassed in 1981 – does the pressure ease. Just before the road swings sharp left to cross the River Croquet is the Northumberland Arms, a perfect wayside inn, with its riverside beer garden. Two bridges stand side by side here. The old fifteenth-century stone one manages to be elegant as well as solid, the 1926 one is merely functional, with an ugly forest of supporting concrete struts. The old bridge, closed to traffic, comes in handy for village celebrations, such as wassailing at Christmas.

Like the other points that have been bypassed, this was a bottleneck. Lorry drivers hated the steep drop to the river and the sharp right angle just before it, which meant they could not get a run-up to tackle the climb through Felton, and the long grind up the ridge that divides the valley of the Coquet with that of the next river, the Aln.

Like Morpeth, Felton has known some argy bargy. During the Wars of the Roses, 1455-1487, armies from both sides passed through on what was then a wooden bridge. It was the strategic importance of this crossing that led to the construction of the stone one. In 1644, during the Civil War, the Royalist army attempted to destroy the bridge as it retreated south, to hinder the pursuing Scots. However, it is said that women villagers put up such a formidable resistance that they were frightened off. If that's true, the women must have even more terrifying than the Scottish army.

Six years later, alliances had changed. After the Scots proclaimed Charles II as king, Oliver Cromwell led the Parliamentary army north over the bridge on his way to defeat them at the Battle of Dunbar. Cromwell stayed overnight at the Angel Inn, at No. 6 Main Street, which is now a private house.

From 1712, when the first stage coaches ran from Edinburgh to London, Felton began to benefit from the road, and its story is a common one for once-obscure hamlets that the Great North Road passed through.

Those first coaches took 13 days to reach London but, by 1786, improved roads allowed an express coach to make it in hours, and two years later the single-carriageway bridge was widened to allow all the extra traffic generated to pass on it.

A string of coaching inns opened on Main Street, one of which – the Widdrington Inn – survives as the Running Fox, an outstanding cafe and bakery, which has a queue outside it today. A group of bikers is wolfing pies from paper bags beside the river. There's a pub, the Fox's Den, in the basement.

Half a dozen other inns sprang up which vied to offer entertainment to tempt travellers. The Widdrington hosted cock fighting tournaments on which huge sums were bet, and the Red Lion had a theatre which hosted companies of travelling players.

The Great North Road brought work not just for inn-keepers but for all trades needed to serve travellers: blacksmiths, harness and saddle makers, butchers, bakers, and grocers. As Felton got rich from the road, the cottages lining the route were replaced with the substantial stone houses I see today.

In 1847, the rail link from London to Edinburgh was completed, with the opening of the Newcastle to Berwick section, and the coaching trade withered. But, unlike many comparable villages, Felton didn't suffer a cataclysmic decline during the century in which travellers switched from road to rail. And the only unpleasant legacy from the sixty bottleneck years when the A1 ran through it is that ugly concrete bridge. Felton has, however, been an altogether more peaceful place since the bypass relieved it in 1981.

I follow the old route out of Felton to the A1, which is now dual carriageway all the way to Alnwick. I have to perform a tricky manoeuvre, in heavy traffic, to avoid joining it.

First I must make it to the central reservation, then turn right into the stream of cars and trucks and, in 200 yards, swing left to regain the old road, signposted Swarland, which runs alongside the new to Newton on the Moor. The manoeuvre is worth it for the further five miles of respite from traffic that it wins me.

Beside the road in another 200 yards is a curious sight. Silhouetted against the sky at the top of Rushy Cap is a white stone obelisk, standing like an alien craft among the trees in this otherwise unremarkable spot. It's the Nelson Monument, erected in 1807, two years after the admiral's death. It was placed there by his friend Alexander Davison, who lived in the now demolished Swarland Hall.

The monument is hidden from the rushing traffic on the A1 by a belt of trees and, now, only locals and those who seek out this surviving loop in the old road get to see it. I resist the signs urging me back on the new road and continue on the old to the pretty little village of Newton on the Moor. From the Cook and Barker Inn I take a moment to enjoy the sweeping views of the Northumberland coast and the Cheviot hills from this elevated spot, before taking another deep breath and re-joining the new road.

On the outskirts of Alnwick I can turn off again, following the old road, now the A1068 and then the B6346. This wins me another six miles off the new road, but just about every other car is doing the same and, in Alnwick Street, we slow to a crawl.

This is my first traffic jam on the old Great North Road, and I wonder what causes it. After not moving more than a few yards in 15 minutes I notice a drive-way climbing off to my left to what looks like an old railway station, and a sign, Barter Books. I've heard of this, one of the largest bookshops in the country, and give up on the traffic. I squeeze into their car park and walk in.

It is an old railway station, the terminus on the branch from the main line at Alnmouth, opened in 1887 and closed in 1968 under the Beeching cuts. It is very grand, built to replace the original 1850 station in case of royal visits to the Percys of Alnwick Castle.

The place has been beautifully restored. Inside, beneath the vaulted glass roof of the old station concourse, where steam engines once hissed, ranks of bookcases rise well above head height. There are dozens of them, holding tens of thousands of books. There are sofas and, in winter, roaring fires. Over the heads of browsers, tin toy trains from the 1950s rattle, their rails supported by the bookcases and the gaps spanned by green-painted bridges.

There are literary quotes painted on boards and, on the end wall, a 36ft-wide mural featuring thirty-three of co-owner Mary Manley's favourite authors – Shakespeare, Jane Austen, Oscar Wilde, Hemingway, Shaw and Dickens among them – all looking very animated and attending what appears to be a literary party in this very bookshop.

I hunt out bookcase B6, Maps and Atlases, on the off-chance there might be something on the Great North Road. There is: a 1920s map of the northern half of the road, designed for cyclists, a neat strip map, folded concertina-like within a red card cover.

I take my purchase through to the old station buffet, now the bookshop cafe, for a closer look.

It's an ingeniously designed little thing. Open it one way and you get the map, with elevations running in a separate strip above it, open it the other and you get points of interest, town street maps and alerts to danger points. I notice a warning of a hilly section at Alnwick, and that 'the surface is rather bumpy' here and at Berwick.

Alongside the books, Stuart and Mary Manley do a roaring trade in Keep Calm And Carry On posters and mugs. Stuart found a rare surviving original in a box of books he bought in 2000. He put the folded, torn and time-worn poster on the wall, and customers liked it so much that he started printing copies, selling up to 9,000 a month and ploughing the profits into restoring the station.

Outside, the road is still gridlocked, so I cheekily leave my car (well, I did spend 24 quid) and walk on into town, the traffic inching along beside me. At Bondgate I find the cause of the holdup.

26. The Narrow Way North
– Alnwick to Berwick –

So that's what's causing the problem. Two solid lines of opposing traffic have to take it in turns to funnel through the low, narrow fifteenth-century arch beneath Bondgate Tower.

Which is exactly what traffic had to do for centuries at this point on the Great North Road. But then, busy as it might have been, the old road never saw anything like the crowds flocking to Alnwick Gardens on sunny days. The whole of the North East seems to be here.

In contrast, a century ago, Uncle Charlie found Alnwick a quiet place, 'a town with a great past and a somnolent present. There are yawns at every turn, echoes with every footfall, and grass growing unbidden in the streets.' Not today there aren't.

Beyond the tower, on Inner Bondgate, is the White Swan, the principal coaching inn. The traffic is peeling off left into Market Street, and after it the Great North Road, now

Narrowgate, becomes blocked not with traffic but tables and chairs, cordoned off by planters filled with red geraniums.

There are plenty of lunching places to choose from, and I pick the eighteenth-century Black Swan, counterpoint to the White at the other end of town. The Scottish poet Robert Burns, who only left his homeland three times, spent a night in this inn in 1787, on one of those rare forays south. In his diary he recorded crossing the Tweed and 'traversing the moors through a wild country'.

Narrowgate bends around Alnwick Castle, home of the Percy family. The castle is vast, the town no more than a pimple on its big round backside. I'm intrigued by the figures on the battlements. Such figures were originally added in the fourteenth century, to confuse attackers, but these were added during restoration in the eighteenth century, and are more fanciful than fearsome.

Some are dressed like soldiers, but don't look remotely warlike. One sits dangling his legs over the side, another has his arm up like a cricket umpire. It makes the place look like an overgrown toy fort.

Round the corner I see one who looks like he's undoing his codpiece for a wazz onto the town. A Percy pointing his percy over the parapet, you might say. Another figure raises a great block of something above his head prior to lobbing it on the visitors strolling below.

After Castle Square the road plunges down to the River Aln, crossed by the Lion Bridge. In the centre on the eastern plinth stands the Percys' lion emblem, its tail stuck straight out behind it. There are meadows up and down river, with the castle's northern flank guarding the way south, a scene that looks like the establishing shot in a Netflix historical drama. I half expect a CGI army to come galumphing from the north, to be met by canon fire, and a hail of arrows.

From here, the old road ascends as the B6341 on a prolonged

three-mile rise to reach 450ft, which my newly-purchased map shows me was one of the hardest climbs on the Great North Road. It's time to pick up the car, skirt the town to the east and re-join the old road a little way up the hill ahead of me. It's either that or plough through the folk enjoying lunch in Narrowgate.

I have a few further miles reprieve from the modern A1 ahead of me, and there is a powerful Border monument along the way. Malcolm's Cross, a mile uphill from the river, marks the spot where, in 1093, Malcolm Caenmore, king of Scotland, was killed while besieging Alnwick Castle. A Percy who, he believed, was surrendering and delivering the keys to the castle, instead stabbed him in the eye with a spear.

The road climbs to the summit of Heiferlaw Bank, on which is a ruined fifteenth-century peel tower, built to provide early warning of attack from Scotland. It stands against the backdrop of a pine wood, a great solid rectangle of white stone, softened by yellow-green lichen, the walls 4ft thick and standing 23ft tall. A rough keyhole-shaped opening allows me in, to look up at a block of sky where the roof and parapet once were.

The tower is a couple of hundred yards to the west of the old road, on the margin of a field in which the wheat is just turning golden. It's a peaceful spot today, but this was once a stretch of wild and dangerous moorland across which threat could flood at any time. One of the fields up here was called Blawweary, a name that evokes bleakness, toil and strife.

From Heiferlaw the old road descends and levels out on the approach to North Charlton, before which I must re-join the A1, single-carriageway once more, and another awkward manoeuvre given the line of speeding traffic and the lack of a run-in.

There is another loop of old road to the west of the A1 at North Charlton, at the end of which is a further ruined monument, this time to the great days of the motoring age: a derelict former Little Chef. It's hidden in the undergrowth these days, a couple of hundred yards through the over-hanging trees on a dead-end stretch of the old road. But all is not lost. Just before the loop re-joins the A1 is another cafe that is very much alive: Carnaby's. It's that rare thing, a thriving modern, clean and welcoming independent cafe on the old Great North Road. I'd begun to expect no more than a caravan in a lay-by shovelling food into truckers, but this is a restaurant, serving 'Ottolenghi-inspired salads' and 'Slow-cooked lamb ragu with potato gnocchi.' I go for the home-made pork sausage roll, a wholesome cylinder of meatiness, with a pair of those salads.

Carnaby's also has the finest smelling gents I've ever been in. I thought the scent was due to the pine panelling until I realised it came from the hand soap, which was called Whisky and Water. So when I spotted they stocked it out in the gift section I bought a bottle, even after I discovered it cost 20 quid. Which feels like more than I've spent on soap in the rest of my life. But worth it.

Carnaby's is owned by the Haggerston family, which has farmed in the area for 400 years, and named after an ancestor, Sir Carnaby Haggerston. It's quite a find on the road: a truly decent cafe. It's packed with locals, who obviously feel it's worth a drive out from Alnwick and points north.

I set out, hands smelling better than they ever have.

I press on to the old coaching town of Belford, where South Road, the old route, takes me to a village with a wide main street that marks it out as a coaching halt and where, in the market place, is the inn, the ivy-covered Blue Bell Hotel, with its little blue and white portico.

This was a traffic-clogged spot until bypassed in the 1980s. Berwick-bound lorries belched black smoke and trailed a string of cars as they crawled up the steep incline of North Bank and headed out of the village. Today it's another very pleasant stopping place, peaceful without being too quiet, in fine country.

To the west rise the Kyloe Hills. Four miles to the east is the incomparable Northumberland coast, with Bamburgh Castle commanding the shores from its red-rock summit. Beyond it lie the Farne Islands, once a hermitage for St Cuthbert, now a nature reserve and home to seals, puffins and 100,000 seabirds.

North of Belford, my three-mile breather over, I re-join the A1, once again on the course of the old road.

William Cobbett recounts a tale about Scottish vagrants who had been picked up in Newcastle to be returned to their villages in Scotland. They were given what was known as a cart pass, which entitled them to transport home. A contractor, paid £2-2s per journey, brought them by cart to the parish of Kyloe, which centres on the village of Fenwick, five miles north of Belford.

Here they were handed over to a police officer, who had them transported on to the parish in Scotland named on their pass. England was attractive for poverty-stricken Scots because, under its poor laws, they got food and shelter, while large swathes of Scotland had no such provision.

Cobbett is told that some individuals had been driven back to Scotland ten or twelve times, but defends the policy, saying: 'Before any quack be impudent enough to propose to abolish English poor laws, let him stop the pass-carts, which are constantly in movement to carry out of England, and to toss back upon their own soil, the destitute people of Scotland.'

At West Mains, where the Lindisfarne Inn stands beside a petrol station and a hostel, the road is within a mile of the coast. At this point a lane runs down to the shore and, via a tidal causeway, to Holy Island, Lindisfarne. I haven't checked the state of the tides and have no idea if I can cross, but head down the lane anyway, keen to complete one theme I have encountered on the Great North Road: that of St Cuthbert.

I'm in luck. The digital board on the shoreline tells me I am OK for an hour, so head on, driving over the seabed towards sand dunes that fringe what Uncle Charlie describes as a miniature St Michael's Mount. The causeway guides me along the flank of the dunes before cresting the lip of the island. I find the red-stone ruined Norman priory alongside twelfth-century St Mary's church.

Parts of that church are seventh century, and it is probably on the site of the original monastery founded by St Aidan. Aidan was a missionary from Iona, and established the monastery here with the blessing of the warrior king Oswald, bringing Christianity to Northumberland. There is a strikingly lifelike elm sculpture, called *The Journey*, depicting six monks carrying St Cuthbert's coffin.

Back on the road, at Haggerston, I come across a name encountered earlier at the roadside restaurant, Carnaby's. Here, Sir Carnaby Haggerston created Haggerston Castle, a nineteenth-century imitation peel tower, on the site of a medieval fortification. It is now at the centre of a holiday park.

Haggerston has another claim to fame: it was here that two types of cypress were cross-pollinated, creating the Leylandii, the towering conifer that is the cause of so many disputes between neighbours.

At Screamerston, where the Berwick bypass begins, I turn off the A1 for my final English loop along the old road, now the A1167. I have been climbing for the past six miles, but now descend to Tweedmouth and Berwick, which are laid out in the valley below me: the North Sea sparkling grey-ly to the east, the twenty-eight giant viaduct arches of the railway-bearing Royal Border Bridge describing an elegant arc to the west.

27. The King's Arse

– Berwick –

A funny thing happens to me in Berwick. I go to sleep in the King's Arms and wake up in the King's Head. It's summer when I turn in, and winter when I crawl out of bed. Overnight, that bed has moved 100 yards uphill from the Arms to the Head. If it had slid in the opposite direction I'd be in the King's Arse, should there happen to be such a place, or dangling my legs in the River Tweed. Come to think of it, the King's Arse is not a bad name for a pub.

All of which sounds mighty confusing, until I explain that I visit Berwick twice, on stays six months apart. For continuity's sake, I'd planned to stay both times in the Arms, but being a little fast-fingered on Bookings.com led me to book a place with a similar name but a different ancestry for my second overnight stay. The Arms is a spruced-up old coaching inn, the Head a lively little local with rooms above. Chalk and cheese. Or maybe roast beef and haggis.

I'm glad on both counts: that I come here twice, and that I stay in two places. It means I see two sides to Berwick: the bustling summer tourist town and the hunkered-down winter haven reclaimed by the locals.

As I arrive the first time, a sea mist is rolling in, forming a solid bank of fog blocking off Scotland. When I get out of the car, the air is fresh and briny, quite refreshing after hot Alnwick. It's nice, at the end of my drive, to experience the Brine on the Tweed rather than the Grime on the Tyne that I encountered back at Newcastle. The place is packed with people out and about for the sake of it, now that all lockdown restrictions are off, and not too sure what to do with themselves.

The second time I arrive, freedoms are being restricted once again. Masks are back, there's talk of Covid passports, and fears of a second Christmas being cancelled. (It isn't, thank goodness.) To add to the gloom, I arrive in the aftermath of a storm that has plunged much of Northumberland and southern Scotland into darkness. Trees are down, taking power lines with them. In the countryside, many people have been without power for several days. I arrive after dark, the temperature hovering around freezing.

On the whole I prefer the winter Berwick. Rough weather suits its rugged charm. It's only after my second visit that I venture north on the final leg to Edinburgh. So, from here, I'll stick to what I found on my return.

Of course, on both trips the essentials of Berwick remain the same. The Tweed is spanned, in descending order as you move downriver, by Robert Stephenson's 1850 Royal Border Bridge, carrying the rails of the East Coast Main Line; the 1928 Royal Tweed Bridge, built to cope with traffic on the newly-created A1; and then the venerable seventeenth-century bridge it superseded. I walk out to the middle of the old bridge, and look upriver at its two successors.

The rail bridge is by far the finest. Its twenty-eight elegant stone arches stretch 2,000ft across the valley, carrying trains 130ft above the River Tweed. It was modelled on a Roman viaduct, and formed a truly impressive final link in the line from London to Edinburgh.

The functional, underwhelming 1928 road bridge I arrived on is very much in its shadow. I peer up at its grubby grey undercarriage, and the forest of concrete struts that support its shallow arches. As Uncle Charlie points out, if the rail bridge had been constructed, as the road bridge was, in the meaner twentieth century, 'there can be no doubt that, instead of a long array of graceful arches, half a dozen lengths of steel lattice girders would span the tide.'

The 1828 bridge lost its strategic importance in 1984, when Berwick was bypassed. The A1 now crosses on the River Tweed Bridge, a mile upstream. Fortunately, the red brick medieval bridge I am standing on has survived, and can be driven on, but only heading south. You might call it the Peace Bridge. It was built in 1611, eight years after the crowning of James VI of Scotland as James I of England unified the kingdoms, and was the first collaboration between the two nations. For a century before that, Berwick had existed as an independent buffer state, a neutral Switzerland between Scotland and England. Centuries of sieges, stormings, assaults, massacres and atrocities – and Berwick's role as a border fortress town – finally came to an end in 1639, with a settlement called the Pacification of Berwick. William Cobbett passed the point where I stand with trepidation: 'As I went over the bridge... thinking... of the dreadful menace of the "SCOTSMAN", and of that "national debt of revenge" that he said Scotland owed me... with my mind thus filled, I could not help crossing myself as I passed this celebrated bridge.'

Cobbett reassures himself that, at the time of his journey, Berwick 'is regarded, by law, as being in neither England nor Scotland, but a separate dominion; and, thinking that this was a safe place, I intended to stay here the night.... in order to prepare myself a little before I actually got into Scotland.'

However, Cobbett found the town suffering an outbreak of cholera and, fearing death by disease more than death by Scot, he pressed on. He should have hung around, it's good to pause before crossing the border.

Looking north from the old bridge I can see that conflict is still writ large on this brownstone town, due to the great sixteenth-century walls – the ramparts – that encircle it.

Berwick is quite a contrast to Alnwick: the stone darker, dirtier, the streets tighter, an altogether closed-in and old-fashioned place. Even the car parking is antique. Rather than paying by phone, I have to buy a cardboard disc from a machine and dial in my arrival time.

There are two sides to Berwick: A homely, old-fashioned one, and a bright, modern and affluent one.

The artist L. S. Lowry captured the former. He was fond of Berwick, holidaying here repeatedly from the 1930s until shortly before his death in 1976, and there is a Lowry Trail around town. It seems to have reminded him of home: the Berwick he paints looks just like his Salford.

I walk back to the north end of the bridge, where a board shows me Lowry's painting of Bridge End, in which he peopled the junction where the Great North Road entered the town with his skinny men, women, cats and dogs. Lowry's vision of the North has been embraced not just by the communities he captured on canvas, but by the art world.

As those *Top of the Pop*sters Brian and Michael sing in their 1978 No. 1 hit 'Matchstalk Men and Matchstalk Cats and Dogs', the man who painted 'kids on the corner of the street that were sparking clogs' became so respected as an artist that 'even the *Mona Lisa* takes a bow'. The lyrics to the song, written two years after Lowry's death, go on:

Now he takes his brush and he waits
Outside them pearly gates
To paint his matchstalk men and matchstalk cats and dogs

Which is all very well, except for the fact that this song is an earworm. It's so catchy that, once I've remembered it, I can't get it out of my head. I find myself humming it as I walk on around the town. Bloody Hell. I'll be singing 'Grandma' by the St Winifred's School Choir next. A bunch of chart-toppers who, funnily enough, sang the backing track on Brian and Michael's hit.

Coaches travelling north will have turned right at Bridge End, into Bridge Street, and then left up Hide Hill for the Kings Arms, streets that haven't changed much since coaching days, except that they now form the smart heart of modern, affluent Berwick. I want to see the old side of the town first, so I turn left, pass beneath the 1928 bridge, and climb up onto the ramparts.

These walls, built to protect Berwick and north eastern England from the threat of invasion from the Scots, are now topped with a neat tarmac footpath between clipped grass verges. In the seventeenth and eighteenth centuries they were lined with troops and cannon. As they carry me high above Marygate, there is another Lowry reproduced on a board: looking down Marygate to the town hall.

In the Lowry, as in real life, the town hall looks curiously elongated with its sharp spire and narrow portico, like a lanky teenager afflicted by a sudden growth spurt. More like a skinny church than a town hall. The road beneath me is the route coaches would take as they resumed their way north; the road that I shall follow in the morning.

The ramparts take me around the northern flank of this fortress town (pursued all the way by matchstalk bloody cats and matchstalk bloody dogs) before angling west, offering me a view out over the steel-grey North Sea. Below me, inside the walls, is the Church of the Holy Trinity, where a great tree has been brought down in the storm that swept Scotland and the North a couple of days earlier. It sprawls over gravestones it has tumbled aside, its upper branches resting against the nave. The church dates from 1650 and is one of very few built in the Commonwealth Era, between the reigns of Charles I and Charles II, when Cromwell was the uncrowned king.

Simon Jenkins, in his *England's Thousand Best Churches*, calls it 'a curious amalgam of classical form and Gothic detail' saying that its local red sandstone, lack of a tower or pitched roof makes it look 'dumpy'. It's certainly more Roundhead than Cavalier. It looks pretty eerie at dusk, and should certainly have a string of bats flying out of it, fluttering around that poleaxed tree.

Dusk is falling as I take the next switch, south, and pass the three great, prison-like blocks of Berwick Barracks and Main Guard. They were built from 1717 to house the King's Own Scottish Borderers, who were charged with protecting the town (and the eastern approach to England) during the Jacobite risings, the campaign to restore the Stuart dynasty to the throne.

They were designed by Nicholas Hawksmoor, better known for the six English Baroque-style churches he built in London's

East End. Berwick's were among the first purpose-built barracks. Prior to this, troops were billeted in inns and houses, which can't have been popular.

My elevated circuit brings me back to my starting point at Bridge End, but I haven't quite finished my tour of old Berwick, so for now I avoid Bridge Street and head straight on up cobbled West Street, where a shop sign featuring what looks more like a whale than a cod, reads 'Fish and Chips Restaurant'. An A-board on the pavement offers:

'A. Corvi
Special
Fish + Chips
Tea
Bread'

It's a lovely old-fashioned Italian place, long and narrow, with pale-tiled walls, little old tables stretching back. It doesn't have the sort of menu you get in a modern Italian.

Affogato? Affageddaboutit!

I dogleg round the back of the town hall for Church Street, where there is evidence that, while Berwick's feet might be planted firmly in England, its heart may be in Scotland. Here, a shop called The Sporran has in its window a mannequin wearing the orange and black striped football shirt of Berwick Rangers, the 'Gers, who play in the Scottish League. There are also two half-deflated Arsenal footballs, Liverpool FC pint glasses and a Man United beer-mug-and-bar-towel combo, among many other bits and bobs.

My need for nostalgia satisfied, I hit Bridge Street, for the best of modern Berwick.

Yarn is being spun in Jennie's Wool Studio, and an array of hand-made paper is on multi-hued display in Tidekettle. There's bike hire; the Green Shop ('Greener than Robin Hood's underpants' according to *The Guardian*) offering everything organic, fairtrade, and eco-friendly; the Curfew micropub (twice CAMRA's Northumberland pub of the year) where I sample a creamy oatmeal stout from the Cheviot Brewery. There's Magna Tandoori, Mavi Turkish, and Atelier, a wine bar and bistro where you can line your stomach with a vegan platter or Sri Lankan vegetable soup.

The Kings Head, in Hide Hill, combines old and new Berwick. This was the principal coaching inn a couple of centuries ago. Charles Dickens stayed twice, in 1858 and 1861, on the latter visit giving a reading in the adjoining assembly rooms. The coffee lounge and a dining room are named after him. The hotel is freshly painted in two shades of grey, and has had quite a makeover.

I pop into the Kocktail King Bar, where I could choose a Zombie, A Jammy Sailor, A King's Garden or a King's Kocktail. Perhaps a Pornstar Martini, or a Candyfloss Daiquiri? I settle for a pint of Moretti, take a seat at a low table glowing blue from an internal light, and try to take it all in. The style might be described as eclectic. To my right is a fireplace elevated on a table, with electric coals glowing, backed by a faux brick wall. The blinds on the windows to either side feature destination boards of New York buses. The wallpaper is patterned with Penny Black stamps. The cushions scattered on the banquettes feature dogs in hats and spectacles.

Framed photos show a chimp in headphones, a flamingo with a top hat and briefcase, a monkey with a pocket watch, and a kangaroo in boxing gloves. In one corner is a three-foot-tall wine glass half-filled with giant gold baubles and strings of lights. A curtained classical archway leads to the bar itself, behind which is a floodlit array of alcohol in every conceivable colour.

The only other person here is a bloke in a Guantanamo Bay-style orange jumpsuit and black bandana. Could he be the interior designer? No, he tells me he's with a crew repairing the storm-damaged rail network.

Dickens only did his reading in the assembly rooms after rejecting the 1,000-capacity Corn Exchange – in Sandgate, and now converted into flats – that had been booked for him.

He wrote to his friend and biographer John Forster from the King's Arms, telling him:

> As odd and out of the way place to be at, it appears to me, as ever was seen! And such a ridiculous room designed for me to read in! An immense Corn Exchange, made of glass and iron, round, dome-topp'd, lofty, utterly absurd for any such purpose, and full of thundering echoes; with a little lofty crow's nest of a stone gallery, breast high, deep in the wall, into which it was designed to put – me! I instantly struck, of course, and said I would either read in a room attached to this house [the King's Arms] ... or not at all.

I wonder what he'd think of the Kocktail King Bar?

28. Oldmansocks

– Berwick to Dunbar –

I'm up early to break for the border. Berwick lies under a blanket of wintry fog, but I can smell Scotland in the air. It spurs me on.

The Great North Road takes me along Marygate and Castlegate, passing another surviving coaching inn, the Castlegate Hotel, until I meet the end of the Berwick bypass at Newfields. Here, a Travelodge, a McDonalds and a Morrisons cluster alongside the roundabout that takes me back onto the A1.

I'm no more than 700 yards from the sea, the climb out of town taking me into a zone where the rising sun is creating a yellow-twinged twilight in the fog. It's a bleak clifftop stretch, the road heeled in half-way down the slippery slope to the lip of the cliffs. I feel like leaning left against its drag.

I pass Meadow House, the first and last pub in England, and wind turbines that are whipping up a fog fondue. At Conundrum, a farm and wedding venue beside the road revives the old tradition of border marriage. Well, not exactly. Once, runaway couples raced for the border to marry at the toll house just over it, now altogether less hurried nuptials take place here, just south of the border.

The border itself, at Lamberton, is underwhelming. Just a lay-by with a big blue saltire on a sign that reads: 'Welcome to Scotland'.

I nose past a string of trucks, their overnighting drivers not yet stirring, to pull up by Adi's diner. A sign on the van offers a 'Welcome to the Border' but its shutter is stoutly padlocked, scuppering my plans to toast my border crossing with a mug of tea and a bacon sarnie.

The now demolished Old Toll House stood just beyond the border. Photographs show a white rendered, barn-like building with a wooden sign above the door: 'Toll House Original Marriage house for the east of Scotland'. Another read: 'Ginger beer sold here and marriages performed at reasonable terms'.

Runaway couples headed here from 1754, when the law in England was changed so that the parent of a child under 21 could veto a marriage they disapproved of. In Scotland, boys could marry at 14, girls at 12, without parental consent. Almost anyone could conduct a marriage, provided they could rustle up two witnesses, so the first bloke you come across when stepping from England into Scotland was ideally placed. That changed in 1858, when Scots law caught up, and a nice little side line for the toll keeper was ended. So that just left the ginger beer business.

Not that you'd know any of this now. As Norman Webster

remarked in the 1970s: 'There is a strange contrast between the Border scenes at Gretna and Lamberton; at the former the crossing is an event, for there are varied signs reminding the traveller of the transition, old marriage houses and new souvenir shops, a rash of cafes and accoutrements of modern road travel, and the sound of recorded bag-pipes.'

The most historically significant marriage to take place in Lamberton was not between a pair of runaways at the toll house, but in the now ruined kirk, and between a Scottish king and an English princess.

Here, in 1503, Margaret Tudor, daughter of Henry VII, met representatives of James IV of Scotland, and was married to him by proxy. She had travelled up the Great North Road staying, as I mentioned in Chapter 15, at inns along the way, including one at Tuxford, north of Newark. Knights from England and Scotland marked the occasion with a tournament here on Lamberton Moor.

The union was short lived, as I'll discover later on my journey, because James was killed in the Battle of Flodden in 1513. However, Scotland and England did finally get it together, in 1603, when James VI of Scotland became also James I of England, on the death of Elizabeth I.

As I cross the border I'm reminded of William Cobbett who, as his chaise rattled through, prayed: 'Angels and ministers of grace defend me!' Perhaps, as he passed into what was for him enemy territory, he remembered having earlier said this: 'Seeing Scotland, madam, is only seeing a worse England. It is seeing the flower gradually fade away to the naked stalk.'

At this point, if he were my travel companion, I'd make him put on a T-shirt with that quote printed on it, and see whether he made it to Edinburgh.

The kirk that witnessed the royal marriage, and served the scattering of farms and hamlets on Lamberton Moor, is just up the first lane on the left past the border. Only the nave and part of the chancel survive.

Seventy-odd years ago, Norman Webster was able to write that: 'The northern hundred miles of the Great North Road lack as yet the attentions paid to the highway in the south. The improvements are of a modest nature with no stretches of motorway and no detours round congested towns. The result is that much of the road north of the Border has changed little since mail-coach days.'

Things have moved on since then. Less than 60 per cent of the Great North Road has been pressganged into service as the A1. Which means there is a good deal more turning off to trace the old route than I had expected. Indeed, almost immediately, the Great North Road leaves the A1's dual carriageway for an oxbow loop past Lamberton.

Six miles north of the border I leave the A1 again, but on a side trip of my own choosing, to Burnmouth. As I near the cliff edge I cross the railway line, alongside which there was a station until 1962. Why a station in such a lonely spot? The answer is down at Burnmouth's little harbour.

Immediately after the railway I turn sharp right for a precipitous single-track descent, alongside a burn. I pass a sign declaring this 'Scotland's First Harbour' to find a couple of fishing boats, among them the Freya from Leith, and piles of lobster pots, nets and a rocky shore on which the seaweed has been piled in the recent storm. A row of tiny cottages stretches out along the foreshore, rendered grey as if soaking up the sea spray like cotton wool.

This was a busy herring port in the nineteenth century. Each year a great harvest of 'silver darlings' was gutted, salted and packed into barrels, to be hauled up the cliff and loaded onto trains which stopped here for that one reason. In 1962 the loss of the herring trade led to the closure of the station.

I only linger a few minutes, but it's my first atmospheric taste of old Scotland. As I drive back up from the harbour, I could take a right turn onto a narrow lane that is an older, clifftop route of the Great North Road. That lane would take me to the A1107 and through Eyemouth, sticking closer to the coast.

Instead, I turn back to the A1, and pass the First and Last, counterpart of the Meadow House on the English side of the border. Until 2006, a pub called The Flemington Inn stood here. It bore on its gable end the counterpart to the boast of the Meadow Bank in England, of being 'First Pub and Last Pub', in Scotland. It burned down in 2006 and was demolished, but the First and Last carries on the tradition.

After less than a mile on the A1, the old road departs again, for a two-and-a-half-mile loop through the village of Ayton. This became the Great North Road's route in about 1817.

This road is much more sheltered than the older coastal one, and I can see why coachmen preferred it to being buffeted by gales howling over the clifftops. Back on the modern A1, road and rail plait their way along the narrow, shallow valley of the Eye Water river, taking a sheltered course along the eastern fringes of the Lammermuir Hills, climbing gently, for Reston and Grantshouse.

This is not always a benign place. The Eye Water can become a raging torrent, and not just in winter. In August 1948, torrential rain so engorged the river that seven bridges were swept away in the five miles between Reston and Grantshouse. The floodwaters destroyed a long stretch of embankment, leaving rails and sleepers suspended in mid-air. It was weeks before trains could run again.

Halfway between Reston and Grantshouse is the hamlet of Houndwood, where, before the railway killed it off, the Houndwood Inn served travellers. The little place is now bypassed by the A1, and sits on rising ground to the north of the new road.

William Cobbett was impressed with Houndwood, and the inn: 'I liked the look of the place so well, the house seemed convenient and clean, and the landlord so civil and intelligent a man, that I resolved to stop here all night.' Is he revising his view of Scotland and the Scots?

Apparently not. He's still banging on about his beef with them. He pauses his journey here, in order, he says: 'to steady my head a little, and to accustom it to that large and fresh supply of "antalluct" which it had been imbibing ever since I crossed the Tyne, and more particularly since my crossing the Tweed.'

He leaves next morning: 'My heart thumping against my ribs, off I dashed at as round a rate as I could prevail on the post-boy to drive. For about five miles the land continued the same as before; a little sort of moor, in which they dig peat, the valley narrow, the hills on the side rocky, cultivated here and there a little, the rest of the ground growing scrubby firs; but great numbers of the Cheviot Hill sheep feeding on them; and very pretty sheep these are.'

There are still sheep on the hills as I leave Houndwood on what feels like a quiet country road rather than the main route between capital cities. I'm enjoying a relaxing drive until I get a van up my jacksie. So I remember the advice from my speed awareness course: let them stew, don't worry about it, concentrate on your own driving, not theirs. Fortunately, as I pass the Cedar Cafe, on a loop of old road, my pursuer pulls off for a plate of testosterone.

Grantshouse, also on a loop of old road, is a watershed: the highest point on the railway line between London and Edinburgh. The Eye Water, which has followed the road since Ayton, gives way to Pease Burn, which flows north. This scattering of cottages round a former inn is easily overlooked, but is an historic spot. There was a Mr Grant who, Uncle Charlie tells me: '...was the contractor who made the road from Berwick to Edinburgh [in 1817], building a cottage for himself in this then lonely spot, which only in later years became the Grant's House Inn.' That inn closed some years ago, and is now a holiday let.

After Grantshouse I look out for a sign to Penmanshiel, a cul-de-sac of old road, now a lane, which will take me to a very poignant memorial. Where the lane swings right I park, and walk along the track ahead of me into woods. This was once the A1. At this point the railway used to enter a 250-yard-long tunnel, scene of the 1979 Penmanshiel Tunnel Disaster. While the floor of the tunnel was being lowered, the roof collapsed, entombing two of the fifteen workmen. Rather than excavate the collapsed section, and recover the bodies, it was decided to reroute the railway. The main line was closed for several months while a cutting was dug to the west.

This is a moving spot today. On the hilltop, a low stone wall encloses a square of paving, in the centre of which stands a stumpy obelisk. Its faces bear a cross, and tributes to the two men who died: Gordon Turnbull from Gordon, 20 miles away, and Peter Fowler from Eyemouth, who was just 21 and married with a child. Peter's tribute describes a man 'whose short life was surrounded by love', Gordon's that he was 'always gentle, always kind'.

The new alignment of the railway cut through the A1, causing it to also be re-routed to the west, and the old course of the road, now cut off by the rail line, is crumbling away in the woods on the other side.

The old road leaves the new again a few miles on, at Cockburnspath. Once, says Norman Webster, it 'climbed dangerously by a curving hill' on a snaking course over a stream and past a ruined border castle, Cockburnspath Tower.

Uncle Charlie says: 'The mouldering old tower [was] beautifully situated for preying upon occasional travellers, the glen and the foaming torrent below have no doubt received the bodies of many a one who in the old days was rash enough to pass within sight of the old tower.'

Cromwell saw it as a dangerous place when he came this way in the 1650s, intent on avenging Scotland's acceptance of the exiled Charles II as king. In a dispatch, he described it as a place 'where one man to hinder is better than twelve to make way'. I take a more navigable intermediate path, on the nineteenth-century alignment of the Great North Road into Cockburnspath. I go left into the village square, with its market cross and round-towered church. I've seen such churches in East Anglia, but there the round tower stands proud to one end of the nave. Here it's been wrapped into the church and rises through the roof like a factory chimney.

That royal wedding back at the border comes back into the story here. This land was part of the dowry given by James IV to Margaret Tudor. Their 'Marriage of the Thistle and the Rose', is marked on the market cross with carved roses (for England) on two faces and a thistle (for Scotland) on the others.

On the other side of Cockburnspath the old road crosses Dunglass Burn, tumbling along the bottom of a steep ravine. There are another four bridges here, for the railway and other courses of the Great North Road. Downstream of me are, in order: the rail bridge, a 1932 alignment of the A1; a second alignment, used when a roundabout was put in; and Dunglass Old Bridge, carrying the earliest known alignment of the old road.

James VI came this way in 1617, on his only visit north of the border after succeeding to the English crown. I don't even want to think what Cobbett would read into that. In anticipation of his visit, roads were improved, bridges including this one either repaired or rebuilt, and vagabonds cleared off the streets. He spent his first night in his homeland in Dunbar, nine miles ahead of me.

I walk beneath the newer bridges in search of the oldest. It's still there, so obscured by trees and shrouded in ivy that you can walk the narrow path it carries almost without realising you are on it. If I had time, I could follow a walk Uncle Charlie took beyond that bridge and discover 'a scene of rare beauty. The walk by the zigzagging path among the thickets and the trees, down to where the sea comes pounding furiously into a little cove, a quarter of a mile below, [is] wholly charming. Away out to sea is the lowering bulk of the Bass Rock, a constant companion in the view approaching Dunbar.'

Just after the bridge I turn off left for the climb up a track to Dunglass Collegiate Church. It's a striking place, the most heavily-built church I have ever seen. More like a fort, with its great stone-vaulted slab roof, the squares placed in overlapping rows, and squat central tower. It's been desecrated: the windows blinded when it was turned into a barn in the eighteenth century, the end wall of the choir ripped out to allow horses and carts to enter.

From the hill I get something of the sea view Charlie talked about, including of Bass Rock, which stands like a grubby iceberg in the Firth of Forth. Droppings from the 150,000 gannets that nest here have turned it dirty white. This rock, with its ruins of a chapel, a lighthouse, and castle-turned-prison is described by Sir David Attenborough as 'one of the 12 wildlife wonders of the world'.

Robert Louis Stevenson, author of *Treasure Island*, described it as 'just the one crag of rock... but great enough to carve a city from.'

There have been so many reasons to interupt my drive today that dusk is coming as I bounce back down the track to the old road. It's very rutted on this stretch, as if it might peter out at any moment, but does takes me to the modern A1, which I follow for four miles. Along the way I misread a sign to Oldhamstocks as pointing to Oldmansocks, which makes me think I might have been on the road too long.

At Torness, within 100 yds of the sea, is the looming box of Torness Nuclear Power Station, the same colour as Bass Rock, and then a cement works, its chimney billowing a similar shade of off-white.

I turn off onto the A1087 for Dunbar, where twin signs tell

me I am following both the East Lothian Coastal Trail, and Scotland's Golf Coast Road. That's the last time I shall need to drive the new road for 28 miles. Not until the last 1.25 miles in Edinburgh will I be back on the A1.

I pass a monument to the Battle of Dunbar just after Broxburn. Here it was that, in 1650, Cromwell engaged the Scottish army. It was the New Model Army's first victory in the invasion of Scotland, and there's a Cromwell Mount in the grounds of the Broxmouth Park estate where the battle took place.

Today, the eighteenth-century mansion is yet another wedding venue. What with the runaways and royals, weddings have been a bit of a theme on this stretch of the drive.

29. The Last Leg

– Dunbar to Edinburgh –

There are those historians who say the Great North Road bypassed Dunbar, but from the accounts of many travellers it would seem it did go into this harbour town. Uncle Charlie certainly came this way, and called Dunbar 'the first characteristically Scottish place to which we come'.

I've been looking forward to it, not least because, from here, I do not touch the A1 again until I am right in the city of Edinburgh. I'm inspired also by the five-star review of Thomas Carlyle, the Scottish historian and essayist who wrote:

> The small town of Dunbar stands high and windy, looking down over its herring-boats, over its grim old castle, now much honeycombed, on one of those projecting rock-promontories with which that shore of the Firth of Forth is niched and vandyked as far as the eye can reach.

Uncle Charlie adds to the superlatives, saying: 'Its streets are wondrously cobble-stoned, those whinstone rocks are red and give a dull, blood-like coloration to the scene, and the curious old whitewashed Tolbooth in the High Street is the fullest exemplar of the Scottish architectural style.'

That 1550 Tolbooth, now known as Dunbar Town House, is still a distinctive landmark halfway up the High Street. It's a curious, cream-rendered building with an octagonal tower, topped by a witch's hat roof. It sports both a clock and a pair of sun dials, as if this was a town really keen not to miss an important appointment.

I walk on up a pleasant main street, where a former bank is now the Sweetie Bank, past Ristorante Umberto and Adriano's fish and chips, with a Buon Natale neon sign on the roof, and on to Victoria Street. On the corner is a pub called Black Agnes, from the nickname of a fourteenth-century Countess of Dunbar. It bears a sign commemorating a Dunbar battle the English didn't win.

I read: 'The legend of Black Agnes. Fondly remembered for her gallant defence of Dunbar castle from a combined English army during the winter of 1337. Along with a small garrison of archers and servants she courageously defended her castle, and ... eventually defeated the enemy.' Obviously there weren't enough women around when Cromwell came calling.

Next morning I take a walk along the beach, where the ash-blonde sand is buried beneath a head-high blanket of storm-ripped seaweed. Delighted dogs are digging down into it in search of breakfast.

I walk north to the Old Harbour, built by Cromwell, who was unimpressed by the muddy creek he found. In the nineteenth century a second – Victoria Harbour – was added, beyond the causeway that runs out to a great rock on which Dunbar battery stands. There are just a few fragile boats – the *Jenny-Lee* and the *Valhalla* among them – sheltering within the great ramparts, like a stone eggbox around eggshells. Building Victoria Harbour meant cutting through the red sandstone of the headland, and the remains of Dunbar Castle, of Black Agnes fame, teeter above it.

Bearing in mind Charlie's comment that Dunbar is the first characteristically Scottish place you come to after leaving England, I decide I should mark my visit here by sampling two of Scotland's most characteristic products. Whisky and haggis? No. Irn Bru and Tunnock's Tea Cakes.

I've had neither before, and am beginning to feel it's remiss. Sampling them is an essential part of my research. So, on my way down to the harbour I popped into a convenience store and got a plastic bottle of the one and a box of the other. I sit on the wall between the two harbours and rummage in my flimsy blue-plastic carrier bag.

You can't get more Scottish than Irn Bru. It's been the nation's top-selling soft drink for a century, beating even Coca Cola. It has its own tartan, a mix of – predominately – orange, blue and mauve. They used to market it with the slogan 'Made in Scotland from girders', but stopped, on account of it wasn't. Made of girders, I mean. It does have a trace of ammonium ferric citrate, but that's the closest thing to iron in it, plus a lot of sugar, caffeine, and a spot of quinine. It represented Scotland as the only soft drink on sale at COP26, the 2021 United Nations Climate Change Conference. So drinking it is pretty much the law north of the border.

I have high expectations as I pop the cap and take a swig. The most distinctive thing about it is its glowing orange hue. It looks a lot like a very trendy but, to my mind, underwhelming Italian aperitif that everyone seems to be drinking all of a sudden. But it's sweeter. A lot sweeter. A new slogan to replace the girders one occurs to me: 'Irn Bru, the Aperol Spritz of Scotland'.

Now for a Tunnock's. What the Yorkie bar is to York, the

Tunnock's Tea Cake is to its home nation. It combines a biscuit base with a filling of white marshmallow and a coating of milk chocolate. I eat one, then another, and another. I find I like shoving them whole into my mouth then pressing up with my tongue, collapsing them against the roof of my mouth. This is bad news, as there are ten in the box.

Tunnock's also play a central role in Scottish life. Dancers dressed as teacakes performed at the opening ceremony of the 2014 Commonwealth games in Edinburgh, while singing 'I'm a little teacake short and stout, you can stuff me down your spout'. Only the last bit of that sentence is made up.

A retired RAF bomber pilot called Tony Cunnane told the *Daily Record* that they became a favourite ration snack for Scotland-based V-bomber nuclear deterrent crews during the Cold War, especially when they realised they not only tasted good, but expanded entertainingly at high altitude. Then some exploded. Tony told the *Record*: 'Chocolate and shredded marshmallow splattered all over the windscreens, the flight instruments and the pilots' flying suits. This rather distracted the pilots from the immediate emergency actions they were supposed to take for aircraft and aircrew safety. Thereafter marshmallows were banned.'

I decide to harness the massive sugar rush the Irn Bru and the Tunnock's (six now consumed and counting) have given me by powering on through my final approach to Edinburgh. At Dunbar the Great North Road has reached its most northerly point. For the final 30 miles into Edinburgh it runs west and slightly south, in a long arc at the foot of the Lammermuir Hills.

Today's drive is on a flat coastal plain, and a contrast to the clifftop rollercoaster of yesterday. To my left the Scottish Tyne weaves its way through the meadows, shadowing my path for miles. The other contrast is the way in which I can avoid the A1. At Beltonford it seems I will have to re-join it, but the old road sidesteps it and, as the A199, runs on alongside the new to East

Linton. Here, the B1377 follows the Great North Road's route through town, the Tyne plunging beneath the road bridge, then re-joins the A199, which continues along the northern flank of the A1 before leaping to cross it and into the little town of Haddington.

Haddington, bypassed in the 1930s, had been a busy town and a major halt for Edinburgh coaches. It was the first town in Scotland to look like the major coaching towns in England, with its large market place and wide high street. The foremost inn, the George, is no longer a hotel, but this curious faux castle at the eastern end of the High Street has been reborn. It had been empty for several years when, in 2017, it was restored, painted in heritage shades of pale grey and powder blue. Now flats, a cafe and shop occupy the space beneath its turrets and battlements.

Haddington's a pleasant place today, nestled in a dip, with riverside walks along the Tyne, which snakes through town. I'd stay longer only Edinburgh – just 17 miles away now, is calling.

I follow the B6471 out of town and onto the A199 again, which takes me on the old route through Gladsmuir and Tranent, leaping the A1 on its way to Musselburgh. On the approach I pass another sign commemorating a battle site, this one the Battle of Pinkie Braes. So-called because combatants were allowed to fight using only the small finger, or pinkie, on their left hand. OK, I made that up, but it should have been the rule. A lot less bloodshed that way.

Actually it was the site of a very bloody, catastrophic defeat for the Scots. It came about in 1547, when Henry VIII sought an alliance with Scotland through the marriage of the infant Mary, Queen of Scots, with his young son, the future Edward VI, a period euphemistically known as the Rough Wooing. When diplomacy failed, invasion followed. This was the last pitched battle between the two countries before the Union of the Crowns in 1603.

The traffic grinds to a halt in Musselburgh, where I encounter a sign proclaiming it 'The Honest Toun', a roundabout decorated with a giant golf ball on a tee, and a sculpture of a giant silver mussel shell studded with barnacles. A sign announces 'End of Coastal Trail', and I swap the A199 for the B6415 to drive along the shore through Joppa to Portobello, which bills itself as Edinburgh's seaside.

Portobello is snarled up with traffic, exacerbated by temporary traffic lights but not helped by the fact there is so little parking that cars hover alongside anyone who looks remotely like they might, sometime in the next few hours, relinquish a space. I finally locate one and walk down to the prom, beside a broad dark-sand beach, everyone muffled up against the wind, almost everyone towing or being towed by a dog.

Bins along the prom carry the slogan 'Keep Porty Tidy'. A man walks past swearing at his dog, which suggests to me he needs his own slogan: 'Watch your Porty Mouth'.

Charlie's a bit snooty about Portobello, noting that, while it 'calls itself the Brighton of Scotland... Brighton does not return the compliment, and has not yet begun to style itself the Portobello of England.' A notice board tells me this has been the favourite resort of Edinburgh middle class from the late 1700s. It seems the same today. There's certainly a lot of brunching going on.

On the prom I find yet another battle commemorated, this one a conflict much more favourable to the Scots, at an amusement arcade called Fun City. It's painted like a castle but, incongruously, rising to the rear is Portobello's oldest building, The Tower, built in 1785 and said to incorporate stones taken from medieval Edinburgh landmarks.

Above the entrances are paintings of a swordsman on horseback, an archer before a castle and the name: Bannockburn. That battle, in 1314, saw victory for Robert the Bruce during the First War of Scottish Independence.

Moving on, I take the A1140 up to Meadowbank. Here, the London Road goes straight on, and looks like a dead cert for being the Great North Road. It has claims to having been a former route, but it's not the A1. That designation belongs to Regent Road, which takes me the last 1.25 miles into Edinburgh city centre.

This has been the route followed by the Great North Road since 1814. Uncle Charlie says neither is the original:

The so-called London and Regent Roads that now lead directly into the New Town of Edinburgh are modern improvements upon the old approach through Canongate into the Old Town. If steep, rugged, and winding, the old way was at least more impressive, for it lay within sight of Holyrood Palace and brought the wayfarer into the very heart of [the novelist Sir Walter] Scott's own romantic town, to where the smells and the dirt, the crazy tenement-houses and the ragged clouts hanging from dizzy tiers of windows, showed [quoting Burns] "Scotia's darling seat" in its most characteristic aspects.

Canongate is best explored on foot, so for now I take the modern A1, passing grand Georgian Montrose Terrace and Regent Terrace, with views across to Arthur's Seat, the extinct volcano which forms the main peak of the group of hills beneath Edinburgh. For Uncle Charlie it was 'a district slowly emerging from the reproach of a disreputable past, when footpads and murderers haunted the muddy roads, or took refuge amid the towering rocks of Arthur's Seat.'

The A1 runs to the north of the furrow through the city that ought by rights to have a river at the bottom of it, but in fact holds the railway line to London.

The road skirts Calton Hill, the city centre at my feet. Calton Hill is littered with grand monuments, among them: a memorial to those killed in the Napoleonic Wars, modelled on the

Parthenon and intended as a tribute to 'the past and incentive to the future heroism of the men of Scotland'; a classic Grecian-style observatory; and the candy twist Nelson Memorial.

The road drops down to Waterloo Place and Princes Street, Edinburgh's main drag, where it reaches its modern destination, outside Waverley Station.

I'm tantalisingly close to that point, but traffic lights hold me in Waterloo Place for what feels like an age. At least it gives me time to take in a demonstration by members of the Scottish Socialist Party, waving red and yellow flags and holding up placards that demand an 'Independent Socialist Scotland'.

After all the reminders of a fraught but glorious and romantic past that I've experienced since crossing the border, it's interesting to encounter a dream of a glorious future.

30. The End of the Road

– Edinburgh –

The first person I meet in Edinburgh is a drunk. I'm sorry. I feel guilty just saying it. Perpetuating a malign Scottish stereotype is wrong. But, in my defence, it's nothing but the truth. And he was the only one I met. Everyone else, without exception, was stone cold sober. I mention him not to do Scotsmen down, but because the second person I met, and the humanity he showed his drunken countryman, was truly inspiring.

It was in the Tollbooth Tavern in Canongate that I came across the pair, an encounter I'll return to in a moment. I'd traced the old route of the Great North Road on foot, back from where it leaves Regent Road and drops down, as Abbey Mount, to pass the ruins of Holyrood Abbey and the spanking new Scottish Parliament building before entering Canongate.

Up until the eighteenth century, Canongate had been

Edinburgh's most fashionable residential area but, by the 1770s, it had deteriorated into a place of poverty and squalor. It was certainly no way to enter a proud capital city. So the monied, and the money, migrated a short way north, over the city's central fissure, to what is still called the New Town.

Princes Street, Scotland's new main drag, was laid out from 1778, and the link to the Great North Road was completed in 1814, cutting a path along the southern fringe of Calton Hill. Now, the mail and other coaches swept in on high ground, passengers enjoying a view of Arthur's Seat to the south, and rounding Calton Hill for a truly theatrical reveal: Edinburgh Castle, that embodiment of national power and pride, ahead of them on Castle Rock.

This path became known as the noblest approach to any European city. But enough of that. Before 1814, travellers rattling along Canongate to the Old Town found themselves in the midst of squalor.

Charles Dickens cited the Old Town as the place where he 'saw more poverty and sickness in an hour than people would believe in, in a life'. At one house he discovered, in 1841, 'in an old egg box which the mother had begged from a shop, a little, feeble, wan sick child. With his little wasted face, and his bright attentive eyes'. When Dickens later gave a speech in support of plans to establish the Great Ormond Street Hospital for Sick Children, he recalled the encounter: 'I can see him now, as I have seen him for several years, looking steadily at us... he lay there, seeming to wonder what it was a' aboot... God knows, I thought, he had his reasons for wonder.'

Canongate was still pretty grim in the early twentieth century. Uncle Charlie reported 'the squalor survives. The poor who live here [hang out] their domestic washing, fluttering in the breeze from every window, at the end of long poles, and how poor they are may be judged from the condition of the clothes they consider worth keeping.'

Today, Canongate is fashionable, but manages to retain its brown-stone sombreness. The tall terraces making the street a cobbled urban canyon are no longer slums. They house smart shops, hotels, restaurants, media companies and apartments.

Just before I reach the Tollbooth Tavern, I pause to take a look at Canongate Kirk. It's a plain, austere place, like so many Scottish churches, and vaguely sinister, its facade a distorted face in which two arched windows hang like drooping eyes above the lolling tongue of a bright red door. A rose window punctures the forehead like a third eye.

Behind the window on the left is a nativity scene, Joseph and Mary beside the manger with the shepherds. Within the one on the right are the three kings, in their gold and finery, gifts in hand, walking towards Bethlehem.

On a stone plinth beside the door is a black iron strongbox with a keyhole for a very big key.

When Charles Dickens came here he noticed a gravestone commemorating one Ebenezer Lennox Scroggie, who had died in 1836, and thought something along the lines of: 'hmm, Scroggie? Might be able to use that name. Maybe change it a little. Scrooge? Yep, make a note of that, could come in handy.'

Two years later, when he was writing *A Christmas Carol*, it did indeed come in handy. It's also possible he misread the gravestone inscription, in which Scroggie is described as a 'meal man', meaning a corn merchant, as 'mean man' which, indeed, Scrooge was.

The real Scroggie was nothing like Scrooge, other than that both were rich. Scroggie was no miser. He had a reputation for being what was then called a 'roister doister' which roughly translates as 'piss artist and groper'. He enjoyed illicit liaisons with serving girls in churchyards including this one, and was expelled from the General Assembly of the Church of Scotland for putting his hand up an aristocratic lady's skirt.

His grave stone was removed in the 1930s, robbing

Canongate of a very handy tourist attraction / target for #metoo anger.

Scroggie has another claim to fame. He was close friends with William Smellie (now there's another great name for you, Dickens), the inventor of the *Encyclopaedia Britannica*. Smellie credited Scroggie with the idea of gathering all the world's information into one massive source of reference, creating the Wikipedia of its day.

The Tollbooth, which I move on to, was the original departure point for London-bound coaches. In a dark, cobbled street slick with rain and saturated with yellow street-lamp light, it looks like something from a *Harry Potter* set. The building dates from 1591 and, as well as hosting and collecting tolls from travellers, it housed a prison, council chamber and police court. Executions were conducted outside. Cromwell stayed twice while in town to fight Royalists.

The Tollbooth looks like a castle of glowering, Norman stolidity, but its great tower is adorned with the sort of tourelles (subsidiary turrets), that might decorate a French chateau. An enormous illuminated clock set into a big black box juts out over the road, and the tower is pierced by a stone-arched carriage entryway.

It only became a pub in 1820, and inside feels pretty much like any old boozer, with its dull mulberry walls and scuffed carpet. But it has a fine, heavily carved bar with matching whisky display shelves behind it. At the bar sits the drunk. Above his head, a screen shows the bar as seen from four different security cameras. I take him in: shaven head, three-day stubble, shapeless black leather jacket, skinny legs lost in baggy jeans, one foot pumping, cheeks sunken: a sad case.

Dickens came here, perhaps after spotting Scroggie's gravestone, and is said to have worked on the plot for *A Christmas Carol* in the bar.

A heavily illuminated betting machine is tattooing a

migraine-inducing pattern of flashing lights on the back of my eyeballs as I order at the bar. The drunk sees me glance at it and says: 'Dinna tru tha wa, paw, subandit.' It takes me a while, but I'm eventually able to translate his words as 'Dinnae trust tha' one, pal, it's a bandit.'

I assure him I won't, and take a seat, but it turns out our conversation isn't over. It's moved on to the background music. I'm a little better attuned to his accent now, so I can make out he says 'Tha's Coldplay,' which it is, and adds: 'Ah no ma music, am ah righ'?'

I assure him he is right, as does the barman, when asked the same question. As do the Italian couple who come into the bar at that point.

I can see the barman has been having some problems. He tells the drunk politely a few times to 'keep the noise down' when he sings along to the tracks playing, and 'leave the customers alone' when he asks one of us whether he's right. We all assure him that he is. Finally, though, the barman says, still very politely: 'Sorry, but you've had enough. I've a duty of care to youse, so I can't serve you any more.'

The drunk is temporarily silenced, perhaps by the novel concept of someone feeling they have a duty of care over him. The barman has to repeat it several times, eventually giving up, and saying: 'Enjoy your drink, but when you've finished: it's on your way.'

But none of this is really having any effect. After a few more rounds of singing and 'am ah righ'?, a man who has been sitting along the bench seat from me, hunched over his phone, gets up, says 'This is taking the piss,' and goes over to the drunk. I expect him to do something like take him by the collar and sling him out into the street, but he does nothing of the kind. Instead, he sits on the stool next to him and asks him where he's from.

It's a remarkably effective intervention. The two are still sitting there chatting when I finish my pint and head on out into

Canongate. I've always suspected drunks in pubs of looking for a fight. It turns out that this one, at least, just wanted someone to talk to. Which was a lesson to me, and why I think it's ok to tell the story here.

Anyway, on I go.

Passengers coming this way into Edinburgh would continue up Canongate, which becomes High Street, into the heart of what might now be called Edinburgh's night-time economy.

Going straight on, High Street takes me to Lawnmarket and up Castle Hill toward the castle itself, which is illuminated a very dramatic blood red. But I take a left at St Mary's Street, on a slight detour in search of a spot called Boyd's Entry.

The night has turned icy. There are flurries of snow in the air, and I have to leap into the road to avoid a mini gritter which is barrelling along the pavement, sprinkling salt behind it to counter the beads of ice that are forming on the ground, making it like walking over slippery pin heads.

Boyd's Entry marks the spot where Boyd's Inn once stood, one of several travellers' taverns clustered here. Today there's just a narrow lane between two anonymous buildings. A cistern overflow is dropping water down two storeys to form a treacherous ice rink on the cobbles. It was to this inn that Samuel Johnson came in 1773 to meet up with James Boswell, his biographer and an Edinburgh lawyer, prior to a tour of the Hebrides that Boswell would write up in *Journey to the Western Isles of Scotland*.

Johnson was not impressed with Boyd's Inn. When Boswell joined him he found his friend fuming because he 'asked to have his lemonade made sweeter, upon which the waiter with his greasy fingers, lifted a lump of sugar, and put it into it. The Doctor, in indignation, threw it out of the window'. I saw something similar in a restaurant once. Someone complained to the waiter that their coffee was cold, and he stuck his finger in it, just to check.

₌ch experiences were by no means uncommon. The inns ₌re generally lousy. As Uncle Charlie writes: 'A traveller arriving at Edinburgh in 1774, for instance, had indeed little comfort awaiting him. "One can scarcely form in imagination the distress of a miserable stranger on his first entrance into this city," says one writing at this period. No inn better than an alehouse, no decent or cleanly accommodation, nor in fact anything fit for a gentleman.'

Charlie's traveller goes on: 'You may guess our amazement when we were informed that this was the best inn in the metropolis, and that we could have no beds unless we had an inclination to sleep together, and in the same room with the company which a stage-coach had that moment discharged.'

Back on track, I walk on down the High Street, through what is known as the Royal Mile. It's as impressive a street as I've seen in any city: broad and car-free, lined with smart shops and restaurants, and landmarks such as the 10ft bronze statue of Adam Smith, economist, philosopher, and author of *The Wealth of Nations*, standing on a great granite plinth.

Alongside it is twelfth-century St Giles Cathedral, the High Kirk of Edinburgh. In 1559, the leader of the Scottish Reformation, John Knox, became its minister.

Another statue is to David Hume, the eighteenth-century philosopher. Hume and Smith were leading figures in the Scottish Enlightenment, which saw an outpouring of intellectual and scientific accomplishments.

All this talk of what William Cobbett called 'feelosfee' and 'feelosofers' reminds me of that frightened polemicist, cowering in his carriage as it rolls into Edinburgh in 1832. He had been ridiculing the idea of a Scottish Enlightenment, and Scots in general, in his journalism since 1790. Six Edinburgh newspapers had warned him his arrival would be 'not only mortifying and disgraceful, but even personally perilous'.

As Gordon Pentland writes in *William Cobbett's Scotophobia*:

'...he had some explaining to do... Cobbett had to atone for a remarkably consistent hostility to Scotland and the Scots... He explained this in a predictable way: by claiming that he had found it difficult to unshackle himself from vulgar English prejudices absorbed across his lifetime; by specifying that his hostility had been to particular types of Scots not the Scots qua Scots; and, of course, by claiming that some of his best friends were Scottish.'

This ruse appears to have worked. Cobbett received a welcome that confounded his expectations. It turned out no one wanted to string him up, despite all he had said and written. He said: 'Here, then, I was, in that city, of which I had heard and read so much; of which I had spoken in terms, not one of which was to be retracted as long as I was in it... [and yet] my reception very far exceeded my hopes. Every man that I have met with at Edinburgh has been as kind to me as if he were my brother.'

The glories of Edinburgh win him over: 'This is the finest city that I ever saw in my life... I thought that Bristol, taking in its heights and Clifton and its rocks and its river, was the finest city in the world.' Edinburgh, he decides is superior 'with its castle, its hills, its pretty little sea-port, conveniently detached from it, its vale of rich land lying all around, its lofty hills in the back ground, its views across the Firth.'

Another figure of the Scottish Enlightenment was a promising young poet called Robert Burns, who had arrived in Edinburgh in 1786, penniless and on a borrowed pony, but was immediately accepted among the city's world-renowned philosophers, economists, scientists, engineers, writers and poets. He became Scotland's Bard, and I'm headed for one of his haunts.

Where the High Street becomes Lawnmarket I dog-leg left and right for the Grassmarket. The cobbled street, strung with Christmas lights of bright white snowflakes, descends to level out at a long, cobbled market place, planted with clumps of trees.

, was an important staging post in the eighteenth and
,y nineteenth centuries. Coaches set out for London from the
Cowgate Head, which is gone, and the White Hart and the
Beehive, which survive as pubs.

The Grassmarket teemed with activity. Daniel Defoe
described it in the eighteenth century: 'This street... is generally
full of wholesale traders, and those very considerable dealers in
iron, pitch, tar, oil, hemp, flax, linseed, painter's colours, dyers,
drugs and wood, and such-like heavy goods, and supplies
country shopkeepers, which our wholesale dealers in England
do.' There was a livestock market here too, and a corn exchange.
Ebenezer Scroggie lived above what is now the Beehive Inn, a
handy home for a merchant in corn and other commodities.

A pub called The Last Drop is a reminder that condemned
prisoners were allowed a final tot of whisky before the other last
drop, with the hangman's noose around their necks.

I pop into The White Hart Inn, at No. 34, which claims to be
Edinburgh's oldest, dating from 1516. This was a haunt of
Robert Burns. The beams on the ceiling in this cosy little pub
carry aphorisms and quotations from his work.

Burns stayed here for a week in 1791, on his last visit to
Edinburgh to see Mrs Agnes Maclehose, with whom he had an
unconsummated love affair, and who was about to depart for
Jamaica with her husband. He wrote the beautiful love song, 'Ae
Fond Kiss', about that parting.

It begins:

Ae fond kiss and then we sever
Ae fareweel, alas for ever
Deep in heart-wrung tears I'll pledge thee
Warring sighs and groans I'll wage thee

Appropriately for a pub, several of the quotes on beams deal
with drinking: 'a man may drink and no be drunk'; 'there's some

are fou' [full] of life divine, tho some are fou o brandy'; and 'Then let us toast John Barleycorn, each man a glass in hand and may his great posterity Ne'er fail in old Scotland!'

One, from 'Epitaph on my own Friend' addresses a broader theme: 'If there's another world, he lives in bliss; If there is none, he made the best of this.'

Tonight the pub is busy, packed with mainly foreign visitors. There are menus on the tables and plates being cleared from the one next to mine, but I overhear a Spanish couple at the bar being told 'no food only drink' which is puzzling them, given the evidence to the contrary.

I was going to have the 'Haggis, Neeps and Tatties', which would have been a highly traditional meal to mark my arrival at the end of the Great North Road. Instead, I settle for what turns out to be a very nice French restaurant next door, where I celebrate the end of my journey with a basket of crusty, soft-centred bread, a jug of red wine and a plate of coque au vin.

There's an inevitable sense of anti-climax at the end of a long journey, and this had been an especially long one. For over a year I have journeyed up and down the Great North Road, dodging lockdowns, navigating restrictions on the who, what, when and where of normal life.

For most of the time, things have been getting better, restrictions loosening, life returning to normal. Now, in the days before Christmas 2021, the lights look like they might be going off again: a fourth wave, a new variant, soaring infection rates.

Not that there's any sense of gloom in Edinburgh. The demands for Covid passports and negative test results I've been warned to expect don't materialise. Not that I mind: I've got both. Unlike London, the place is packed with foreign visitors, and a vast outdoor Christmas market in East Princes Street Gardens is doing great business. And, you know, it just doesn't seem worth worrying about. Which turns out to be the right attitude. Because we ride the wave.

Tomorrow it will be time to head home, but there is one more stretch of road to explore on the way: Telford's Road of 1828, intended to form the first stage in a new route for the Great North Road to London. So the journey's not quite over. There's something more to look forward to. And with that thought I order more wine, more bread, and a plate of cheese.

VIII

TELFORD'S ROAD OF 1828
Edinburgh
to Morpeth

EDINBURGH

Dolkeith

Telford's
Road
of 1828

Blackadder

Greenlaw

Coldstream

Wooler

THE
BLACK BULL
INN

Morpeth

It was to have been the first section of a new, improved, alternative path for the Great North Road. It was stage two in a national roads strategy.

In 1811 the great engineer Thomas Telford had been tasked with improving the road from London to Holyhead, and did such a splendid job, driving a new route through mountainous central Wales and bridging the Menai Straits, that he was asked to look next at the Great North Road.

By 1824 the whole route had been surveyed – with innovations including a 100-mile stretch south of York laid out in a perfectly straight line – and construction approved. Work commenced on the most northerly section, from Edinburgh to Morpeth, creating a route that ran inland through Dalkeith, Greenlaw, Coldstream, and Wooler, avoiding the exposed coastal sections of the old road, and cutting 11 miles off the 102-mile total of the route via Berwick.

And then the railways happened.

In 1825 the Stockton and Darlington Railway opened, followed by the line from Liverpool and Manchester. It became clear that rail was the future of transport, and the plans were abandoned. But work was too far advanced on the northern section, which became known as Telford's Road, and it opened in 1828.

Telford's Road never caught on. Stage coaches avoided it because it passed through few towns, and offered little custom, mail coaches because they still needed to serve towns such as Alnwick, Berwick and Dunbar, which it avoided. In any case, it lacked the supporting infrastructure: the inns at which travellers could be fed, and tired horses exchanged for fresh ones, which had built up along the Great North Road over centuries. And, although the road was well engineered, the long moorland climbs it involved were more taxing on horses.

Of course, none of that mattered to me, all I was interested in was discovering whether Telford's Road offered a better drive south to Morpeth.

31. Homeward Bound

I came in to Edinburgh from the East, I leave to the South.

Telford's Road, now the A7, takes me on North Bridge, flying over Waverley Station and crossing High Street to become South Bridge, past Old College and the Festival Theatre and out through the suburbs. This being Edinburgh, the buildings are still six or more storeys high and crowd the road in one solid stone terrace, like a castle wall of flats, with shops under, all the way to East Preston Street. Here I take a left, Arthur's Seat peeking at me from the end of the road, and then a right onto Dalkeith Road. I pass Newington Cemetery which brings a stretch of greenery to the scene, and barrel on towards Dalkeith, the terraces gradually declining in height from four, to three to two storeys.

An expansive and very confusing roundabout at Cameron Toll, which has signs to everywhere but Dalkeith, leads to a stretch of increasingly open country before I cross the City of Edinburgh bypass and take the A6106 Old Dalkeith Road.

In Dalkeith, Robert Burns and Margaret Tudor crop up again. In the High Street is a Victorian cast iron fountain, erected in 1899 to commemorate the centenary of Burns's death. Its canopy has been recently restored, and painted a smart red, black and white.

It's a curious connection between poet and princess. Burns is believed to have visited Dalkeith in 1787, and wrote a poem called 'Sae Far Awa' (So Far Away) set to a traditional tune called 'Dalkeith's Maiden Brig'. That tune refers to the brig, or bridge, over which the maiden (Margaret Tudor, daughter of Henry VII and sister of Henry VIII) crossed on her way to meet James IV of Scotland, her future husband. The bridge spans the River South Esk, which flows just to the south of the town centre, through what is now Newbattle Golf Course.

Margaret, you will remember, is said to have been married to James by proxy at the border kirk at Lamberton, which I passed on my way north from Berwick, and the poem fits her story, but with the sexes of the protagonists reversed. It is spoken by a man leaving his native land for the sake of a lover and starts:

> O sad and heavy should I part,
> But for her sake, sae far awa;
> Unknowing what my way may thwart,
> My native land sae far awa.

In the second verse the speaker seems to be asking God to give him strength not to forsake his country for his 'fair' maiden:

> Thou that of a' things maker art,
> That form'd this fair sae far awa,
> Gie body strength, then I'll ne'er start
> At this my way sae far awa.

The poem was written while Burns was touring the Borders, passing into England for the first time. So he is something of a companion on my drive south, and I'll bump into him again when I cross the border, which I head for now on the A68.

The day is icy cold, but the sky clear and a brilliant blue, the lowest of winter suns dazzling me. There is a scattering of snow on the fields and chunks of traffic-blackened ice on the road margins

The road on the four miles to Pathhead gets far more rural as I approach one of the engineering triumphs of Telford's Road. The evidence of the terrible storm of a few days ago is all around, trees tumbled in the woodland alongside the road, the highway littered with leaves and branches. Several times on my drive south I am stopped at temporary traffic lights, set up by road gangs chainsawing off the boughs of trees that have fallen onto the road.

At times I see strings of telegraph poles toppled over in the fields, and for a while follow a truck loaded with their replacements. Telford's dead-straight road descends at a steady, gentle gradient past Oxenfoord Castle, which started life in the sixteenth century as a fortified tower house and is now inevitably, a 'unique castle wedding venue', and the Stair Arms Hotel.

This was once a coaching inn, built in 1831 in anticipation of profiting from the traffic that never really came to this brand new route. Quite a few investors must have caught a cold, speculating on the success of Telford's Road, but the Stair Arms survived, and is now a very nice hotel which references its origins in the horse-drawn coach on its roadside sign.

Just past it is that Telford triumph: the Lothian Bridge, which spans the deep ravine at this point so effectively that I can hardly tell where land becomes bridge and bridge land. To achieve this, and avoid a precipitous plunge down to cross the Tyne, Telford ran lofty embankments in from either side and built a tall and graceful five-arch bridge, rising 49ft above the river bed.

He did the same over two other deep ravines that would have disrupted my smooth decent to this point, at Cotty Burn and Cranston Dean. I didn't notice crossing them at all.

Traffic on the road up to Pathhead slows and it's a bit of a grind, locked in a line of trucks, through this place of mainly single-storey stone cottages, one of them a pub called The Foresters. Pathhead gets its name from its position at the highest point on the route from Edinburgh to Lauder, 500ft above sea level.

The line this stretch of the road follows predates Telford by close to two thousand years. It was Roman Dere Street, and ran north from Corbridge, on Hadrian's Wall, into country the

Roman's never managed to subjugate. It ran via Lauder to Pathhead, then on to the fortress at Inveresk, in today's Musselburgh. I have been roughly on its line since I picked up the A68 after leaving Dalkeith. It was also an important route in medieval times, as I shall discover in a few miles.

High country persists to the south of the village, with Fala Moor to my right and frequent lay-bys in which to pause to enjoy the fine valley views. Tweedy, muted colours dominate, the landscape all muddy greens and browns, the colour scheme of a country gent's suit.

The road swings left at Soutra Hill, diverging from the line of Dere Street. A half-mile diversion on the B6368 brings me to Soutra Aisle, the ruins of the House of the Holy Trinity, a medieval church that was part of a friary, and one of the most important medieval hospitals in Scotland.

It was founded by Malcolm IV in 1164, when the road through here was called the Via Regia, and was the main route from Edinburgh to the Borders abbeys of Jedburgh, Melrose, Dryburgh, and Kelso. A document from 1444 states that it was 'the founders intention to found there a hospital for the reception of the poor rather than a religious place... the church is built at the top of a hill near a public way where there are often fierce winds and frequent cold spells'.

Excavations have revealed rare seeds and traces of medicinal herbs from across the then-known world, and it was estimated that – at its peak from the twelfth to the mid-fifteenth centuries – around 300 people lived here, caring for travellers and the sick.

It was confiscated by the Crown in the 1460s, following a scandal involving the master of the hospital, and fell into disrepair. Most of the stone was removed and, today, just the rough-hewn stone chapel, roofed in turf, still stands. It only survived because it became the burial place of the local Pringle family in 1686, and gets the name Soutra Aisle from the Church of Scotland decree, in 1590, that no monuments to the dead should be allowed in churches. Hence, separate burial vaults, or aisles, were established. It's looking its best today, under a low sun and bright blue sky, but is still a lonely, eerie place, and I sense many ghosts.

Back on Telford's Road there are vast windfarms to either side, swathes of them planted beneath the line of the road so that their windmilling arms appear to dig into the land. They all face north, but swing languidly, becalmed after the storm.

My map shows a section of track to the west called both Kings Road and Dere Street. It heads south east from Soutra Aisle through the wind turbines, with Telford's Road running parallel to the east of it. It's a brilliant day, with stunning views east over the moors to the sea. The landscape undulates, and I get a second, overtaking lane on the ascents, relinquishing it to north-bound traffic whenever the road descends.

Telford's Road descends into Lauderdale, but avoids Lauder itself, leaving the old Roman and medieval route at Carfraemill. The inn at this junction served coaches running between Kelso and Edinburgh from the 1800s, and is now a thriving hotel.

Here, the route switches designations from A68 to A697, soon making a sudden, sharp change in direction from south-east to east. This is clearly the less-favoured route, devoid of trucks, and much quieter. It feels like a forgotten country road, in contrast to the well-maintained A68.

It winds and twists its way over the Lammermuirs, the pastures blanketed white, the furrows of the few ploughed fields lined black and white. I pass a farm where the yard is piled with cylinders of hay baled in shiny white plastic, and later another where the hay wears black, like two styles of farmer's fetishwear. There's slush on the margins and at the centre of the road, and the few trucks I encounter fling a wheelful at my windscreen as they pass.

Just a few hamlets line the lonely 15 miles between

Carfraemill to Greenlaw, which is the first town I've encountered since Pathhead. It's a long slow descent, yellow gorse giving way to Christmas tree plantations and then pasture as I tick off tiny places – Houndslow, Hexpath, Rumbletonrig – cross the bridge over Blackadder Water and pull up in the rugged, tough little high-country town of Greenlaw. It stands at a crossroads: the A6105 between Galashiels and Berwick crossing Telford's Road. There were two coaching inns here. The Cross Keys is long closed, but the Blackadder Inn still thrives.

The menu displayed outside – Stornoway black pudding and haggis wedges among the starters, Scottish salmon and Balmoral chicken among the mains – make me wish it was lunch time. As its only mid-morning I pop next door for coffee in the Amaretto Tea Room, whose pastel shades are a contrast to the white render and black stone window frames of the Blackadder.

I have my coffee to take away and wander around town. There is absolutely no one around, and hardly any cars on the main road, but the signs to Blackadder Holiday Park, just over the green, suggest that this must be a busy place in season.

Over the road from the inn is a grand and strangely out of place building, very imposing, neo classical, colonnaded and domed, like a vast mausoleum. Could it commemorate some great Scottish statesman? There are no clues, just a tiny brass plate on the door: 'Coldingham Investments Limited Registered Office'.

I walk around it and see – through sometimes broken windows – desks, chairs, but no other signs of habitation. It turns out this is a town hall, and there's a story of misplaced ambition behind it.

It is part of the rivalry between Greenlaw and Duns. Both are in Berwickshire but when the English captured the county seat, Berwick, in 1482, another county town was needed. Greenlaw got the job, then lost it to Duns, then got it back again. This to-and-fro went on for four centuries. In 1829, in a bid to put Duns out of the running for good, the Earl of Marchmont commissioned a magnificent new County Buildings and Court House (now referred to as the Town Hall).

It didn't work, Duns finally winning the crown for good in 1903. So Greenlaw had a vast building they didn't know what to do with. A Polish tank regiment was billeted here during World War II, and in the 1970s it was converted into a swimming pool. Then Duns built a bigger and better pool. The bastards. In 2006 the building was one of three Scottish contenders for a contest, featured in a BBC series, *Restoration*, but was unsuccessful. Then, in 2011, the Scottish Historic Buildings Trust stepped in, £2m was spent and the town hall reopened for community use. But, today, at least when I come through, it is disused once more.

Norman Webster, who passed this way in the 1970s, says: 'The harsh appearance of Greenlaw town is softened by the beauty of the surroundings and by the sparkling waters of the Blackadder, a river as beautiful as its name is repellent.'

Norman was writing well before Blackadder gave its name to the classic BBC comedy in which Rowan Atkinson played a character called Edmund Blackadder, so he can't have known that someone else found the use of that name repellent, despite the fact it apparently means, innocuously enough, 'deep, winding river'.

At *Mail Online* where I – like all serious authors – do the bulk of my research, I find a story headlined: 'Blackadder made our lives a misery, says widow of GP: Scottish doctor's surname gave rise to ridicule and rejected table bookings'.

So, obviously I have to read on. I learn that, in 1982, when Rowan Atkinson, Richard Curtis and John Lloyd were working on the first series of the hit show, they were taken by the name of Dr Eric Blackadder, the BBC's chief medical officer, and used it, slightly adapted, for their lead character.

Dr Eric had no idea this had happened until, the story says,

'BBC colleagues started teasing him in the management dining rooms'. The account goes on: 'I remember asking my secretary to see if she could find out if my name was being used in television.'

When told it was, Eric was not amused. In an effort to win him round, he and his wife were invited to a screening of the first two episodes, followed by dinner with the cast.

The doctor was not won round, and tried to persuade Alasdair Milne, then the BBC director general, to rename the show. When Milne declined: 'I spoke to the BBC solicitors but was told that I had no copyright in my name.'

Nuisance callers would ring up while the show was being screened, asking to speak to Baldrick, which led to Eric keeping a referee's whistle beside the phone, so he could give them an ear-splitting blast. He suffered taxi drivers and restaurants thinking bookings were a hoax, and shop assistants sniggering over the name on his credit card.

Mrs Blackadder said: 'I can say from the bottom of my heart that the side-effects have all been adverse. We started off with a respectable name but all of this has changed our lives.'

I cross Blackadder Water once more on my route out of town, and then the road climbs again – a wet ribbon of dazzling, reflected sun between brown hedges – angling south east as it approaches the River Tweed, and the border.

Just after that change in direction I pass a brown sign to Richard Hillary Memorial, and decide to take a look. I drive down the B6460 to arrive at a crossroads in a wood. Here stands a grey granite plinth, against which two poppy wreaths lean.

Hillary was a remarkably brave Spitfire pilot in the Battle of Britain, flying with 603 (City of Edinburgh) Squadron. In just one week, he shot down five enemy planes and damaged three more, experiences he recounted in *The Last Enemy*. His luck ran out when he was shot down over the English Channel. Unable to bail out of his blazing plane, he suffered terrible burns and blacked out. But, before his plane hit the water, he fell out of it. Hillary regained consciousness as he was tumbling through space, and was able to open his parachute. He was rescued by the Margate lifeboat, undergoing three months of surgery on his face and hands.

Despite being barely able to lift a knife and fork, he returned to active service. Hillary's story ended here, close to what was then RAF Charterhall, when the Bristol Blenheim bomber he was piloting on a night flight in atrocious weather came down in fields, killing him and his navigator.

The memorial records Hillary's death on 9 January 1943. Set into the ground behind it is a landing light from the airstrip at Charterhall. The old runways are still visible as a darker, Saltire-like cross in the green of the fields.

Moving on, the road descends onto a wide open plain, where the biggest retail outlets are the tractor dealers. On the approach to Coldstream the road runs east, parallel to the Tweed, which forms the border between Scotland and England.

Coldstream means guards, and this is that regiment's home. To give them their full name, they are the First Regiment of Foot and, dating from 23 August 1650, are the oldest continuously serving regiment of the regular British Army, best known for their role guarding the monarch, and performing ceremonial duties in their tall black busbies and red jackets.

They were formed as part of Cromwell's New Model Army by General Monck, his military governor in Scotland and, eleven days later, helped defeat Scottish royalist forces at the Battle of Dunbar. However, ten years later, Monck had changed sides, and led his forces across the Tweed on their way to London, forcing the restoration of Charles II to the crown.

I half expect to see off-duty guards about town, busbees pushed back, red jackets unbuttoned, but no. Apart from the Guards Rest Army Surplus store I see no military presence as I drive through.

Soaring into the sky above the town is a great memorial column with a little man on the top. I assume it commemorates a great guardsman, or perhaps a famous victory, but no. It's not even to Coldstream's most famous son (all things are relative) Alec Douglas-Home, who became Prime Minister when Harold Macmillan resigned, and who is buried here. Alice, as *Private Eye* delighted in calling him, lasted just a year, from October 1963 until the general election of October 1964, when he came across as an out of touch aristo against Labour's pipe-smoking, mac-wearing Scouse leader Harold Wilson, and lost. Home's family seat is at the Hirsel, just north of the road I took through town.

In fact, the little man on the very tall column turns out to be Charles Albany Marjoribanks (1794-1833) a Scottish Liberal MP who, the monument inscription tells me, was a man of 'high talents, amiable qualities and political principles'. The statue had to be replaced in 1873 when it was struck by lightning. I mean, if you're going to stick your head that far above the parapet... Part of the original statue, nicknamed Old Charlie's Leg, is on display in the Coldstream Museum.

Leaving town, the A697 bends right to cross the Tweed on another wonderful bridge, not Telford's this time, but John Smeaton's elegant six-arch creation of 1763-6. Just before it, tucked to the side, is the Old Marriage House, a little stone bungalow where weddings were conducted until 1856, couples joining hands over a limestone boulder as a final part of the ceremony.

The Tweed marks the border and, as I pass over it without ceremony, I wonder idly what changes I'd find here if Scotland won independence. On the far side is a rather scruffy old sign, a red cross on a silver shield, and the one word: ENGLAND. Looking back, the 'SCOTLAND Welcomes You' sign is much bigger, much bolder, more modern. Prouder maybe? It certainly suggests that the border holds more significance for the Scots than the English.

I pull off the road and walk back above the great, wide, whisky-brown waters. Coldstream is a cluster of dark stone in the distance, Charlie striding along the treetops on his enormous monument. Far below me an angler is casting his line, competing with a cormorant, fishing just upstream of him.

Rabbie Burns came this way in 1787. His soaring popularity as a poet made him suddenly flush, and he decided to spend some of it exploring Scotland. Along the way he was able to pick up cash from those who had placed orders for his latest edition, making the trip something of a victory parade, and a bit of an earner in itself. He carried three dozen copies of an engraved portrait of himself, to hand out to his super-fans.

Burns's guide was a young apprentice lawyer, Robert Ainslie, who knew the Borders well. To look the part of the rich, fashionable young author, Burns blinged himself up, splashing out on a new suit, and spending £4 on a mare, which he named Jenny Geddes, after a fiery Edinburgh market-trader who is said to have sparked a revolt against English rule.

Geddes apparently hurled a stool at the head of the minister in St Giles Cathedral in protest at the first use of the *Scottish Episcopal Book of Common Prayer*. A riot ensued and the Civil War followed.

The day before he got to Coldstream, Burns demonstrated his way with the ladies when, attending church with Ainslie's parents and sister Rachel, he wrote a flattering verse on the flyleaf of her Bible. Rachel had become upset at the sermon on sinners and Burns, sitting next to her, took the good book and wrote:

Fair maid, you needna take the hint
Nor idle texts pursue;
'Twas guilty sinners that he meant
Not angels such as you!

When Burns and Ainslie got to the point I am now standing, and the poet stepped from Scotland into England for the first time, he was himself overcome with emotion.

To Ainslie's surprise Burns threw off his hat, knelt down and lifted his hands to heaven. With great passion he prayed for and blessed Scotland, and declaimed part of his poem 'A Cottar's Saturday Night', which begins:

O Scotia! my dear, my native soil!
For whom my warmest wish to Heaven is sent!
Long may thy hardy sons of rustic toil
Be blest with health, and peace, and sweet content!

The Coldstream Burns Club marks Burns's crossing with an annual ceremony on the anniversary in May. Another historic figure to come this way south from Coldstream was James IV, who I'll catch up with in a moment.

The first village in England is Cornhill on Tweed, where the Georgian Collingwood Arms was a distinguished coaching inn, and where the Clas farm-equipment dealer has been busy decorating tractors with Christmas lights. Making him Santa Clas. A lonely road follows, through the hamlet of Barelees, and then, three miles into England, a brown sign points a mile south to Flodden Field, near the village of Branxton. An Aberdeen granite Celtic cross, commemorating the battle, is just visible across the fields, standing on the top of Pipers Hill.

In September 1513, James IV marched south from Coldstream on his invasion of northern England. Just ten years before, James's marriage to Margaret Tudor was intended to cement peace between the two nations but, clearly, diplomacy had failed.

James acted in support of Scotland's old ally, the French, with whom Henry VIII was at war, and brought with him most of Scotland's nobility, and 10,000 troops. His aim was not to take territory, but to persuade the English king to withdraw his troops from France. At Flodden Field the Scots met their match, and were slaughtered, the king among them. This was the biggest military catastrophe to befall the Scots in their centuries of battles with the English.

Is all forgiven now? The base of the cross, erected in 1910, reads: 'To the brave of both nations'.

I press on, through Crookham – with another former coaching inn, the Blue Bell – on my way to Wooler, the only substantial town on the English section of Telford's Road. On the approach, the plain I have been crossing since the border comes up against the Cheviots hills, and the road bears left at their foot. I follow Borders Bus No. 267 into town alongside the weirs of Wooler Water, the once-bright day now overcast and grim.

Wooler is charming, the sort of town that wins Best Place to Live awards in newspaper property pages. I stroll up the High Street, past the Black Bull, once a coaching inn. In 1910 a black and white turret was suspended from its four-storey stone face, like an elongated false nose. Next to it another venerable old inn, the more humble two-storey Angel, has its own very modest bay above the main entrance.

Wooler has all the stores needed to make up a proper town. I window shop at the Chocolate Box, and St Cuthbert's Retreat book shop, the window full of volumes about the Borders, Northumberland and Hadrian's Wall. There's the Wooler Wool Shop, T. R. Johnson Family Butchers' – with sausages made locally from rare-breed pigs – The Good Life shop, and, in Glendale Paints, a real hardware store, its window signage offering 'wall coverings, paint, woodstains, household, electrical, ironmongery'.

Yep. Wooler joins Thirsk, and one or two other towns I have encountered, as a place where I can imagine living a good life. After it, I'm very much on the home straight. All the time I am closing in on the route of the Great North Road, and signs pointing down lanes to my left would take me to towns on it in a couple of miles, Alnwick among them.

The road drops down to cross the River Breamish for Powburn, after which Telford's Road bumps up against another Roman road, the Devil's Causeway, following it for a couple of stretches before climbing over Framlington Common, at 800ft above sea level far higher than anything on the Great North Road.

At Weldon I cross the River Coquet, last encountered on by way north at Felton, the road then running straight and fast through the village of Longhorsley until, finally, it rises to vault the A1 and drops me down to join the south-bound carriageway.

It'll be the modern A1 all the way home now. A succession of motorway sections and boring bypasses. For the first time I feel like letting someone else do the driving. Better still, having a car that would run on automatic pilot. I could ask it to wake me up when I get to London, then close my eyes.

Failing that, I keep myself alert by reflecting on the many highlights of my journey on the Great North Road and its offshoots.

I think of Buckden, with its bishop's palace, and Stilton with its inn, the Bell, and its cheese; of the wonderful town of Stamford, with The George, and Grantham's Angel and Royal. Of the Pilgrim Fathers' home village of Scrooby.

On the York Road there was Selby Abbey, with the faces hidden in stone, and the boozy old city of York itself. I think of the bridges of Newcastle; of St Cuthbert and St Bede in Durham, and of the Angel of the North. Of Morpeth, Berwick and the badlands; and of Edinburgh itself, a place with an atmosphere more powerful than any I have encountered.

Not to mention the many London highlights: Smithfield Market and the former inns at Hicks Hill; the revolutionaries' haunt of the Red Lion and the *Monopoly* board's famed Angel;

of Archway and The Kinks. Of Shakespeare and Marlowe at Norton Folgate on the Old North Road. Of Cromwell, at Huntingdon and just about everywhere else.

And of my companions, who I invite now to take a bow. Let's hear it for the ByngAdvisor, Fletch, Celia Fiennes, Drunken Barnaby, Rabbie Burns and William Cobbett, who I guess I have to accept was a companion, albeit an obnoxious one. And, most of all, for Uncle Charlie, who was with me every step. Thanks for keeping me company on the road, for pointing the way and showing me what to look out for.

All in all, it's been a remarkable journey: peopled with heroes, villains and plenty of ghosts. When I set out I couldn't be sure what I'd find. Looking back, I can see clearly now. I uncovered an old England (plus a bit of old Scotland).

And those are very nice places to be.

BIBLIOGRAPHY

I have consulted the following books, websites and academic papers during my research, and acknowledge my debt to their authors.

Anonymous *British History Online* (british-history.ac.uk)

Bradley, Tom *The Old Coaching Days in Yorkshire* (London, EP Publishing, 1968)

Braithwaite, Richard *Barnaby's Four Journeys to the North of England* (Poland, Palala Press, 2015)

Burke, Coleman *Matchstalk Men and Matchstalk Cats and Dogs* (London, EMI Music, 1978)

Byng, John *The Torrington Diaries* (London, Eyre and Spottiswood, 1954)

Cobbett, William *Rural Rides* (London, Penguin, 2001)

Cooper, Chris *The Great North Road Then and Now* (Old Harlow, Battle of Britain International, 2013)

Defoe, Daniel *A Tour through the Whole Island of Great Britain* (London, Penguin, 2005)

Bibliography

Defoe, Daniel *The Fortunes and Misfortunes of the Famous Moll Flanders* (London, Penguin, 1978)

Fiennes, Celia *Through England on a Side Saddle* (London, MacDonald, 1982)

Fletcher, Joseph Smith *Darrington: A Yorkshire Parish* (London, Lane, 1917)

Fletcher, Joseph Smith *Nooks and Corners of Yorkshire* (London, Everleigh Nash, 1910)

Harper, Charles G. *Stage-coach and Mail in Days of Yore* (London, Chapman & Hall, 1903)

Harper, Charles G. *The Great North Road* (London, Cecil Palmer, 1901)

Hawthorne, Nathaniel *The English Note-books* (gutenberg.org)

Hillary, Edmund *The Last Enemy* (London, Pan, 1974)

Hodgeson, John *History of Morpeth* (Morpeth, Newgate Press, 1999)

Jenkins, Simon *England's 1,000 Best Churches* (London, Penguin, 1999)

Lumley, Edith *Story of Our Village* (croftontees.co.uk)

Outram, Tristram, W. *Coaching Days and Coaching Ways* (London, Macmillan, 1888)

Pentland, Gordon *William Cobbett's Scotophobia* (academia.edu)

Pepys, Samuel *Diaries* (gutenberg.org/ebooks/4200)

Smollett, Tobias *Humphry Clinker* (London, Penguin, 2008)

Trent, Christopher *Motorists' Companion on the Highways of England* (London, Newnes, 1955)

Webster, Norman W. *The Great North Road* (Bath, Adams and Dart, 1974)

Investigate our other titles and
stay up to date with all our latest releases at
www.scratchingshedpublishing.co.uk